Calm the Chaos

A Parent's Polyvagal Guide to Neurodivergent
Parenting

Doreen Anna Richmond

First Edition

Paperback ISBN: 978-1-923604-16-2

eBook ISBN: 978-1-923604-17-9

This book is for educational and informational purposes only and is not intended as medical, psychological, or therapeutic advice. The information contained herein should not be used as a substitute for professional medical care or mental health services. Always consult with qualified healthcare providers, licensed therapists, or your child's pediatrician before implementing any strategies discussed in this book.

The author is not a licensed medical doctor, psychologist, or therapist. While the content is based on established research and clinical approaches, individual results may vary. The strategies presented may not be appropriate for all children or families.

Names Mentioned Disclaimer: All case studies and family examples in this book use fictional names and composite scenarios to protect privacy. Any resemblance to actual persons, living or deceased, is purely coincidental. References to researchers, clinicians, and published works are cited for educational purposes and do not imply endorsement of this book by those individuals or their institutions.

The author and publisher disclaim any liability for adverse effects arising from the use or application of the information contained in this book.

Table of Contents

Chapter 1: The Neurodivergent Nervous System:

Why Traditional Approaches Fail

Sarah had tried everything. Time-outs, reward charts, taking away privileges, even bribing her eight-year-old son Marcus with his favorite video game time. Nothing worked. In fact, the harder she tried to "fix" his behavior, the worse things got. The meltdowns became more intense, the defiance stronger, and the distance between them wider.

What Sarah didn't know was that Marcus's brain was wired differently. His autistic nervous system was constantly scanning for threats, operating from a place of survival rather than learning. Every traditional parenting strategy she'd been taught was actually making his nervous system feel less safe, not more regulated.

This scenario plays out in millions of homes every day. Parents of neurodivergent children find themselves caught in exhausting cycles of behavioral interventions that don't just fail—they often make things worse. The problem isn't the parents or the children. The problem is that we've been approaching neurodivergent behavior through the wrong lens entirely.

Understanding Polyvagal Theory for Parents

Polyvagal theory, developed by Dr. Stephen Porges, revolutionizes how we understand the human nervous system (Porges, 2011). Instead of viewing our nervous system as simply "on" or "off," polyvagal theory shows us that we have three distinct operating systems, each designed for different situations:

The *newest system* is our **social engagement system**. When this system is online, children can learn, connect, and handle daily challenges with flexibility. They can hear your voice, make eye contact, and access their thinking brain. This is the state where traditional parenting strategies actually work.

The *middle system* is our **fight-or-flight response**. When children's nervous systems detect danger (real or perceived), this system takes over. Kids might become hyperactive, argumentative, or aggressive. They might run, hide, or explode. Their body is literally preparing them to fight or flee from threat.

The *oldest system* is our **shutdown response**. When fight-or-flight doesn't resolve the threat, or when a child's nervous system becomes overwhelmed, this system activates. Children might appear "lazy," "defiant," or "checked out." They're not being difficult—their nervous system has gone offline to protect them from what feels like overwhelming danger.

Here's what changes everything: **neurodivergent children spend much more time in these protective states than neurotypical children**. Their nervous systems are more sensitive to threat detection and slower to return to the calm, connected state where learning and cooperation are possible.

Dr. Mona Delahooke, a child psychologist specializing in neurodevelopmental differences, explains that "behavior is merely the tip of the iceberg" (Delahooke, 2019). What we see on the surface—the tantrums, defiance, or withdrawal—is actually our child's nervous system doing exactly what it's designed to do: protect them from perceived threat.

How Neurodivergent Nervous Systems Differ from Neurotypical Ones

Understanding these differences isn't about making excuses—it's about working with your child's neurobiology instead of against it.

Threat Detection Systems Run Hot

Neurodivergent nervous systems often have what researchers call "hypervigilance" (Van der Kolk, 2014). Imagine your child's nervous system as a smoke detector that's incredibly sensitive. While a neurotypical child's detector might only go off for actual fires, your neurodivergent child's detector sounds the alarm for burnt toast, candles, or even the neighbor's barbecue three houses down.

This isn't a character flaw—it's neurobiology. Research shows that autistic individuals have differences in their amygdala (the brain's alarm system) that make them more likely to perceive neutral situations as potentially threatening (Herrington et al., 2017). For children with ADHD, differences in their prefrontal cortex mean they have less ability to regulate these alarm responses (Shaw et al., 2012).

Sensory Systems as Information Highways

For neurotypical children, sensory information flows like cars on a well-organized highway. For neurodivergent children, it's more like rush-hour traffic with multiple accidents—information gets backed up, overwhelms the system, or takes unexpected detours.

Dr. Lucy Jane Miller's research on sensory processing differences shows that over 75% of autistic children have significant sensory processing challenges (Miller et al., 2007). These aren't preferences or quirks—they're neurological differences that directly impact nervous system regulation.

Consider ten-year-old Emma, who has both autism and sensory processing differences. The fluorescent lights in her classroom don't just bother her—they trigger her fight-or-flight response. The sound of pencils on paper doesn't just annoy her—it sends danger signals to her nervous system. By lunchtime, her nervous system has been in protective mode for hours, making it impossible for her to access the calm, learning state her teachers expect.

Recovery Time Works Differently

When neurotypical children get upset or overstimulated, they typically return to baseline relatively quickly. Neurodivergent children often need much longer recovery periods. Dr. Ross Greene's research shows that children with executive function challenges (common in ADHD and autism) can take 45 minutes to several hours to fully regulate after a stressful event (Greene, 2014).

This extended recovery time isn't stubbornness—it's neurobiology. The neurodivergent nervous system processes stress hormones like cortisol and adrenaline differently, and it takes longer to clear these chemicals from their system.

Why Punishment-Based Discipline Backfires with Dysregulated Children

Traditional discipline assumes that children misbehave because they choose to, and that consequences will teach them to choose better next time. This approach can work for regulated, neurotypical children whose social engagement system is online. But for dysregulated neurodivergent children, punishment activates their threat detection system even more.

The Discipline Trap

When Marcus had a meltdown about homework, his mother Sarah would send him to his room for a time-out. In her mind, this gave him time to "think about his choices" and calm down. But Marcus's nervous system interpreted the isolation as abandonment—a primal threat that triggered even more distress.

Time-outs, which are designed to help children self-regulate, actually require skills that dysregulated children don't have access to in the moment. It's like asking someone having a panic attack to solve a math problem. The capacity simply isn't there.

Consequences vs. Connection

Dr. Daniel Siegel's research on brain development shows that children need to feel safe and connected before they can access their learning brain (Siegel and Bryson, 2012). When we lead with consequences instead of connection, we're trying to teach children whose nervous systems are in survival mode.

Research by Dr. Bruce Perry demonstrates that "you cannot reason with a dysregulated nervous system" (Perry & Szalavitz, 2007). When children are in fight-or-flight or shutdown, their prefrontal cortex—the part of the brain responsible for thinking, reasoning, and learning—is offline.

The Shame Spiral

Repeated punishment doesn't just fail to improve behavior—it often creates shame spirals that make regulation even harder. Children begin to internalize messages that they're "bad," "difficult," or "broken." This shame triggers the nervous system's threat response, creating a cycle where the child becomes increasingly dysregulated and the parent becomes increasingly frustrated.

Twelve-year-old Jake with ADHD described it perfectly: "Every time I get in trouble, my brain gets even more scrambled. Then I mess up worse, and everyone gets madder, and my brain gets more scrambled." Jake's description captures the neurobiological reality that shame and fear make executive function challenges worse, not better.

The Cost of Chronic Nervous System Activation in Neurodivergent Kids

Living in a constant state of nervous system activation isn't just uncomfortable—it has serious long-term consequences for neurodivergent children's development, learning, and mental health.

Academic Impact

When a child's nervous system is chronically activated, learning becomes nearly impossible. The stress hormone cortisol actually impairs memory formation and recall (McEwen & Sapolsky, 1995). Children who spend their school days in fight-or-flight mode aren't just struggling behaviorally—they're literally unable to access their learning capacity.

Research from the National Institute of Mental Health shows that chronic stress in childhood can permanently alter brain development, particularly in areas responsible for executive function, emotional regulation, and social skills (Lupien et al., 2009). For neurodivergent children who already have differences in these areas, chronic nervous system activation compounds their challenges.

Physical Health Consequences

Chronic nervous system activation takes a toll on physical health too. Dr. Gabor Maté's research shows that children in constant stress states have higher rates of autoimmune disorders, digestive issues, and sleep problems (Maté, 2003). Many parents notice that their neurodivergent children get sick more often, have frequent stomachaches, or struggle with chronic fatigue—all signs of an overworked nervous system.

Mental Health Implications

Perhaps most concerning, chronic nervous system dysregulation in childhood sets the stage for anxiety and depression later in life. Research published in the Journal of Autism and Developmental Disorders found that autistic children who experienced chronic stress and trauma symptoms had significantly higher rates of anxiety disorders in adolescence and adulthood (Gotham et al., 2015).

The tragedy is that much of this chronic activation is preventable when we understand how to support neurodivergent nervous systems instead of inadvertently triggering them.

Shifting from Behavior Management to Nervous System Support

The transformation begins when we stop asking "How do I get my child to behave?" and start asking "What does my child's nervous system need to feel safe right now?"

Safety First, Everything Else Second

Dr. Stephen Porges emphasizes that safety is not the absence of threat—it's the presence of connection and predictability (Porges, 2017). For neurodivergent children, creating nervous system safety requires intentional environmental modifications, predictable routines, and adults who understand their unique wiring.

This doesn't mean permissiveness or avoiding all challenges. It means creating conditions where your child's social engagement system can come online, making learning and cooperation possible.

The Power of Regulation Before Reasoning

Instead of jumping straight to problem-solving or consequences, nervous system-informed parenting prioritizes regulation first. This might mean:

- Offering co-regulation through calm presence instead of lectures
- Modifying the environment to reduce sensory overwhelm
- Providing movement or sensory input to help the nervous system reset
- Using connection and empathy to activate the social engagement system

Behavior as Communication

When we view behavior through a nervous system lens, everything changes. A child who won't do homework isn't being defiant—their nervous system might be overwhelmed by the transition from school to home. A child who has meltdowns during bedtime isn't being difficult—their nervous system might need more predictability and co-regulation to feel safe enough to let go of consciousness.

This shift from judgment to curiosity transforms not just your parenting, but your child's experience of themselves and the world.

Case Studies: Before and After Nervous System-Informed Parenting

Case Study 1: Marcus - From Meltdowns to Connection

Before: Eight-year-old Marcus would have explosive meltdowns several times a week, usually triggered by homework or transitions between activities. His parents used time-outs, privilege removal, and reward charts. The meltdowns were getting more frequent and more intense.

Sarah would find herself yelling, Marcus would escalate further, and both would end up exhausted and disconnected. Sarah felt like she was failing as a parent, and Marcus began saying things like "I'm stupid" and "nobody likes me."

After: Once Sarah understood Marcus's autistic nervous system, everything changed. She learned to recognize his early warning signs—the way he'd start scripting from movies or flapping his hands more intensely. Instead of dismissing these as "stimming," she understood them as his nervous system's way of trying to regulate.

She created a "regulation station" in their living room with a weighted blanket, fidget toys, and noise-canceling headphones. When she saw early signs of dysregulation, she'd offer co-regulation: "I notice your nervous system is working hard right now. Want to reset together?"

Instead of time-outs, she provided time-ins—staying close while Marcus regulated, offering deep pressure hugs or simply sitting nearby. The meltdowns didn't disappear overnight, but they became less frequent and less intense. More importantly, Marcus began trusting that his mom understood him.

Six months later, Marcus could identify when he needed a break and would often go to his regulation station on his own. His teachers noticed improved focus and fewer classroom difficulties. Most significantly, the connection between Marcus and Sarah was restored.

Case Study 2: Emma - School Success Through Nervous System Support

Before: Ten-year-old Emma was labeled "school-phobic" and "attention-seeking" because she would have meltdowns every morning and frequently asked to go to the nurse's office. Her parents tried behavior charts, rewards for school attendance, and consequences for "fake" illness complaints.

Emma's anxiety was increasing, her academic performance was declining, and she began having nightmares about school. Her parents felt helpless and frustrated, especially when teachers suggested she was manipulating the system.

After: When Emma's parents learned about sensory processing and nervous system regulation, they realized her morning meltdowns and frequent nurse visits weren't behavioral—they were neurobiological. Emma's sensory system was overwhelmed by the school environment, and her nervous system was in constant protective mode.

Working with an occupational therapist trained in polyvagal theory, they developed a comprehensive support plan. Emma got noise-reducing headphones, a weighted lap pad for her desk, and scheduled sensory breaks. Her parents taught her teachers about her nervous system needs and provided a "regulation kit" for the classroom.

At home, they implemented nervous system-supportive morning routines: a warm bath before school to activate her parasympathetic nervous system, a breakfast smoothie with protein for blood sugar stability, and a few minutes of deep breathing exercises together.

The change was remarkable. Within a month, Emma's morning meltdowns stopped. Her nurse visits became occasional check-ins rather than desperate escape attempts. Her academic performance improved as her nervous system felt safer in the school environment.

Most importantly, Emma began to understand her own nervous system. She'd tell her parents, "My nervous system needs a break" instead of saying "I can't do this." This self-awareness became the foundation for lifelong regulation skills.

Case Study 3: Jake - From Shame to Self-Advocacy

Before: Twelve-year-old Jake with ADHD was in a constant cycle of forgetting assignments, rushing through work, and getting in trouble for hyperactive behavior. His parents used privilege removal and grounding, while teachers employed behavior charts and detention.

Jake was developing learned helplessness and depression. He'd say things like "I'm just dumb" and "nothing I do matters anyway." His self-esteem was plummeting, and his family relationships were strained.

After: Jake's parents learned that his "impulsive" and "hyperactive" behaviors were actually his nervous system's attempts to regulate. His constant movement wasn't defiance—it was his body's way of managing an under-aroused nervous system.

Instead of trying to eliminate his movement, they worked with it. Jake got a standing desk, a fidget bike for homework time, and regular movement breaks. His parents stopped taking away physical activities as consequences, understanding that movement was medicine for his nervous system.

They also addressed the shame spiral that had developed. Instead of focusing on what Jake did wrong, they celebrated his efforts and progress. They taught him about his ADHD brain, helping him understand that he wasn't broken—just different.

Jake learned to advocate for his needs, asking teachers for movement breaks and using fidget tools during lessons. His academic performance improved not because his ADHD went away, but because his environment finally supported his nervous system's needs.

The transformation in Jake's self-concept was profound. Instead of seeing himself as "the problem kid," he began to understand himself as someone whose brain worked differently and needed different supports to succeed.

The Foundation for Everything That Follows

Understanding your child's neurodivergent nervous system isn't just the first step—it's the foundation that makes everything else possible. When you understand that behavior is communication from the nervous system, that safety must come before learning, and that regulation is a prerequisite for connection, you're equipped to support your child in ways that actually work.

This doesn't mean parenting becomes easy. Neurodivergent children will still have challenges, difficult days, and moments that test every bit of patience you have. But when you're working with your child's nervous system instead of against it, you're building skills that will serve them for life.

The strategies, tools, and approaches in the following chapters all build on this foundation: your child's behavior makes sense when viewed through the lens of nervous system safety, and your job as a parent is to become a co-regulator who helps their nervous system feel safe enough to learn, grow, and connect.

Your child isn't broken, difficult, or defiant. Their nervous system is doing exactly what it's designed to do—protect them from perceived threats. Once you understand this, everything changes. Not just your parenting, but your child's entire relationship with themselves and the world around them.

Chapter 2: Recognizing Your Child's Window of Tolerance

Nine-year-old Sofia seemed like two different children. Some days, she'd wake up ready for anything—chatting happily at breakfast, transitioning smoothly between activities, handling unexpected changes with flexibility. Other days, the slightest deviation from routine would send her into complete meltdown mode, or she'd shut down entirely, becoming what her parents called "unreachable."

Sofia's parents couldn't predict which version of their daughter they'd get each day. They tried to maintain consistency, but even their most reliable strategies would work perfectly one day and fail spectacularly the next. What they didn't understand was that Sofia wasn't being unpredictable—her nervous system was.

Every human being has what's called a "window of tolerance"—a zone where we can handle life's challenges with relative ease. For neurodivergent children, this window is often narrower and more variable than for their neurotypical peers. Understanding your child's unique window of tolerance is like having a roadmap for their nervous system, helping you recognize when they're cruising comfortably, when they're approaching their limits, and when they've moved outside their capacity to cope.

Understanding the Window of Tolerance Concept

The term "window of tolerance" was coined by Dr. Dan Siegel to describe the zone of optimal arousal where we can think clearly, feel our emotions without being overwhelmed by them, and respond to challenges with flexibility (Siegel, 1999). Inside this window, children can learn, connect with others, and handle the normal stresses of daily life.

Think of your child's window of tolerance as the comfortable zone on a thermostat. Just as a room can become uncomfortably hot or cold when the temperature moves outside the ideal range, children become dysregulated when their arousal level moves outside their window of tolerance.

Inside the Window: The Green Zone

When children are within their window of tolerance, they have access to what Dr. Stephen Porges calls their *social engagement system* (Porges, 2011). In this state, children can:

- Think clearly and solve problems
- Communicate their needs effectively
- Handle transitions and changes with relative ease
- Connect emotionally with others
- Learn new information and skills
- Show flexibility when things don't go as planned

This is the zone where traditional parenting strategies work best because children can actually hear what you're saying and access their thinking brain to make different choices.

Outside the Window: Red Zones

When children move outside their window of tolerance, they enter what many therapists call "the red zone." There are actually two red zones, corresponding to the two protective responses of the autonomic nervous system:

Hyperarousal (Fight-or-Flight): Children become overly activated— anxious, hyperactive, aggressive, or oppositional. Their system is flooded with stress hormones, preparing them to fight or flee from perceived danger.

Hypoarousal (Shutdown): Children become under-activated—withdrawn, "spacey," lethargic, or seemingly unresponsive. Their system has essentially gone offline to protect them from overwhelm.

Dr. Bessel van der Kolk's research shows that when children are outside their window of tolerance, the rational, thinking part of their brain goes offline (Van der Kolk, 2014). This is why reasoning, consequences, and traditional behavior management strategies don't work when children are dysregulated—they literally cannot access the part of their brain that would allow them to respond to these interventions.

Windows Aren't Fixed

Here's what many parents don't realize: windows of tolerance change constantly based on a multitude of factors. Sleep, nutrition, sensory load, stress levels, routine changes, illness, growth spurts, seasonal changes, and even the nervous system state of the adults around them all impact the size and stability of a child's window.

For neurodivergent children, these factors can have an even more dramatic impact. A child who handles morning routines beautifully when they're well-rested might have a complete meltdown over the same routine when they're sleep-deprived. This isn't inconsistency—it's neurobiology.

Hyperarousal vs. Hypoarousal in Neurodivergent Children

Understanding the difference between hyperarousal and hypoarousal is crucial because each state requires different support strategies. Many parents recognize hyperarousal (the explosive, aggressive, hyperactive responses) but miss hypoarousal, which can look like compliance or even laziness.

Hyperarousal: When the System Runs Too Hot

Children in hyperarousal are in survival mode. Their nervous system has detected threat (real or perceived) and is preparing them to fight or flee. In neurodivergent children, hyperarousal might look like:

Physical signs: rapid breathing, increased heart rate, sweating, muscle tension, inability to sit still, aggressive movements, or repetitive behaviors that seem more intense than usual.

Emotional signs: explosiveness, rage, panic, extreme defiance, inconsolable crying, or emotional responses that seem disproportionate to the trigger.

Cognitive signs: inability to think clearly, forgetting familiar rules or routines, black-and-white thinking, catastrophic interpretations, or repetitive thoughts and worries.

Behavioral signs: aggression toward others or objects, running away, hiding, arguing, refusing to cooperate, or engaging in high-intensity stimming behaviors.

Eleven-year-old David with ADHD would enter hyperarousal whenever his routine changed unexpectedly. If his usual teacher was absent, David's nervous system would interpret this as a threat. He'd become hyperactive, argue with the substitute teacher, and sometimes even try to leave the classroom. Teachers saw defiance, but David's nervous system was simply trying to escape what felt dangerous.

Hypoarousal: When the System Shuts Down

Hypoarousal is often misunderstood because it can look like compliance. Children in this state have moved beyond fight-or-flight into what's sometimes called "freeze" or "fawn" mode. Their nervous system has essentially shut down non-essential functions to conserve energy and protect against overwhelming input.

In neurodivergent children, hypoarousal might look like:

Physical signs: low energy, slumped posture, slow movements, difficulty with coordination, falling asleep at inappropriate times, or appearing "floppy" or disconnected from their body.

Emotional signs: numbness, emptiness, disconnection, inability to access emotions, or seeming "flat" or unresponsive.

Cognitive signs: difficulty concentrating, memory problems, feeling "foggy" or "spacey," inability to make decisions, or giving up easily on tasks.

Behavioral signs: withdrawal from social interaction, decreased communication, lack of initiative, appearing to "zone out," or going through motions without engagement.

Eight-year-old Maya with autism would enter hypoarousal when the sensory demands of her environment became overwhelming. During crowded family gatherings, she'd become quiet and compliant, sitting wherever adults placed her and following directions without her usual questions or resistance. Her family thought she was "being good," but Maya's nervous system had actually shut down to protect her from sensory overwhelm.

The Flip Between States

Many neurodivergent children flip rapidly between hyperarousal and hypoarousal, sometimes within the same day or even the same hour. This can be confusing for parents who might see explosive behavior followed by complete withdrawal.

This flipping isn't a behavioral choice—it's a nervous system trying to find regulation. When hyperarousal strategies don't resolve the threat, the system may shut down instead. Understanding this pattern helps parents recognize that both states indicate dysregulation and need nervous system support.

The Three States: Calm-Alert, Fight-or-Flight, and Shutdown

While it's useful to think about windows of tolerance, it's even more practical to understand the three basic states your child's nervous system can be in at any given moment. Dr. Stephen Porges describes these as the three circuits of the autonomic nervous system, each designed for different survival needs (Porges, 2017).

State 1: Calm-Alert (Social Engagement)

This is your child's optimal state—what we want to see most of the time. When children are calm-alert, they can:

- Make eye contact and respond to facial expressions
- Hear and process verbal communication
- Show curiosity and interest in their environment
- Handle age-appropriate challenges and frustrations
- Connect with others emotionally
- Access learning and problem-solving abilities

What it looks like: relaxed body posture, natural breathing, appropriate energy level for the situation, flexible thinking, cooperative behavior, and genuine engagement with people and activities.

How to support it: predictable routines, appropriate sensory input, connection with caring adults, manageable challenges, and environments that feel safe.

State 2: Fight-or-Flight (Mobilized Defense)

This is the state of hyperarousal where children's systems are preparing for action against perceived threat. The key word is "mobilized"—children in this state have energy and will use it to try to escape or fight off what their nervous system perceives as dangerous.

What it looks like: increased movement and energy, heightened emotions, oppositional behavior, difficulty with transitions, sensory sensitivity, and responses that seem disproportionate to the trigger.

How to support it: remain calm yourself, provide safe movement outlets, reduce sensory input, offer co-regulation through your presence, avoid reasoning or consequences until regulation returns.

State 3: Shutdown (Immobilized Collapse)

This is the state of hypoarousal where children's systems have shut down non-essential functions. The key word is "immobilized"—children in this state don't have the energy to fight or flee, so their system conserves resources and waits for the threat to pass.

What it looks like: low energy, withdrawal from social interaction, appearing "checked out" or disconnected, difficulty initiating activities, slowed responses, and what might look like depression or apathy.

How to support it: gentle, non-demanding presence, patience with slow responses, activities that gently activate the nervous system (like swinging or gentle music), and avoiding overwhelming stimulation.

Learning Your Child's Unique Nervous System Patterns

Every neurodivergent child has their own unique patterns of regulation and dysregulation. Learning these patterns is like becoming fluent in your child's nervous system language—it allows you to anticipate needs, prevent crises, and provide targeted support.

Identifying Personal Triggers

While every child is different, common triggers for neurodivergent nervous system dysregulation include:

Sensory triggers: specific sounds, textures, lighting, crowds, or overwhelming sensory environments *Transition triggers:* changes in routine, unexpected events, switching between activities, or time pressure *Social triggers:* group situations, performance pressure, conflict, or social demands that exceed current capacity *Internal triggers:* hunger, tiredness, illness, hormonal changes, or emotional overwhelm *Environmental triggers:* new places, unpredictable adults, chaotic environments, or lack of structure

Ten-year-old Alex with autism had very specific patterns. Fluorescent lighting was a major trigger that would push him toward hyperarousal within 20 minutes. Sudden loud noises would send him immediately into fight-or-flight. When overwhelmed, he'd first become hyperactive and then, if the trigger continued, shut down completely.

His parents learned to recognize that hand-flapping was an early sign he was approaching his window's edge, scripting from movies meant he was working hard to regulate, and going nonverbal was a sign he'd moved into shutdown. This knowledge allowed them to intervene early and prevent full dysregulation.

Recognizing Early Warning Signs

Most children show subtle signs before moving into full dysregulation. Learning to read these early warning signs allows for proactive support rather than reactive damage control.

Early hyperarousal signs might include:

- Increased stimming or repetitive behaviors
- Higher pitched or faster speech
- Increased movement or restlessness
- Beginning to argue or negotiate more than usual
- Sensory seeking behaviors (spinning, jumping, crashing)
- Difficulty with tasks that are usually manageable

Early hypoarousal signs might include:

- Decreased eye contact or social engagement
- Slower responses to questions or directions
- Appearing tired or lethargic without obvious cause
- Decreased initiation of activities or conversation
- Looking "glazed over" or disconnected

- Increased need for adult prompting

Understanding Recovery Patterns

Just as every child has unique triggers and early warning signs, every child has their own recovery patterns. Some children bounce back quickly from dysregulation, while others need extended time to fully return to their window of tolerance.

Dr. Bruce Perry's research shows that recovery from nervous system activation follows predictable stages, but the timing varies greatly between individuals (Perry & Szalavitz, 2007). Some children need 20 minutes to fully regulate, while others may need several hours or even overnight.

Understanding your child's recovery pattern helps you plan appropriately and avoid the common mistake of expecting normal functioning before regulation has returned.

Daily Tracking Tools and Observation Guides

Systematic observation helps you identify patterns that might not be obvious day-to-day. When you track your child's nervous system patterns over time, you begin to see connections between seemingly unrelated events and responses.

Simple Tracking Methods

You don't need complex systems to track nervous system patterns effectively. Simple, consistent observation is more valuable than elaborate tracking systems that become burdensome.

The Three-State Check-In: Several times throughout the day, simply note whether your child seems to be in calm-alert, fight-or-flight, or shutdown. You can use symbols (green circle, red triangle, blue square) or simple words. Look for patterns around timing, activities, or environmental factors.

Trigger and Response Log: When dysregulation occurs, briefly note:

- What was happening before the dysregulation began?

- What did the dysregulation look like?

- How long did it take for regulation to return?

- What helped (or didn't help) the recovery process?

Energy and Regulation Ratings: Using a simple 1-10 scale, rate your child's energy level and regulation capacity at key times of day (morning, after school, evening). This helps identify patterns related to time of day, sleep, meals, or activities.

The Window of Tolerance Map

Creating a visual map of your child's window of tolerance helps both you and your child understand their nervous system patterns. This can be as simple as a drawing or as detailed as a chart.

Green Zone (Inside the Window): List what your child looks like, sounds like, and is capable of when regulated. Include their strengths, interests, and the conditions that support this state.

Red Zone - High (Fight-or-Flight): Describe your child's hyperarousal signs, including physical, emotional, and behavioral indicators. Note what triggers this state and what helps them return to regulation.

Red Zone - Low (Shutdown): Describe your child's hypoarousal signs and triggers. Note what this state looks like and what supports recovery.

Twelve-year-old Jordan worked with his parents to create his window of tolerance map using colors and drawings. He drew himself as a green superhero in his regulated state, a red tornado in fight-or-flight, and a gray ghost in shutdown. This visual helped Jordan understand his own patterns and communicate his needs to adults.

Environmental Factor Tracking

Since environmental factors significantly impact nervous system regulation, tracking these alongside your child's states can reveal important connections:

Physical environment: lighting, noise levels, crowding, temperature, air quality *Social environment:* who was present, group size, social demands, conflict levels *Routine factors:* schedule changes, transitions, time pressure, predictability *Internal factors:* sleep quality, meal timing, illness, medication effects, hormonal changes *Activity factors:* cognitive demands, physical demands, sensory input, novelty levels

Building Awareness Without Judgment

The goal of tracking and understanding nervous system patterns isn't to judge or criticize your child's responses—it's to build compassionate awareness that leads to better support.

Approaching Patterns with Curiosity

When you notice patterns in your child's nervous system responses, approach them with genuine curiosity rather than frustration. Instead of "Why does he always melt down after school?" try "What might his nervous system be experiencing that leads to this pattern?"

This shift from judgment to curiosity changes everything. It moves you from seeing your child as problematic to seeing their nervous system as communicating important information about their needs and capacity.

Normalizing Nervous System Responses

Help your child understand that having a narrow window of tolerance or specific triggers isn't a character flaw—it's neurobiology. Many neurodivergent individuals have nervous systems that are more sensitive to their environment, and this sensitivity can actually be a strength in many contexts.

Dr. Elaine Aron's research on highly sensitive individuals shows that sensory sensitivity often comes with increased creativity, empathy, and awareness of subtleties others miss (Aron, 2013). Helping your child see their nervous system differences as variations rather than deficits builds self-acceptance and reduces shame.

Teaching Self-Advocacy Skills

As children develop awareness of their own patterns, they can begin to advocate for their needs. This might sound like:

- "I notice my nervous system is getting overwhelmed. I need a break."

- "Fluorescent lights make it hard for me to think. Can I wear my sunglasses?"

- "I'm in my yellow zone right now. I might need extra help staying regulated."

- "My nervous system needs some movement before I can sit and focus."

This self-awareness and advocacy becomes a lifelong skill that serves neurodivergent individuals well into adulthood.

Celebrating Regulation Efforts

Focus on celebrating your child's efforts to regulate rather than just their success at staying regulated. When children are working hard to manage their nervous system responses, that effort deserves recognition even if they don't achieve perfect regulation.

"I noticed how hard you worked to stay regulated during that transition. Your nervous system was working really hard, and you used your strategies well."

This approach builds intrinsic motivation for regulation while acknowledging that regulation is an ongoing process, not a perfect state.

Building Your Child's Regulation Toolbox

Understanding your child's window of tolerance is just the first step. The next step is building a toolbox of strategies that help them stay within their window or return to it when they've become dysregulated.

Prevention Strategies

The most effective regulation strategies are preventive—they help children stay within their window of tolerance rather than trying to get them back in after dysregulation occurs.

Environmental modifications: Change the physical environment to reduce known triggers and support regulation (noise-reducing headphones, fidget tools, comfortable seating, appropriate lighting).

Routine supports: Create predictable routines around transitions, meals, bedtime, and other potentially challenging times.

Sensory diet: Work with an occupational therapist to develop a "sensory diet"—planned sensory activities throughout the day that help maintain optimal arousal levels.

Co-regulation opportunities: Build in regular connection time where your child can borrow your regulated nervous system state.

Early Intervention Strategies

When you notice early warning signs that your child is approaching the edge of their window, quick interventions can prevent full dysregulation.

Movement breaks: Brief physical activity to help regulate arousal levels *Sensory input:* Weighted lap pads, fidget tools, music, or other sensory supports *Connection:* Brief moments of focused attention and empathy *Environmental modifications:* Quick changes to reduce sensory load or increase predictability

Recovery Strategies

When dysregulation does occur, having a plan helps both you and your child navigate the recovery process more smoothly.

Safety first: Ensure physical and emotional safety for everyone involved *Co-regulation:* Offer your calm presence without demands *Sensory support:* Provide regulating sensory input appropriate to your child's current state *Time and patience:* Allow adequate recovery time without rushing the process

Your Child's Nervous System Makes Sense

Understanding your child's window of tolerance transforms how you see their behavior. What once seemed unpredictable, defiant, or attention-seeking begins to make perfect sense when viewed through the lens of nervous system regulation.

Your child isn't choosing to have meltdowns, shut down, or struggle with daily activities. Their nervous system is responding exactly as it's designed to—protecting them from what it perceives as threatening or overwhelming. Your job isn't to eliminate these responses but to understand them, support regulation when possible, and provide safety and connection during dysregulation.

This understanding changes everything. It reduces your frustration because behavior makes sense. It reduces your child's shame because their responses are normal for their nervous system. It increases connection because you're working with your child's neurobiology instead of against it.

Most importantly, it gives you a roadmap for supporting your child's development in ways that actually work. When you know your child's patterns, triggers, and recovery needs, you can create environments and relationships that help them thrive within their unique nervous system design.

The window of tolerance isn't fixed—with the right supports, it can expand over time. But first, you must meet your child where they are, understanding and respecting their current capacity while gently supporting their growth. This is the foundation for everything that follows: a deep, compassionate understanding of how your child's nervous system works and what it needs to feel safe enough to learn, grow, and connect.

Chapter 3: Sensory Processing Through a Polyvagal Lens

Seven-year-old Mia would have complete meltdowns in Target. Not tantrums—full-blown nervous system collapse that would leave her shaking and nonverbal for the rest of the day. Her parents tried everything: shopping when she was well-rested, bringing snacks, promising treats, even attempting to bribe her with new toys. Nothing worked.

What Mia's parents didn't understand was that Target wasn't just overwhelming for her—it was physiologically threatening. The fluorescent lights triggered her visual system, the squeaky cart wheels activated her auditory processing issues, the smooth floor challenged her vestibular system, and the crowded aisles overwhelmed her sense of space and safety. By the time they reached the toy section, Mia's nervous system had been in fight-or-flight mode for twenty minutes.

Mia wasn't being difficult. Her eight sensory systems were sending danger signals directly to her brainstem, bypassing her thinking brain entirely. Understanding sensory processing through a polyvagal lens changes everything about how we support neurodivergent children in a world that often feels unsafe to their nervous systems.

How Sensory Sensitivities Trigger Nervous System Responses

Traditional approaches to sensory processing focus on helping children tolerate or adapt to sensory input. A polyvagal understanding reveals something more fundamental: sensory experiences directly influence nervous system state, often triggering protective responses before conscious awareness even occurs.

The Sensory-Nervous System Highway

Dr. Stephen Porges explains that sensory information travels through our nervous system along multiple pathways, with some routes bypassing conscious awareness entirely (Porges, 2011). This means that sensory input can trigger fight-or-flight responses before a child even consciously registers what's happening.

For neurodivergent children, this pathway is often hyperactive. Their nervous systems interpret neutral sensory experiences as potential threats, activating protective responses that neurotypical children's systems would never trigger.

Consider the difference between neurotypical and neurodivergent responses to a fire drill:

Neurotypical child: Hears the alarm, recognizes it as a drill, feels mild annoyance or excitement, follows procedures, returns to normal activity quickly.

Neurodivergent child: The alarm sound triggers an immediate fight-or-flight response, heart rate spikes, thinking brain goes offline, may freeze or try to escape, needs significant recovery time even after understanding it was just a drill.

The neurodivergent child's response isn't wrong or overreactive—their nervous system processed the sudden loud sound as a threat and responded accordingly.

Neuroception and Sensory Safety

Dr. Porges introduced the concept of *neuroception*—our nervous system's unconscious detection of safety or threat in our environment (Porges, 2004). This detection system evaluates sensory input millisecond by millisecond, determining whether our current environment supports social engagement or requires protective responses.

For many neurodivergent children, common sensory experiences trigger neuroception of threat:

- Fluorescent lights → visual system stress → nervous system activation

- Background noise → auditory overwhelm → fight-or-flight response

- Unexpected touch → tactile threat detection → shutdown or aggression

- Strong smells → olfactory overload → nausea and withdrawal

- Crowded spaces → proprioceptive confusion → panic response

These aren't preferences or behaviors children can simply choose to change. They're neurobiological responses happening below the level of conscious control.

The Cumulative Effect

Sensory triggers don't operate in isolation—they accumulate throughout the day. Dr. Lucy Jane Miller's research on sensory processing disorder shows that sensory-sensitive children experience what she calls "sensory overload buildup" (Miller et al., 2007).

Think of your child's nervous system like a cup filling with water. Each sensory experience adds drops to the cup. For neurotypical children, the cup is large and has good drainage. For neurodivergent children, the cup is smaller and the drainage is poor. By mid-day, what appears to be a minor sensory experience (like a tag in their shirt) can cause the cup to overflow into complete dysregulation.

This explains why children often have meltdowns over seemingly minor triggers at the end of the day. It's not really about the tag—it's about the accumulation of sensory stress throughout the day finally exceeding their nervous system's capacity.

The Eight Sensory Systems and Their Impact on Regulation

Most people know about the five traditional senses, but occupational therapy recognizes eight sensory systems that all contribute to nervous system regulation. Understanding each system helps you identify which sensory experiences support your child's regulation and which trigger dysregulation.

1. Visual System (What We See)

The visual system processes light, color, movement, and spatial relationships. For many neurodivergent children, visual processing differences create significant nervous system challenges.

Common triggers: fluorescent lights, bright sunlight, busy visual patterns, moving objects in peripheral vision, too much visual information in one space.

Regulation supporters: dim lighting, solid colors, organized visual environments, sunglasses, visual schedules that reduce uncertainty.

Nine-year-old Emma's visual system was so sensitive that classroom fluorescent lights would trigger migraines and meltdowns within an hour. When her teacher allowed her to wear tinted glasses and sit near a window with natural light, Emma's behavior problems virtually disappeared. The intervention wasn't behavioral—it was neurobiological.

2. Auditory System (What We Hear)

The auditory system processes sounds, but for neurodivergent children, it also plays a crucial role in nervous system safety assessment. Dr. Porges notes that specific sound frequencies directly influence vagal tone and nervous system regulation (Porges, 2017).

Common triggers: sudden loud noises, background noise, certain frequencies (like hand dryers or microphones), overlapping conversations, echoing spaces.

Regulation supporters: predictable sounds, nature sounds, specific music, noise-canceling headphones, quiet spaces for recovery.

Twelve-year-old Jordan with autism could predict his meltdowns by paying attention to sound accumulation. The morning announcements, hallway noise, pencil sharpeners, and cafeteria chaos would build up until his nervous system hit overload. Noise-reducing headphones allowed him to stay regulated throughout the school day.

3. Tactile System (What We Touch and Feel)

The tactile system includes light touch, deep pressure, temperature, and texture. This system is closely connected to emotional regulation because touch experiences directly influence our sense of safety and connection.

Common triggers: unexpected touch, light touch, rough textures, wet or sticky substances, temperature changes, clothing tags or seams.

Regulation supporters: deep pressure, weighted materials, soft textures, warm baths, massage, predictable touch experiences.

Five-year-old Marco would have explosive reactions to getting his face washed or hands cleaned. His parents thought he was being defiant, but occupational therapy revealed severe tactile defensiveness. The light, unpredictable touch of a washcloth triggered his fight-or-flight response. Deep pressure and predictable washing routines transformed daily hygiene from a battle to a manageable routine.

4. Proprioceptive System (Body Awareness)

Proprioception tells us where our body is in space and how our joints and muscles are positioned. This system is crucial for emotional regulation—many people unconsciously use proprioceptive input to calm their nervous systems.

Common challenges: poor body awareness, difficulty gauging personal space, appearing clumsy or uncoordinated, seeking intense physical experiences.

Regulation supporters: heavy work activities, weight-bearing exercises, deep pressure, swimming, playground equipment, fidget tools that provide resistance.

Ten-year-old Sam seemed to be in constant motion, crashing into furniture and people, appearing hyperactive and unfocused. Rather than trying to get him to sit still, his occupational therapist recommended proprioceptive input breaks every 30 minutes. Push-ups against the wall, carrying heavy books, or using a weighted lap pad gave Sam's nervous system the input it needed to regulate and focus.

5. Vestibular System (Balance and Movement)

The vestibular system, located in the inner ear, processes information about head position, movement, and balance. This system has direct connections to emotional regulation centers in the brain.

Common challenges: motion sickness, fear of heights or movement, seeking intense spinning or swinging, difficulty with balance activities.

Regulation supporters: gentle swinging, rocking, controlled spinning, balance activities, specific movement patterns that match the child's needs.

Eight-year-old Lily would shut down completely during any activity involving movement or height. Playground equipment, riding in cars, and even walking up stairs would trigger her freeze response. Gentle vestibular input through therapy swings and controlled movement activities gradually expanded her window of tolerance for movement experiences.

6. Olfactory System (Smell)

The olfactory system is directly connected to the limbic system (emotional brain), making smells powerful triggers for nervous system responses. Many neurodivergent children have heightened smell sensitivity that can trigger immediate fight-or-flight responses.

Common triggers: perfumes, cleaning products, food smells, bathroom odors, car exhaust, certain personal scents.

Regulation supporters: essential oils (carefully chosen), fresh air, removing trigger scents from the environment, having a "smell escape plan."

Eleven-year-old David couldn't enter the school cafeteria without gagging and feeling panicked. The mixture of food smells, cleaning products, and packed bodies created olfactory overload that his nervous system interpreted as threat. Eating lunch in a quieter classroom with fewer competing smells allowed him to actually enjoy his meal and socialize with peers.

7. Gustatory System (Taste)

Taste sensitivity often overlaps with other sensory systems and can significantly impact nutrition and social experiences around food.

Common challenges: extreme food selectivity, strong reactions to certain tastes or textures, difficulty trying new foods, gagging or vomiting responses to non-preferred foods.

Regulation supporters: respecting food preferences while gradually expanding options, focusing on nutrition within preferred foods, reducing pressure around eating.

Six-year-old Maya's food selectivity was so severe that family meals became battlegrounds. Understanding that her gustatory system was sending threat signals for most foods changed the family approach from force to understanding. Working with her preferred foods and very gradually introducing new options reduced everyone's stress and actually expanded Maya's diet over time.

8. Interoceptive System (Internal Body Signals)

Interoception is our ability to sense internal body signals like hunger, thirst, need for bathroom, heart rate, breathing, and emotional states. Many neurodivergent children have interoceptive differences that make it hard to recognize their body's needs.

Common challenges: not recognizing hunger or thirst until extreme, difficulty identifying emotions, not noticing when they need the bathroom, unable to sense illness symptoms early.

Regulation supporters: regular check-ins about body signals, visual aids for identifying internal states, structured meal and bathroom times, teaching body awareness through mindfulness activities.

Thirteen-year-old Alex would go from seeming fine to having explosive meltdowns with no warning. Occupational therapy revealed that he couldn't sense his internal stress signals until they reached crisis levels. Learning to identify early internal warning signs (tense shoulders, faster heartbeat, stomach tightness) gave him tools for early intervention.

Sensory Seeking vs. Sensory Avoiding Behaviors Explained

Understanding the difference between sensory seeking and sensory avoiding behaviors is crucial for supporting regulation. Both are attempts by the nervous system to achieve optimal arousal levels for social engagement.

Sensory Seeking: When the System Needs More Input

Some neurodivergent children have nervous systems that are under-responsive to sensory input. Their systems crave intense sensory experiences to reach an optimal level of arousal where they can focus and connect.

Sensory seeking behaviors might include:

- Crashing into furniture or people

- Seeking loud sounds or music

- Spinning, jumping, or other intense movement

- Chewing on non-food items

- Seeking tight squeezes or heavy blankets

- Looking for bright lights or visual stimulation
- Touching everything in their environment

These behaviors aren't attention-seeking or disruptive—they're regulation-seeking. The child's nervous system needs more intense input to function optimally.

Seven-year-old Tyler seemed hyperactive and disruptive, constantly moving, making noise, and touching things. His teachers saw behavioral problems, but an occupational therapist recognized sensory seeking. Providing structured opportunities for intense sensory input (obstacle courses, weighted vests, fidget tools) transformed Tyler from "disruptive" to focused and engaged.

Sensory Avoiding: When the System Needs Less Input

Other neurodivergent children have nervous systems that are over-responsive to sensory input. Their systems become overwhelmed by typical sensory experiences, leading to avoidance behaviors designed to reduce input.

Sensory avoiding behaviors might include:

- Covering ears or eyes
- Refusing to touch certain textures
- Avoiding crowded or noisy places
- Having strong reactions to clothing, food, or personal care
- Withdrawing from social situations
- Appearing "picky" or "difficult"
- Shutting down in overwhelming environments

These behaviors aren't defiance or manipulation—they're protection strategies. The child's nervous system is trying to prevent overload by reducing input.

Ten-year-old Grace was labeled "difficult" because she refused to participate in many family activities. She wouldn't go to restaurants, avoided birthday parties, and had meltdowns about clothing choices. Understanding her sensory avoiding patterns helped her family make modifications that allowed her to participate in ways that felt safe to her nervous system.

Mixed Patterns: The Reality for Many Children

Many neurodivergent children don't fit neatly into seeking or avoiding categories. They might seek certain types of sensory input while avoiding others, or their needs might change based on their current regulation state.

Twelve-year-old Isaiah sought proprioceptive input (loved rough play and heavy work) but avoided auditory input (needed quiet environments to focus). His sensory profile was complex, requiring individualized supports that honored both his seeking and avoiding needs.

Creating Sensory Profiles for Your Child

A sensory profile is like a map of your child's unique sensory nervous system. It identifies which sensory experiences support regulation, which trigger dysregulation, and what your child's optimal sensory environment looks like.

Observing Across Environments

Children's sensory responses can vary dramatically across different environments. A child who seems regulated at home might struggle significantly at school due to different sensory demands.

Home environment observations:

- Which rooms does your child prefer?
- What activities naturally calm them?
- What sensory experiences cause problems?

- How do they respond to household sounds, lights, smells?
- What clothing choices do they make when given options?

School environment observations:

- How do they handle classroom lighting and noise?
- What's their response to cafeteria, gym, or outdoor environments?
- How do they manage school supplies and materials?
- What time of day do sensory challenges peak?

Community environment observations:

- How do they respond to stores, restaurants, or public spaces?
- What's their tolerance for car rides or public transportation?
- How do they handle crowds, waiting areas, or new environments?
- What strategies help them succeed in challenging sensory environments?

Identifying Patterns Across Time

Sensory tolerance changes based on regulation state, time of day, stress levels, and other factors. Looking for patterns across time helps you understand when your child's sensory system is most vulnerable.

Daily patterns: Many children have lower sensory tolerance at certain times of day (often late afternoon or evening when they're tired).

Weekly patterns: Some children show decreased tolerance by the end of the school week when their systems are depleted.

Seasonal patterns: Changes in daylight, temperature, or routine can affect sensory processing.

Stress patterns: During high-stress periods, children often become more sensitive to sensory input.

Working with Professionals

Occupational therapists trained in sensory processing and polyvagal theory can provide comprehensive sensory evaluations. They can help you understand your child's unique patterns and develop targeted interventions.

When choosing an occupational therapist, look for someone who:

- Understands the connection between sensory processing and nervous system regulation

- Takes a strengths-based approach rather than trying to "fix" sensory differences

- Works with families to create sustainable environmental modifications

- Recognizes that sensory differences are neurobiological, not behavioral

Environmental Modifications for Nervous System Safety

Once you understand your child's sensory profile, you can make targeted environmental modifications that support nervous system regulation. Small changes can have dramatic impacts on your child's ability to stay regulated throughout the day.

Home Environment Modifications

Lighting adjustments: Replace fluorescent bulbs with LED or incandescent options, use lamps instead of overhead lighting, add dimmer switches, provide access to natural light.

Sound modifications: Identify and eliminate unnecessary background noise, use sound-absorbing materials like rugs or curtains, create quiet spaces for regulation, consider white noise or nature sounds for some children.

Visual organization: Reduce visual clutter, use solid colors instead of busy patterns, organize belongings in ways that reduce visual overwhelm, create calm visual spaces for regulation.

Tactile considerations: Remove tags from clothing, provide preferred textures in common areas, offer alternatives for necessary but unpleasant tactile experiences (like bathtime modifications).

Movement opportunities: Create spaces for safe sensory seeking (indoor swings, trampolines, crash pads), ensure access to heavy work opportunities, provide fidget tools and movement options.

School Environment Modifications

Working with your child's school team to implement sensory supports can dramatically improve their regulation and learning:

Classroom modifications: preferred seating (away from high-traffic areas, near natural light), access to fidget tools, movement breaks, alternative work spaces for overwhelming times.

Transitional supports: visual schedules to increase predictability, warning systems for unexpected changes, designated quiet spaces for regulation.

Cafeteria and gym modifications: alternative lunch locations if needed, modified PE activities that honor sensory needs, access to regulation tools during challenging activities.

Community Environment Strategies

Shopping and errands: shop during less crowded times, use noise-reducing headphones, bring regulation tools, plan for sensory breaks, have exit strategies for overwhelm.

Social events: prepare your child's nervous system in advance, identify quiet spaces for breaks, bring familiar comfort items, respect your child's tolerance limits.

Travel and transportation: plan for sensory needs during travel, bring regulation tools, prepare for different sensory environments, maintain familiar routines when possible.

Working with Occupational Therapists from a Polyvagal Perspective

Not all occupational therapists understand the connection between sensory processing and nervous system regulation. Finding a therapist who works from a polyvagal-informed perspective can make a significant difference in your child's progress.

What to Look for in a Polyvagal-Informed OT

Philosophy: They view sensory differences as neurobiological variations rather than problems to fix. They understand that sensory experiences directly impact nervous system state.

Approach: They prioritize nervous system safety and regulation over compliance with activities. They recognize that forcing sensory experiences can be traumatizing for sensitive nervous systems.

Family involvement: They work with families to understand sensory patterns and implement supports across environments. They provide education about the nervous system connection to sensory processing.

Individualization: They recognize that every child's sensory system is unique and develop highly individualized intervention plans.

Questions to Ask Potential Therapists

- How do you understand the relationship between sensory processing and nervous system regulation?

- Do you use polyvagal theory to inform your intervention approaches?

- How do you handle situations where a child refuses to participate in sensory activities?

- What role do you see parents playing in sensory intervention?

- How do you measure progress beyond compliance with therapy activities?

Red Flags in Sensory Intervention

Forcing sensory experiences: Therapy that pushes children through sensory activities despite distress can be traumatizing to sensitive nervous systems.

Ignoring child's responses: Good sensory intervention constantly monitors the child's nervous system state and adjusts accordingly.

One-size-fits-all approaches: Every neurodivergent child's sensory system is unique—effective intervention must be highly individualized.

Focusing only on tolerance: While building tolerance can be helpful, the primary goal should be supporting nervous system regulation and finding ways for children to thrive with their sensory differences.

The Sensory-Informed Family

Understanding sensory processing through a polyvagal lens transforms not just how you support your neurodivergent child, but how your entire family approaches daily life. When you recognize that sensory experiences directly impact everyone's nervous system state, you can create family environments that support regulation for all family members.

Sensory-Aware Daily Routines

Morning routines: Consider each family member's sensory needs when planning morning schedules. Some children need quiet, slow mornings, while others need movement and stimulation to regulate for the day.

Transition supports: Build sensory regulation into transitions between activities. This might mean deep breathing before homework, movement breaks between tasks, or sensory input before challenging activities.

Evening routines: Create sensory-supportive bedtime routines that help nervous systems transition from daytime alertness to nighttime calm.

Family Sensory Accommodations

Not every sensory accommodation requires individual solutions. Many modifications support the entire family's regulation:

- Reducing overall household noise levels
- Using lighting that's comfortable for sensitive eyes
- Creating calm, organized spaces that feel peaceful
- Having regulation tools available for anyone who needs them
- Planning family activities with everyone's sensory needs in mind

Teaching Sensory Self-Advocacy

As children understand their own sensory patterns, they can begin advocating for their needs:

"My ears need a break from the noise. Can I use my headphones?"

"This light is making it hard for me to think. Can we dim it or move to a different spot?"

"My body needs some heavy work before I can sit and focus."

This self-awareness and advocacy becomes a lifelong skill that serves neurodivergent individuals well into adulthood.

Understanding Changes Everything

When Mia's parents understood that her Target meltdowns were neurobiological responses to sensory overwhelm rather than behavioral choices, everything changed. They stopped trying to force tolerance and started supporting her nervous system.

They shopped during less crowded times, brought noise-reducing headphones, planned for sensory breaks, and respected her sensory limits. When they needed to shop during busier times, they prepared Mia's nervous system in advance and had a plan for regulation support.

Most importantly, they stopped seeing Mia as difficult and started seeing her as having a nervous system that needed specific supports to feel safe in sensory-overwhelming environments. This shift from judgment to understanding transformed not just their shopping trips, but their entire relationship with their daughter.

Your child's sensory responses aren't behavioral choices—they're neurobiological reactions happening below the level of conscious control. When you understand sensory processing through a polyvagal lens, you can create environments and supports that help your child's nervous system feel safe enough to engage, learn, and connect.

This doesn't mean avoiding all challenging sensory experiences—it means building your child's capacity gradually, with their nervous system safety as the foundation. When children feel safe in their sensory environments, they can access their full potential for learning, growth, and connection.

The sensory world will always be more challenging for your neurodivergent child than for neurotypical peers. But with understanding, modifications, and nervous system-informed supports, they can learn to navigate sensory experiences successfully while maintaining regulation and connection. This is the foundation for lifelong thriving in a sensory-complex world.

Chapter 4: The Parent-Child Co-Regulation Dance

Fifteen minutes into Maya's homework session, everything was falling apart. Again. The eight-year-old sat at the kitchen table, tears streaming down her face, pencil thrown across the room. "I can't do this! It's too hard! I'm stupid!"

Maya's mom, Jennifer, felt her own heart racing. Her first instinct was to fix the problem: "It's just math, Maya. You know how to do this. Just calm down and try again." But as Jennifer's voice got louder and her suggestions more urgent, Maya melted down further.

What Jennifer didn't understand was that Maya's nervous system was in full fight-or-flight mode, making learning impossible. And Jennifer's own activated nervous system—trying to solve, fix, and control the situation—was actually making Maya's dysregulation worse. Both mother and daughter were caught in a dysregulation spiral that would end with everyone exhausted and disconnected.

This scenario plays out in countless homes every day because most parents don't understand one of the most fundamental principles of nervous system regulation: you cannot regulate a dysregulated person from a dysregulated state. Co-regulation—the process of one person's regulated nervous system helping another person's nervous system find regulation—is the foundation of all emotional development and learning.

Understanding Co-Regulation vs. Self-Regulation

The ability to self-regulate—to manage our emotions, attention, and behavior independently—is often seen as the goal of child development. But neuroscience reveals that self-regulation actually develops through thousands of co-regulation experiences with caring adults. We learn to regulate our nervous systems by borrowing the regulation of others.

Co-Regulation: The Foundation of Development

Dr. Allan Schore's research shows that children's nervous systems literally develop through co-regulation experiences (Schore, 2003). When a calm, regulated adult attends to a dysregulated child with presence and attunement, the child's nervous system begins to mirror the adult's regulated state.

Think of co-regulation like a tuning fork. When you strike a tuning fork and hold it near another fork of the same frequency, the second fork begins to vibrate at the same frequency. Similarly, when your regulated nervous system is present with your child's dysregulated nervous system, your child begins to attune to your regulation.

This isn't metaphorical—it's measurable. Research shows that during co-regulation, children's heart rate, breathing, and stress hormone levels begin to match those of the regulating adult (Feldman, 2012).

Why Self-Regulation Strategies Often Fail

Many parenting approaches focus on teaching children self-regulation strategies: "Take deep breaths," "Count to ten," "Use your words." While these strategies can be helpful for regulated nervous systems, they often fail during dysregulation because they require access to the prefrontal cortex—exactly the part of the brain that goes offline during stress responses.

Dr. Dan Siegel explains that when children are "flipping their lid" (his term for nervous system activation), the rational, thinking brain becomes disconnected from the emotional brain (Siegel and Bryson, 2012). Asking a dysregulated child to use self-regulation strategies is like asking someone having a panic attack to solve algebra problems—the capacity simply isn't available.

The Developmental Progression

Self-regulation develops through a predictable progression that requires thousands of co-regulation experiences:

Infancy: Complete dependence on caregiver co-regulation
Toddlerhood: Beginning awareness of internal states with intensive co-regulation support
Preschool: Developing some self-regulation skills with frequent co-regulation backup *School age:* Increasing self-regulation capacity with co-regulation support during stress *Adolescence:* Mostly self-regulated with co-regulation needed during high stress or transitions *Adulthood:* Independent regulation with ongoing need for co-regulation in relationships

For neurodivergent children, this progression often takes longer and requires more intensive support. Their nervous systems may need co-regulation support well beyond the typical age ranges, and that's completely normal for their neurobiology.

How Your Nervous System Affects Your Child's

One of the most powerful and challenging aspects of parenting neurodivergent children is recognizing that your nervous system state directly impacts your child's regulation. Children are constantly monitoring the adults around them for cues about safety, and neurodivergent children are often hypervigilant to these cues.

Nervous System Contagion

Dr. Stephen Porges describes how nervous system states are "contagious"—we unconsciously pick up and mirror the nervous system states of people around us, especially people we're emotionally connected to (Porges, 2017). This is why walking into a room where people are stressed makes you feel stressed, even if you don't know why.

For neurodivergent children, this contagion effect is often heightened. Their sensitive nervous systems pick up on subtle cues that indicate stress, threat, or dysregulation in their caregivers.

The Parent's Dilemma

Here's the challenge: parenting a neurodivergent child is genuinely stressful. Frequent meltdowns, daily struggles with basic tasks, social challenges, and the constant advocacy required to meet your child's needs all create legitimate stress in your nervous system.

But when you approach your dysregulated child from your own dysregulated state, you inadvertently amplify their distress. Your stressed nervous system signals danger to their already activated nervous system, creating escalation rather than regulation.

This doesn't mean you need to be perfectly regulated all the time—that's impossible and unnecessary. It means developing awareness of your nervous system state and learning to find enough regulation to offer co-regulation to your child.

Recognizing Your Nervous System States

Signs you might be in fight-or-flight:

- Feeling urgent, impatient, or irritable

- Speaking faster or louder than usual

- Feeling like you need to fix or control the situation immediately

- Physical tension, rapid heartbeat, or shallow breathing

- Thinking in black-and-white terms ("This always happens," "Nothing works")

Signs you might be in shutdown:

- Feeling overwhelmed or emotionally numb

- Wanting to escape or avoid the situation

- Feeling hopeless or defeated

- Physical fatigue or feeling "heavy"

- Difficulty thinking clearly or making decisions

Signs you're regulated and available for co-regulation:

- Feeling present and connected to your body

- Breathing deeply and naturally

- Able to stay curious rather than judgmental

- Physical sense of groundedness and stability

- Able to hold complexity and uncertainty

Building Safety and Connection Before Correction

Traditional parenting wisdom suggests that discipline and correction should happen immediately when children misbehave. But nervous system science reveals that learning and behavior change can only happen when a child's social engagement system is online—which requires safety and connection first.

The Safety-Connection-Learning Sequence

Dr. Bruce Perry's research demonstrates that the brain develops and functions in a hierarchical way: survival first, then emotional regulation, then learning and thinking (Perry & Szalavitz, 2007). This means that until a child feels safe and connected, attempts at teaching, correcting, or reasoning will be ineffective.

Safety: The child's nervous system perceives the environment and relationships as non-threatening *Connection:* The child feels emotionally attuned to and understood by their caregiver *Learning:* The child can access their thinking brain for behavior change, skill development, and growth

When children are dysregulated, they're stuck in the safety layer. Until that's addressed, connection and learning are impossible.

What Safety Looks Like for Neurodivergent Children

Safety isn't just the absence of threat—it's the presence of specific conditions that signal safety to a sensitive nervous system:

Environmental safety: Predictable routines, manageable sensory input, organized spaces, clear expectations *Relational safety:* Adults who understand their neurodivergent needs, predictable responses from caregivers, absence of criticism or judgment about their neurological differences *Emotional safety:* Permission to have big feelings, understanding that their responses make sense, no pressure to be someone they're not

Connection Before Correction in Practice

When ten-year-old Sam threw his homework across the room and declared "This is stupid! I hate math!" his dad's first instinct was to address the behavior: "We don't throw things when we're frustrated. Pick up your papers and try again."

But Sam's dad had learned about nervous system regulation. Instead, he recognized that Sam's nervous system was in fight-or-flight mode—the homework had triggered overwhelm, and Sam's thinking brain was offline.

Rather than correcting immediately, Sam's dad focused on connection: "Wow, your nervous system is really working hard right now. That math must feel overwhelming." He sat down near Sam, not hovering but making his calm presence available.

Sam's initial response was more anger: "It IS overwhelming! I can't do any of it!" But instead of trying to solve the math problem, his dad stayed with the feeling: "It makes total sense that your nervous system would feel overwhelmed by this. Math can be really hard when our brains are tired."

Within a few minutes, Sam's breathing slowed and his body relaxed slightly. Only then did his dad offer support: "What do you think would help your nervous system feel ready to try again? We could take a movement break, get a snack, or maybe try just one problem at a time."

The correction—about throwing papers—came later, when Sam was regulated and connected. And because Sam felt understood rather than judged, he was actually able to hear and internalize the guidance about expressing frustration more appropriately.

The Importance of Parental Presence and Attunement

Co-regulation isn't about fixing, solving, or eliminating your child's distress. It's about offering your regulated nervous system as a resource for your child's dysregulated nervous system. This requires presence and attunement—two skills that go against many parents' instincts to help by doing.

Presence vs. Problem-Solving

Presence is the ability to be fully with your child's experience without needing to change it immediately. It's the difference between "Let me fix this for you" and "I'm here with you while you experience this."

Most parents struggle with presence because it requires tolerating your child's distress without immediately jumping into action. But for dysregulated nervous systems, presence is often more regulating than problem-solving attempts.

Attunement: Matching Your Child's Internal Experience

Attunement is the ability to accurately perceive and reflect your child's internal emotional state. Dr. Daniel Siegel describes attunement as "feeling felt" by another person (Siegel and Bryson, 2012).

Attunement might sound like:

- "Your whole body is telling me this feels impossible right now."

- "I can see how frustrated your nervous system is with this situation."

- "It looks like your brain is working really hard and feeling overwhelmed."

Notice that these responses focus on the child's internal experience rather than the external problem. When children feel accurately seen and understood, their nervous systems begin to regulate.

Common Attunement Mistakes

Minimizing: "It's not that big of a deal" or "You'll be fine" dismisses the child's genuine experience and can increase dysregulation.

Rushing to solutions: "Let's just figure this out" or "Here's what you should do" skips the crucial step of acknowledging the child's current state.

Taking it personally: "Why are you being so difficult?" or "You're ruining our whole evening" makes the child responsible for the parent's emotional state.

Comparing: "Other kids don't have this problem" or "Your sister handles this just fine" invalidates the child's unique nervous system needs.

Practical Co-Regulation Techniques for Daily Use

Co-regulation is both an art and a science. While the basic principle—offering your regulated nervous system to support your child's dysregulated nervous system—remains constant, the specific techniques vary based on your child's age, temperament, and current state.

Environmental Co-Regulation

Sometimes the most powerful co-regulation happens through environmental modifications that support both nervous systems:

Lighting: Dim, warm lighting often supports regulation better than bright overhead lights *Sound:* Soft background music, nature sounds, or simply reducing competing noises *Space:* Creating physical closeness without crowding, having comfort items available

Movement: Gentle swaying, rocking, or walking together can be deeply regulating

Physical Co-Regulation

For children who tolerate and seek physical input, body-based co-regulation can be very effective:

Deep pressure: Firm hugs, weighted blankets, or gentle squeezing (always with the child's consent) *Rhythmic movement:* Rocking, swaying, or gentle bouncing *Breathing together:* Matching your child's breathing and gradually slowing your own *Progressive muscle relaxation:* Tensing and releasing muscle groups together

Twelve-year-old Emma found that lying under a weighted blanket with her mom nearby was the most effective co-regulation strategy. Her mom didn't try to talk through the problem or offer solutions—she just provided calm presence while Emma's nervous system borrowed her regulation.

Verbal Co-Regulation

The words you use during co-regulation matter less than the tone and intention behind them:

Validation: "This is really hard for you right now" *Normalization:* "It makes sense that your nervous system would react this way" *Partnership:* "We'll figure this out together" *Time orientation:* "This feeling won't last forever" *Capacity acknowledgment:* "Your nervous system is working as hard as it can"

Breathing as Co-Regulation

One of the most accessible co-regulation tools is your own breathing. When you consciously slow and deepen your breathing in your child's presence, their nervous system often naturally begins to match your rhythm.

You don't need to instruct your child to breathe differently—just focus on your own breathing and let their nervous system do the attunement naturally. This works because breathing patterns directly influence vagal tone and nervous system state.

Creative Co-Regulation Strategies

Art and creativity: Drawing, coloring, or creating together while processing difficult experiences *Music:* Singing, humming, or listening to calming music together *Nature:* Spending time outdoors, observing nature, or caring for plants or animals together *Storytelling:* Creating stories about characters who face similar challenges *Sensory activities:* Play-dough, kinetic sand, or other tactile experiences that engage the nervous system

When Co-Regulation Isn't Working: Troubleshooting Guide

Even with the best understanding and techniques, co-regulation doesn't always work smoothly. When your attempts at co-regulation seem to make things worse, it's usually because one of several common issues is interfering with the process.

Issue 1: You're Not Actually Regulated

The most common reason co-regulation fails is that you're trying to offer regulation you don't actually have. Children's sensitive nervous systems quickly detect when adult "calm" is forced or superficial.

Signs you might not be regulated:

- Feeling impatient for your child to "get better" quickly

- Using co-regulation techniques while internally frustrated

- Thinking about other things you need to do instead of being present

- Feeling annoyed that co-regulation is taking so long

Solutions:

- Take a few minutes to actually regulate your own nervous system first

- Use breathing, movement, or other techniques to find genuine regulation

- Ask for support from another adult if you're too activated to offer co-regulation

- Remember that co-regulation is a process, not a quick fix

Issue 2: Your Child's Tank Is Too Empty

Sometimes children's nervous systems are so depleted that they can't accept co-regulation until basic needs are met.

Consider whether your child needs:

- Food (blood sugar affects nervous system regulation)

- Sleep (exhaustion makes regulation nearly impossible)

- Movement (some children need physical activity before they can co-regulate)

- Sensory input (specific sensory needs might need to be met first)

- Medical attention (illness, pain, or medication effects can interfere with regulation)

Issue 3: The Approach Doesn't Match Your Child's Needs

Not all children co-regulate in the same way. Some need closeness, others need space. Some need talking, others need silence.

Physical approach mismatches:

- Offering hugs to a child who needs space to regulate

- Staying distant from a child who needs physical connection

- Talking when a child needs quiet presence

- Being silent when a child needs verbal processing

Timing mismatches:

- Trying to co-regulate too early (child still escalating)

- Waiting too long (child has moved into shutdown)

- Rushing the process (nervous systems need time to shift)

- Giving up too quickly (regulation sometimes takes longer than expected)

Issue 4: Environmental Factors Are Interfering

Sometimes the environment itself prevents effective co-regulation:

Sensory interference: Too much noise, light, or activity in the space
Social interference: Other family members, pets, or distractions
Spatial interference: Not enough privacy or too much crowding
Temporal interference: Time pressure or competing demands

Issue 5: Trauma or Trust Issues

For children who have experienced trauma or have had many experiences of adult dysregulation, accepting co-regulation can feel unsafe. These children might need:

- More time to build trust in your regulation

- Very gentle, non-demanding approaches

- Consistency in your responses over time

- Professional support to address underlying trauma

Problem-Solving Co-Regulation Challenges

When co-regulation isn't working, try this troubleshooting sequence:

1. *Check your own nervous system state* - Are you truly regulated enough to offer co-regulation?

2. *Assess basic needs* - Does your child need food, rest, movement, or medical attention?

3. *Evaluate the approach* - Does your co-regulation style match your child's current needs?

4. *Consider environmental factors* - Is something in the environment interfering with regulation?

5. *Review recent patterns* - Has something changed in your child's life that might be affecting their ability to co-regulate?

6. *Seek support if needed* - Sometimes professional help is necessary to understand complex regulation challenges

The Long-Term Benefits of Co-Regulation

When you consistently offer co-regulation to your neurodivergent child, you're not just helping them through individual difficult moments—you're literally building their capacity for self-regulation over time.

Building Neural Pathways for Regulation

Every co-regulation experience creates neural pathways in your child's brain that support future regulation. Dr. Allan Schore's research shows that the right brain develops through relational experiences, particularly co-regulation with caregivers (Schore, 2019).

Over time, children internalize the co-regulation experiences they receive. The calm, regulated voice of a parent becomes an internal resource the child can access independently.

Developing Internal Self-Compassion

Children who receive empathetic co-regulation during distress develop internal self-compassion. Instead of harsh self-criticism during difficult moments, they learn to offer themselves the same kindness they received from caregivers.

Fifteen-year-old Jordan, who had received years of co-regulation support, described his internal process during a stressful exam: "I could hear my mom's voice in my head saying 'Your nervous system is working hard right now, and that makes sense.' It helped me stay calmer instead of getting mad at myself for being anxious."

Strengthening Family Relationships

Co-regulation builds trust and connection between family members. When children experience being truly seen and supported during their most difficult moments, it creates lasting bonds that strengthen relationships throughout life.

Preparing for Adult Relationships

The capacity to both receive and offer co-regulation becomes crucial for adult relationships. Children who learn these skills through family experiences are better equipped to form healthy partnerships and friendships throughout life.

Teaching Your Child About Co-Regulation

As children develop, you can help them understand the co-regulation process, making them active participants rather than passive recipients.

Age-Appropriate Explanations

Ages 3-6: "Sometimes when your feelings are really big, my calm feelings can help your feelings get smaller. That's what families do—we help each other."

Ages 7-11: "When your nervous system gets overwhelmed, my nervous system can help yours remember how to feel safe again. It's like your brain borrowing my brain's calmness."

Ages 12+: "Co-regulation is when one person's nervous system helps another person's nervous system find balance. We all need this throughout our lives—it's not something you outgrow."

Teaching Self-Advocacy

As children understand co-regulation, they can begin asking for it directly:

- "I think my nervous system needs to borrow yours right now"

- "Can you help me regulate? I'm feeling overwhelmed"

- "I need some co-regulation before we try to solve this problem"

This self-advocacy becomes a lifelong skill for accessing support in relationships.

The Parent-Child Co-Regulation Dance

Co-regulation between you and your neurodivergent child is indeed a dance—sometimes flowing smoothly, sometimes stepping on each other's toes, always requiring attention to rhythm, timing, and mutual attunement.

Like any dance, it improves with practice. The more you understand your child's unique nervous system patterns and your own regulation needs, the more skilled you become at offering the specific type of co-regulation your child needs in different moments.

This dance isn't always easy. Parenting a neurodivergent child requires you to be emotionally available during some of your most challenging moments. But the investment pays dividends not just in immediate regulation, but in your child's long-term capacity for emotional health and relationships.

Remember that co-regulation is not about perfection. You don't need to be perfectly regulated all the time, and your child doesn't need to regulate quickly or smoothly every time. What matters is the overall pattern of connection, understanding, and nervous system support over time.

When Maya's mom Jennifer learned about co-regulation, it transformed their homework battles. Instead of trying to fix Maya's math problems while Maya was dysregulated, Jennifer first offered co-regulation: "Your nervous system is telling you this feels impossible right now. That makes total sense."

She sat with Maya, offering her calm presence without trying to solve anything. Only after Maya's breathing slowed and her body relaxed did they address the math homework—and by then, Maya could actually access her thinking brain to engage with the problems.

The homework still wasn't easy, but the relationship was preserved. Maya learned that her mom understood her struggles and would help her regulate before expecting performance. This foundation of safety and connection made future challenges more manageable for both of them.

Your nervous system is one of the most powerful tools you have for supporting your neurodivergent child. When you understand co-regulation and develop your capacity to offer it consistently, you provide your child with the fundamental safety and connection they need to navigate a world that often feels threatening to their sensitive nervous system.

This is the foundation upon which everything else builds: not perfect behavior, but regulated connection. Not elimination of all challenges, but the safety to face challenges together. Not independence at any cost, but interdependence that honors both your needs and your child's unique neurobiology.

Chapter 5: Morning Routines That Set the Nervous System for Success

At 6:47 AM, the Chen household was already in crisis mode. Eight-year-old Marcus sat at the breakfast table in his underwear, tears streaming down his face because his favorite cereal was gone. His mom Jennifer was frantically searching through cabinets while simultaneously trying to pack lunch and find matching socks. His dad David was getting increasingly frustrated as he watched the clock tick toward the school bus arrival.

"Marcus, you need to get dressed NOW!" David called from the hallway. "The bus will be here in ten minutes!"

But Marcus couldn't get dressed. His nervous system had been in fight-or-flight mode since the moment he discovered the empty cereal box, and every adult demand was pushing him deeper into dysregulation. By the time the school bus arrived, Marcus was sobbing, Jennifer was exhausted, and David was questioning every parenting decision they'd ever made.

Sound familiar? For families with neurodivergent children, mornings can feel like navigating an emotional minefield. But here's what the Chen family didn't understand: Marcus's meltdown wasn't really about cereal. It was about a nervous system that woke up already vulnerable and encountered stressor after stressor with no regulation support.

Why Mornings Are Make-or-Break for Neurodivergent Children

Morning routines set the neurobiological tone for the entire day. For neurodivergent children, whose nervous systems are already more sensitive to stress and change, chaotic mornings can create a dysregulation spiral that affects learning, behavior, and family relationships for hours.

The Vulnerable Morning Nervous System

Dr. Matthew Walker's research on sleep and brain function reveals that all nervous systems are more vulnerable upon waking (Walker, 2017). During sleep, our brains process the previous day's experiences, consolidate memories, and reset stress hormone levels. But for neurodivergent children, this reset process is often incomplete or disrupted.

Children with ADHD frequently have differences in their circadian rhythms that make mornings particularly challenging (Coogan & McGowan, 2017). Their natural sleep-wake cycles may be delayed, meaning they're biologically programmed to sleep later and wake later than typical school schedules require.

Autistic children often experience what researchers call "morning cortisol dysregulation"—their stress hormone levels don't follow the typical pattern of being highest in the morning and declining throughout the day (Corbett et al., 2008). This can leave them feeling either overwhelmed by high cortisol or sluggish from low cortisol first thing in the morning.

The Cascade Effect of Morning Stress

When neurodivergent children start their day in a dysregulated state, it creates what Dr. Bruce Perry calls a "cascade effect" (Perry & Szalavitz, 2007). Early morning stress triggers the release of stress hormones that take hours to clear from their systems. This means a difficult morning can affect:

- Attention and focus at school
- Emotional regulation throughout the day
- Social interactions with peers and teachers
- Ability to handle unexpected changes or challenges
- Family relationships in the evening
- Sleep quality the following night

Ten-year-old Sofia's parents tracked her behavior patterns for two months and discovered a clear correlation: difficult mornings predicted difficult days at school, which led to after-school meltdowns, which created bedtime battles, which resulted in poor sleep and more difficult mornings. Breaking this cycle required understanding that morning regulation was the foundation for everything else.

The Window of Tolerance in the Morning

Most neurodivergent children wake up with a narrower window of tolerance than they'll have later in the day. Their nervous systems need time and support to gradually expand this window, but typical morning routines often do the opposite—they bombard children with demands, transitions, and sensory input before their systems are ready to handle them.

Research by Dr. Megan Gerdes shows that children with sensory processing differences are most sensitive to sensory input within the first two hours of waking (Gerdes et al., 2012). The fluorescent bathroom lights that don't bother them at bedtime can trigger dysregulation in the morning. The breakfast sounds that seem normal later in the day can feel overwhelming when their auditory system is still sensitive.

Pre-Wake Nervous System Preparation Strategies

The most effective morning routines actually begin the night before. Preparing your child's nervous system for the morning transition can prevent many regulation challenges before they start.

Environmental Pre-Staging

Creating a sensory-supportive wake-up environment helps your child's nervous system ease into consciousness gradually rather than being jolted into alertness.

Lighting preparation: Install dimmer switches or use lamps instead of overhead lights for gentler wake-up illumination. Many families find that gradual light-awakening alarm clocks help their children's nervous systems transition from sleep more smoothly.

Sound considerations: Minimize jarring alarm sounds. Nature sounds, gentle music, or gradually increasing volume can support nervous system regulation better than sudden, loud alarms.

Temperature comfort: Ensure your child's room is at a comfortable temperature for waking. Being too hot or cold can trigger stress responses before consciousness even returns.

Visual organization: Lay out clothes, backpack, and other morning necessities the night before so your child's visual system isn't overwhelmed by decisions and searching first thing in the morning.

Twelve-year-old Emma's family discovered that her morning meltdowns significantly decreased when they installed blackout curtains with a wake-up light that gradually brightened over 20 minutes. Her light-sensitive nervous system could ease into the day rather than being shocked into alertness.

The Pre-Wake Routine

Many successful families develop pre-wake routines that prepare both the environment and the child's nervous system for morning transitions.

Gentle awakening: Instead of sudden wake-up calls, try sitting near your child's bed and speaking softly, offering gentle touch (if they tolerate it), or using their preferred wake-up method consistently.

Transition time: Build in extra time between waking and first demands. Some children need 10-15 minutes of quiet consciousness before they can handle any requests or decisions.

Predictable sequence: Establish the same wake-up sequence every day so your child's nervous system knows what to expect and can prepare accordingly.

Connection before demands: Offer connection and co-regulation before any task demands. This might be a few minutes of snuggling, sharing something you're looking forward to about the day, or simply sitting together quietly.

Sensory-Friendly Morning Sequences

Traditional morning routines are often sensory disasters for neurodivergent children. Creating sensory-supportive sequences can transform mornings from battles into successful regulation-building experiences.

The Sensory Systems Morning Check-In

Understanding how each sensory system affects your child's morning regulation helps you create targeted supports:

Visual system morning support: Use dim lighting initially, minimize visual clutter, provide visual schedules, offer sunglasses if needed for transitions to brighter environments.

Auditory system morning support: Keep noise levels low, eliminate unnecessary background sounds (like morning news), use preferred music or nature sounds, provide noise-reducing headphones if needed.

Tactile system morning support: Allow for preferred textures in clothing and blankets, provide deep pressure if your child seeks it, respect tactile sensitivities around personal care tasks.

Proprioceptive system morning support: Include heavy work activities like carrying a weighted backpack around the house, doing wall push-ups, or helping carry laundry.

Vestibular system morning support: Incorporate gentle movement like swaying, rocking, or spinning if your child finds it regulating.

Nine-year-old David needed proprioceptive input to regulate his ADHD nervous system in the mornings. His family created a "morning obstacle course" in their hallway—crawling under the dining room table, doing bear walks down the hall, and carrying his heavy backpack to the front door. These activities provided the sensory input his nervous system needed to focus for the day.

Creating Sensory-Smart Morning Spaces

The wake-up space: Your child's bedroom should support gentle transition from sleep to wakefulness. This might mean softer lighting, organized visual spaces, comfortable temperatures, and minimal overwhelming sensory input.

The bathroom space: Many morning battles happen around personal care tasks. Consider the sensory impact of bathroom lighting (often harsh fluorescent), echoing sounds, cold surfaces, and the tactile demands of washing and brushing.

The kitchen space: Breakfast spaces can be sensory overwhelming with appliance sounds, competing smells, bright lighting, and social demands. Think about how to make this space more regulation-supportive.

The transition spaces: Hallways, entryways, and car spaces all have sensory demands. Consider lighting, sound, visual organization, and spatial flow as your child moves through morning transitions.

Accommodating Sensory Preferences

Rather than fighting against your child's sensory needs, morning routines work best when they accommodate and work with these neurobiological differences.

Clothing accommodations: Allow extra time for finding comfortable clothing, remove tags and seams when possible, respect texture preferences, consider seamless socks and soft fabrics.

Food accommodations: Honor food preferences and sensitivities while maintaining nutrition. This might mean having backup preferred foods available, considering textures and temperatures, and avoiding battles over food variety first thing in the morning.

Personal care accommodations: Modify brushing, washing, and grooming tasks to work with your child's tactile system. This might mean different toothbrush textures, adjustable water temperature, or alternative hair-brushing techniques.

Visual Schedules and Predictability Tools

Neurodivergent nervous systems crave predictability. Visual schedules and other predictability tools help children feel safe by knowing what to expect and when to expect it.

The Neuroscience of Predictability

Dr. Lisa Feldman Barrett's research on predictive brain processing shows that our brains are constantly trying to predict what will happen next based on past experiences (Barrett, 2017). When predictions are accurate, we feel safe and regulated. When predictions are wrong, our nervous systems activate stress responses.

For neurodivergent children, whose nervous systems are already more sensitive to uncertainty, predictable morning routines provide crucial nervous system safety. Visual schedules make abstract time concepts concrete and help children prepare mentally for each step of their morning.

Creating Effective Visual Schedules

Age-appropriate design: Younger children might need picture schedules, while older children can handle written schedules or even digital formats. The key is matching the format to your child's current developmental and visual processing abilities.

Individual customization: Generic morning schedules rarely work as well as schedules customized to your family's specific routine and your child's unique needs.

Clear sequence indicators: Use numbers, arrows, or other visual indicators to show the order of morning activities. Some children also benefit from time estimates for each activity.

Built-in flexibility: Include some choice points in your schedule so children feel agency within the structure. This might be "choose breakfast option A or B" or "complete personal care in bedroom or bathroom."

Seven-year-old Marcus's family created a morning visual schedule using photographs of Marcus doing each activity. The schedule included getting dressed (photo of Marcus putting on his shirt), eating breakfast (photo of Marcus at the table), brushing teeth (photo of Marcus with his toothbrush), and getting his backpack (photo of Marcus by the front door). Having this visual roadmap reduced his morning anxiety significantly.

Digital and Interactive Tools

Morning apps: Several apps are designed specifically for morning routines, allowing children to check off completed tasks and see their progress visually.

Voice assistants: Some families use smart speakers to provide gentle reminders and play preferred wake-up music or sounds.

Timer tools: Visual timers can help children understand how much time they have for each morning activity without the anxiety of abstract time pressure.

Checklist systems: Some children respond well to morning checklists they can check off, providing a sense of accomplishment and progress tracking.

Backup Plans and Flexibility

Even the best visual schedules need backup plans for off-days, illness, schedule changes, or when your child's nervous system is having a particularly sensitive morning.

Modified routines: Create abbreviated versions of your morning routine for days when your child's window of tolerance is especially narrow.

Emergency protocols: Have plans for mornings when everything goes wrong—what gets prioritized, what can be skipped, and how to preserve regulation even when running late.

Seasonal adjustments: Morning routines often need adjustment for daylight changes, temperature differences, and seasonal schedule variations.

Nutrition and Nervous System Regulation

The relationship between nutrition and nervous system regulation is particularly important for neurodivergent children, whose systems may be more sensitive to blood sugar fluctuations, food sensitivities, and nutritional deficiencies.

Blood Sugar and Behavior

Research by Dr. Bonnie Kaplan shows that blood sugar instability can significantly impact attention, mood, and behavior regulation, particularly in children with ADHD (Kaplan et al., 2004). Many children wake up with low blood sugar after 10-12 hours without food, and their nervous systems remain dysregulated until blood sugar stabilizes.

Protein-rich breakfasts: Including protein in morning meals helps stabilize blood sugar and provides sustained energy for nervous system regulation. This might be eggs, nut butters, Greek yogurt, or protein smoothies.

Complex carbohydrates: Whole grains, fruits, and vegetables provide steady glucose release rather than the spikes and crashes that come from simple sugars and refined carbohydrates.

Avoiding dysregulating foods: Many families find that artificial colors, high sugar cereals, and processed foods can trigger hyperactivity or other regulation challenges in their neurodivergent children.

Timing and Nervous System States

Early morning nutrition: Some children need small snacks immediately upon waking before they can handle getting dressed or other demands. Others need time to wake up before eating feels comfortable.

Pre-school fueling: Ensuring adequate nutrition before school starts helps maintain nervous system regulation during the cognitive and social demands of the classroom.

Hydration support: Dehydration can significantly impact attention and behavior. Some children need reminders and support to drink adequate water in the morning.

Eleven-year-old Jordan's parents noticed that mornings went more smoothly when he had a protein smoothie within 30 minutes of waking. His ADHD nervous system needed the blood sugar stability that protein provided, and the smoothie format worked with his oral motor preferences better than solid breakfast foods.

Working with Food Sensitivities and Preferences

Many neurodivergent children have strong food preferences that parents worry about nutritionally. However, research shows that fighting food battles in the morning often creates more regulation problems than nutritional solutions.

Honoring preferences: Working within your child's food preferences while gradually expanding options tends to be more successful than forcing variety first thing in the morning.

Nutritional creativity: Finding ways to add nutrition to preferred foods rather than eliminating preferred foods and substituting new ones.

Supplement considerations: Some families work with healthcare providers to address nutritional gaps through supplements rather than forcing food battles every morning.

Eating environment: Consider the sensory aspects of breakfast—lighting, sounds, textures, smells, and social demands—that might be affecting your child's ability to eat comfortably.

Troubleshooting Common Morning Challenges

Even with the best understanding and preparation, morning challenges will still arise. Having troubleshooting strategies helps you respond effectively rather than reactively when things don't go as planned.

The "Nothing is Working" Morning

Some mornings, your child's nervous system is simply too dysregulated for your usual routine to be effective. This might be due to poor sleep, illness, stress from the previous day, or simply nervous system variability.

Recognize early signs: Learn to identify when your child's nervous system is having a particularly vulnerable morning and adjust expectations accordingly.

Have a backup plan: Create simplified morning routines for off-days that prioritize nervous system regulation over completing all typical tasks.

Focus on connection: When routines aren't working, prioritize emotional connection and co-regulation over task completion.

Communicate with school: Develop communication systems with teachers so they understand when your child arrives at school already dysregulated and might need extra support.

The Time Pressure Problem

Running late creates stress for everyone's nervous systems, but it's particularly challenging for neurodivergent children who need extra time for transitions and regulation.

Build in buffer time: Most families underestimate how much time their neurodivergent child needs for morning tasks. Building in extra time reduces pressure for everyone.

Identify time bottlenecks: Track which morning activities consistently take longer than expected and adjust timing accordingly.

Prepare the night before: The more that can be done the evening before, the less pressure exists in the morning time crunch.

Priority systems: Identify which morning tasks are truly essential and which can be modified or skipped if time runs short.

The Sibling Dynamic Challenge

When families have both neurodivergent and neurotypical children, morning routines need to support everyone's needs without creating resentment or additional stress.

Individual accommodations: Different children may need different wake-up times, routines, or supports based on their neurobiological needs.

Sibling education: Help neurotypical siblings understand why their neurodivergent sibling might need different supports without feeling that accommodations are unfair.

Family teamwork: Create morning routines where family members support each other rather than compete for parental attention or resources.

Separate spaces: Sometimes siblings need separate spaces for morning routines to reduce overwhelm and interpersonal stress.

The Transition to School Challenge

The transition from home to school can be particularly difficult for neurodivergent children, whose nervous systems might feel safe at home but threatened by the school environment.

Gradual transitions: Some children benefit from gradual transitions rather than abrupt shifts from home to school mode.

Transition objects: Comfort items, photos, or other connections to home can help ease the nervous system transition to school.

Communication systems: Develop ways for your child to communicate their morning regulation state to teachers so appropriate supports can be provided.

School environment preparation: Work with teachers to ensure the classroom environment supports rather than threatens your child's morning regulation state.

The Morning Regulation Investment

Creating nervous system-supportive morning routines requires investment—in time, energy, environmental modifications, and sometimes significant changes to family patterns. But families consistently report that this investment pays enormous dividends in daily quality of life, family relationships, and their child's long-term development.

Short-Term Benefits

Reduced morning stress: Both children and parents experience less daily stress when mornings support rather than threaten nervous system regulation.

Improved school performance: Children who arrive at school regulated are better able to learn, focus, and interact positively with peers and teachers.

Better family relationships: When mornings aren't battlegrounds, families can connect positively and start each day with love rather than conflict.

Increased confidence: Children who experience morning success develop confidence in their ability to manage daily challenges.

Long-Term Benefits

Self-regulation skills: Children who receive morning nervous system support gradually develop their own internal regulation strategies.

Understanding of personal needs: Through supported morning routines, children learn to identify and advocate for their own nervous system needs.

Positive associations: Creating positive morning experiences helps children develop healthy relationships with daily routines and self-care.

Life skills development: Structured, supportive morning routines teach organizational skills, time management, and personal responsibility within a framework that honors neurobiological needs.

Making Morning Routines Work for Your Family

Remember that there's no perfect morning routine that works for every neurodivergent child or every family. The most effective morning routines are those that honor your child's unique nervous system needs while fitting within your family's practical constraints.

Start Small and Build

Choose one change: Rather than overhauling your entire morning routine, choose one small change that addresses your biggest morning challenge.

Track what works: Pay attention to which modifications support your child's regulation and which don't make a significant difference.

Adjust and refine: Morning routines often need ongoing adjustments as children grow, seasons change, and family circumstances shift.

Celebrate progress: Notice and celebrate small improvements rather than waiting for perfect mornings to acknowledge success.

Individual Family Considerations

Work schedules: Morning routines must work within the reality of parent work schedules and transportation needs.

Multiple children: Families with several children need routines that support everyone without creating additional chaos.

Living situations: Apartment living, shared spaces, or other housing considerations might affect what morning modifications are possible.

Resource limitations: Effective morning routines can be created within any budget by focusing on understanding and accommodation rather than expensive products or major home modifications.

The Chen family from our opening story discovered that Marcus's morning meltdowns weren't really about cereal availability—they were about his autistic nervous system needing predictability and regulation support. They made three simple changes: They prepared breakfast options the night before, created a visual morning schedule, and built in 15 minutes of connection time before any task demands.

Six months later, their mornings transformed from crisis management to connection opportunities. Marcus still had occasional difficult mornings, but they were the exception rather than the rule. More importantly, the whole family started each day feeling connected and confident rather than stressed and exhausted.

Your child's morning behavior isn't defiance or difficulty—it's communication from their nervous system about what they need to feel safe and regulated for the day ahead. When you understand morning routines through a nervous system lens, you can create the supports your child needs to start each day successfully, building a foundation for learning, growth, and positive family relationships that benefits everyone.

Chapter 6: School Transitions and Nervous System Preparation

At 3:15 PM, nine-year-old Riley would transform from the "well-behaved" student her teachers knew into someone her parents barely recognized. The moment she got in the car, the meltdowns would begin. Screaming about homework she hadn't even seen yet. Sobbing about friends who had been perfectly nice to her. Complete emotional collapse over having to put on her seatbelt.

"How can she be so good at school and so difficult at home?" Riley's parents wondered. They began dreading school pickup, knowing that the transition from school to home would trigger hours of dysregulation that would affect the entire family's evening.

What Riley's parents didn't understand was that their daughter had been using every ounce of her nervous system capacity to appear regulated at school all day. By pickup time, her system was completely depleted, and the transition from one environment to another was the final stressor that pushed her into complete overwhelm.

Riley wasn't being manipulative or saving her worst behavior for the people who loved her most. She was experiencing what researchers call "transition shock"—the neurobiological reality that transitions are among the most challenging experiences for neurodivergent nervous systems.

The Hidden Stress of Transitions for Neurodivergent Children

Transitions seem simple to neurotypical brains: finish one activity, move to another location, start a new activity. But for neurodivergent children, each transition involves complex neurobiological processes that can easily trigger stress responses.

The Neurobiology of Transitions

Dr. Ross Greene's research shows that transitions require multiple executive function skills simultaneously: stopping one activity, remembering what comes next, organizing materials, managing time awareness, adapting to new environmental demands, and initiating new behaviors (Greene, 2014). For children whose executive function systems are still developing or function differently, transitions can be overwhelming.

Brain imaging studies reveal that during transitions, multiple brain networks must coordinate effectively. The default mode network must quiet down, the attention network must engage, and the executive control network must manage the shift (Menon, 2011). For neurodivergent brains, this coordination often requires more effort and energy than it does for neurotypical brains.

The Sensory Challenge of Environmental Shifts

Every environment has its own sensory signature—lighting, sounds, smells, textures, spatial organization, and social dynamics. When neurodivergent children transition between environments, their sensitive nervous systems must rapidly adjust to entirely new sensory demands.

Consider the transition from classroom to cafeteria: fluorescent classroom lights to brighter cafeteria lighting, quiet work sounds to loud social chatter, organized desk space to crowded lunch tables, predictable classroom routines to unpredictable social dynamics. For a sensory-sensitive nervous system, this isn't just a change of location—it's a complete sensory system reorganization that can trigger fight-or-flight responses.

The Social and Emotional Load of Transitions

School transitions also involve shifting social and emotional demands. The social rules for hallway behavior differ from classroom rules, which differ from playground rules, which differ from bus rules. Each environment has its own emotional climate, expectations, and interpersonal dynamics.

Dr. Michelle Garcia Winner's research on social thinking shows that neurodivergent children often struggle with the rapid social cognitive demands of transition periods (Winner, 2007). They must quickly assess new social contexts, adjust their behavior accordingly, and navigate interpersonal interactions that change with each environment.

Twelve-year-old Alex described school transitions this way: "It's like my brain has to completely reboot every time we change classes. By the time I figure out what this new place expects from me, we're already moving somewhere else."

Before-School Nervous System Priming Techniques

Preparing your child's nervous system for the school day can significantly improve their ability to handle school transitions successfully. This preparation begins at home and creates a foundation of regulation that supports them throughout the day.

Morning Nervous System Assessment

Before leaving for school, many families find it helpful to do a quick nervous system check-in with their child. This isn't about forcing conversation but about gauging your child's regulation state and adjusting support accordingly.

Green zone indicators: Your child seems calm, can make eye contact, responds to questions appropriately, handles typical morning tasks without significant distress.

Yellow zone indicators: Your child seems slightly more activated or withdrawn than usual, might be more sensitive to sensory input, or shows early signs of stress but is still manageable.

Red zone indicators: Your child is already showing signs of significant dysregulation—hyperactivity, emotional overwhelm, shutdown behaviors, or inability to handle normal morning demands.

When eight-year-old Maya was in her green zone, she could handle typical school preparation and transition. When she was in her yellow zone, her parents would provide extra regulation support and alert her teacher that she might need additional accommodations. When she was in her red zone, they would consider whether she was well enough for a full school day or if modifications were needed.

Pre-School Regulation Activities

Sensory preparation: Some children benefit from specific sensory input before school to help their nervous systems prepare for the sensory demands of the school environment. This might include proprioceptive activities (heavy work), vestibular input (swinging or spinning), or calming sensory activities (deep pressure or soft music).

Connection and co-regulation: Spending a few minutes in connected, regulated interaction with your child can help their nervous system feel safe and supported before facing school challenges.

Predictability support: Reviewing the school day schedule, discussing any changes or special events, and preparing for potential challenges helps the nervous system feel safer about upcoming transitions.

Confidence building: Reminding your child of their strengths, recent successes, and available supports helps them approach the school day from a more regulated, confident state.

The Transition from Home to School

The actual transition from home to school can be supported through specific strategies that honor the nervous system's need for gradual adjustment rather than abrupt shifts.

Car ride regulation: Use the car ride to school as a bridge between home and school environments. This might involve listening to calming music, doing breathing exercises together, or having quiet conversation about the upcoming day.

Arrival preparation: Some children need a few minutes in the car upon school arrival to prepare their nervous systems for the transition into the building. Rushing from car to classroom can trigger dysregulation before the day even begins.

School entry support: Work with school staff to create supportive entry routines. This might involve arriving a few minutes early to avoid crowded hallways, having a designated adult to check in with, or having a quiet space to transition before joining the full classroom environment.

After-School Decompression Protocols

For many neurodivergent children, the end of the school day represents both relief and challenge. Relief that they can stop "masking" or working so hard to appear regulated, but challenge because their nervous systems are often depleted and transitions remain difficult.

Understanding After-School Collapse

Dr. Mona Delahooke explains that many neurodivergent children experience "after-school restraint collapse"—the phenomenon of holding it together all day at school and then completely falling apart at home (Delahooke, 2019). This isn't manipulation or saving bad behavior for parents—it's nervous system biology.

Think of your child's nervous system like a phone battery. They start the day at 100%, but school demands drain the battery throughout the day. By pickup time, they're running on 5% battery, and any additional demand can cause complete system shutdown.

Signs of nervous system depletion:

- Immediate emotional meltdowns upon seeing parents
- Inability to handle simple requests or transitions
- Sensory sensitivity that seems worse than usual
- Physical exhaustion or hyperactivity

- Difficulty communicating needs or experiences

- Regression to younger behaviors

Creating Decompression Time

Most neurodivergent children need significant decompression time after school before they can handle homework, chores, social activities, or family interactions effectively.

Immediate decompression: The first 30-60 minutes after school should focus entirely on nervous system regulation rather than productivity or information gathering. This means no questions about the school day, no demands for homework or chores, and no social expectations.

Environmental support: Create a calm, sensory-supportive environment for after-school decompression. This might involve dim lighting, quiet spaces, comfort items, or preferred sensory activities.

Individual decompression needs: Some children need complete alone time to decompress, while others need quiet connection with parents. Some need movement activities, while others need rest. Understanding your child's unique decompression needs is crucial.

Family education: Help family members understand that after-school decompression isn't optional—it's a neurobiological necessity that benefits everyone by preventing evening meltdowns and family stress.

Ten-year-old Jordan needed 45 minutes of complete quiet time in his bedroom after school before he could handle any family interactions. His parents initially worried that this was antisocial behavior, but they discovered that respecting his decompression needs actually led to more positive family time later in the evening.

The School-to-Home Transition

Car ride decompression: Use the car ride home as transition time rather than information-gathering time. Many parents want to ask about the school day immediately, but children's nervous systems often need quiet processing time first.

Home arrival routines: Create predictable routines for arriving home that support nervous system regulation. This might involve changing into comfortable clothes, having a snack, or spending time in a preferred space.

Delayed information gathering: Wait until your child's nervous system has had time to regulate before asking about their school day. You'll get more accurate and complete information from a regulated nervous system than from a depleted one.

Sibling considerations: If you have multiple children, their after-school decompression needs might conflict. Some families need to create separate spaces or schedules to honor everyone's regulation requirements.

Working with Teachers to Understand Nervous System Needs

Many teachers are well-intentioned but lack understanding of how nervous system regulation affects learning and behavior. Educating your child's educational team about nervous system needs can create more supportive school experiences.

Communicating Nervous System Concepts

Use accessible language: Rather than overwhelming teachers with technical polyvagal theory, focus on practical impacts they can observe and support.

Focus on learning impact: Help teachers understand that supporting nervous system regulation isn't "babying" children—it's creating conditions where learning can actually occur.

Provide specific strategies: Rather than just asking for "understanding," provide specific strategies that teachers can implement within their classroom constraints.

Share success stories: When nervous system supports lead to improved learning or behavior, share these successes with teachers to reinforce the value of the accommodations.

Sample Teacher Communication

"Hi Ms. Johnson,

I wanted to share some information about Emma that might help her succeed in your classroom. Emma has a nervous system that's very sensitive to stress and sensory input. When she feels overwhelmed, she might appear defiant or distracted, but she's actually having trouble accessing her thinking brain.

A few things that help Emma stay regulated for learning:

- A 2-minute warning before transitions
- A quiet space to go when feeling overwhelmed
- Permission to use fidget tools during instruction
- Understanding that her best learning happens when she feels calm and safe

I'm happy to discuss this further and provide any additional information that would be helpful."

Building Collaborative Relationships

Start with strengths: Begin conversations by acknowledging what's working well and the teacher's positive intentions.

Provide education gradually: Rather than overwhelming teachers with information, provide nervous system education in small, applicable pieces over time.

Offer resources: Share articles, books, or training opportunities that might help teachers understand neurodivergent nervous systems better.

Problem-solve together: Approach challenges as collaborative problem-solving opportunities rather than demands for specific accommodations.

IEP/504 Plan Accommodations from a Polyvagal Perspective

Traditional special education accommodations often focus on behavioral management or academic modifications without addressing the underlying nervous system needs that drive both behavior and learning challenges.

Nervous System-Informed Accommodation Categories

Environmental modifications:

- Preferential seating away from high-traffic areas or sensory distractions
- Access to noise-reducing headphones or sunglasses
- Alternative lighting options when possible
- Quiet space access for regulation breaks

Transition supports:

- Advanced warning before transitions (2-5 minute warnings)
- Visual schedules for daily routines and schedule changes
- Transition objects or tools to carry between environments
- Modified transition expectations (extra time, alternative routes)

Regulation supports:

- Scheduled movement breaks throughout the day
- Access to fidget tools or sensory supports
- Permission to take regulation breaks as needed
- Adult check-ins during stressful transitions

Communication accommodations:

- Recognition that behavior communicates nervous system state

- Alternative ways to communicate needs when verbal communication is difficult

- Understanding that compliance difficulties may indicate nervous system overwhelm

- Modified expectations during dysregulated states

Sample IEP/504 Language

Instead of: "Student will remain in seat during instruction." Try: "Student will have access to alternative seating options and movement breaks to support nervous system regulation for optimal learning."

Instead of: "Student will complete transitions within expected timeframes." Try: "Student will receive transition warnings and supports to allow nervous system preparation for environmental changes."

Instead of: "Student will ask for help appropriately." Try: "Student will have multiple ways to communicate nervous system overwhelm and request regulation support."

Advocating for Nervous System Accommodations

Educate the team: Provide information about how nervous system regulation affects learning and behavior.

Connect to academic goals: Show how nervous system supports directly impact your child's ability to achieve academic and behavioral goals.

Provide specific language: Draft accommodation language that reflects nervous system understanding rather than just behavioral compliance.

Monitor and adjust: Regularly review whether accommodations are actually supporting nervous system regulation or if adjustments are needed.

Summer Break and School Year Preparation Strategies

The transition between school years presents unique nervous system challenges. Extended breaks can allow for nervous system recovery but may also create anxiety about returning to school demands.

Summer Nervous System Recovery

Reduced demands: Many families find that removing academic and social pressures during summer allows their child's nervous system to recover from the cumulative stress of the school year.

Intensive skill building: Some children benefit from working on regulation skills during summer when there's less pressure and more time for practice.

Maintaining some structure: While reducing demands is important, maintaining some routine and structure helps prevent the anxiety that can come from completely unstructured time.

Preparation for return: Gradually reintroducing school-like demands as the new school year approaches can help the nervous system prepare for increased expectations.

New School Year Preparation

Environmental familiarization: Visiting new classrooms, meeting new teachers, and becoming familiar with new routines before the school year starts can reduce nervous system activation on the first day.

Communication with new staff: Ensuring that new teachers and staff understand your child's nervous system needs from the beginning of the year.

Gradual schedule increases: Some families find it helpful to gradually increase academic and social demands during the first few weeks of school rather than expecting immediate full capacity.

Support system activation: Ensuring that all support systems (accommodations, communication plans, regulation tools) are in place before challenges arise.

Fifteen-year-old Sam's family learned that he needed a two-week "soft start" to each school year. During these weeks, they focused on helping his nervous system adjust to the sensory and social demands of school while keeping academic expectations minimal. This approach led to much more successful school years than when they expected him to immediately function at full capacity.

Creating School Success Through Nervous System Support

Supporting your neurodivergent child's school transitions isn't about eliminating all challenges or making school effortless. It's about understanding how their nervous system processes transitions and providing the supports they need to access their learning capacity within school environments.

The Long-Term Perspective

Building capacity over time: With appropriate nervous system supports, many children gradually develop increased capacity for handling school transitions and demands.

Self-advocacy development: Children who understand their nervous system needs can learn to communicate these needs to teachers and advocate for appropriate supports.

Positive school associations: When school feels safe to the nervous system, children can develop positive associations with learning and social interaction that benefit them throughout life.

Family stress reduction: Supporting school transitions effectively reduces family stress and improves everyone's quality of life.

The Ripple Effects

When Riley's parents understood that her after-school meltdowns were nervous system depletion rather than behavioral choices, they completely changed their approach. Instead of trying to problem-solve her school day immediately, they created a one-hour decompression protocol: comfortable clothes, preferred snack, quiet music, and no demands or questions.

The results were remarkable. Not only did the after-school meltdowns decrease dramatically, but Riley began sharing information about her school day voluntarily once her nervous system had time to regulate. Her evening homework sessions became more manageable because she wasn't starting from a depleted state. Even her sleep improved because she wasn't going to bed still activated from afternoon stress.

Most importantly, Riley began to understand her own nervous system needs. She started asking for "quiet time" when she felt overwhelmed and learned to recognize when she needed regulation support. These self-awareness skills served her well throughout her educational journey and into adulthood.

Your child's school transition challenges aren't behavioral problems that need to be fixed—they're nervous system communications that need to be understood and supported. When you approach school transitions through a polyvagal lens, you can create the conditions your child needs to access their learning capacity, develop positive school relationships, and build self-regulation skills that will serve them throughout their educational journey and beyond.

The goal isn't perfect transitions or elimination of all school challenges. The goal is understanding your child's nervous system well enough to provide effective support, advocate for appropriate accommodations, and help your child develop their own capacity for navigating the complex sensory, social, and academic demands of educational environments.

Chapter 7: Homework Without the Meltdown

Academic Regulation Strategies

By 4:30 PM, the Henderson kitchen table had become a battlefield. Ten-year-old Ethan sat slumped in his chair, math worksheet untouched, tears streaming down his face. "I can't do this! My brain is broken! I hate math!"

His mom Sarah felt her own stress rising as she looked at the simple addition problems that Ethan had mastered just last week. "Come on, Ethan. You know how to do this. Just try the first one."

But Ethan's response was to push the worksheet away and put his head down on the table. "I can't! My brain won't work! Everything looks wrong!"

What Sarah didn't understand was that Ethan's brain wasn't broken— it was dysregulated. After seven hours of managing his ADHD nervous system in the classroom environment, coming home to immediate academic demands pushed him completely outside his window of tolerance. His thinking brain was offline, making the math problems as impossible as Sarah asking him to solve calculus.

The tragedy is that Ethan actually could do the math when his nervous system was regulated. But traditional homework approaches ignore the neurobiological reality that learning requires a regulated nervous system, and for neurodivergent children, regulation often needs intensive support before academic tasks become possible.

Why Traditional Homework Approaches Fail Neurodivergent Children

Most homework strategies assume that children have regulated nervous systems and just need motivation, structure, or consequences to complete academic work. These approaches often backfire spectacularly with neurodivergent children because they ignore the foundational requirement of nervous system regulation for learning.

The Depletion Reality

Dr. Russell Barkley's research on ADHD shows that sustained attention and executive function require significant mental energy, and this energy becomes depleted throughout the day (Barkley, 2015). For neurodivergent children, a full school day often uses up most or all of their available regulation capacity.

By the time homework begins, many neurodivergent children are operating on what researchers call "cognitive fumes"—they have little to no executive function capacity left for additional academic demands. Asking a cognitively depleted child to complete homework is like asking someone who just ran a marathon to immediately run another five miles.

Signs of cognitive depletion:

- Tasks that were easy earlier in the day seem impossible

- Increased emotional reactivity to minor frustrations

- Difficulty remembering or following multi-step directions

- Physical restlessness or complete lethargy

- Sensory sensitivities that seem worse than usual

- Regression to younger behaviors or communication styles

The Stress-Performance Connection

The Yerkes-Dodson law demonstrates that performance follows an inverted U-shaped curve relative to arousal level (Yerkes & Dodson, 1908). A little arousal improves performance, but too much arousal dramatically impairs it. For neurodivergent children, traditional homework pressure often pushes them far beyond optimal arousal into the zone where learning becomes nearly impossible.

When children are stressed about homework, their bodies release cortisol and adrenaline—stress hormones that impair memory formation, flexible thinking, and problem-solving abilities. This creates a vicious cycle: homework stress makes learning harder, which leads to more homework difficulty, which creates more stress.

The Masking Effect

Many neurodivergent children engage in what researchers call "masking" throughout the school day—using enormous energy to appear neurotypical and meet classroom expectations (Hull et al., 2017). This masking is exhausting and unsustainable, and by homework time, many children simply cannot maintain the facade any longer.

Parents often wonder why their child can "behave" at school but falls apart at home during homework. The answer is that school behavior often represents maximum effort that cannot be sustained, and homework time is when the mask inevitably comes off.

Twelve-year-old Ava described it perfectly: "At school, I use all my brain power to look normal and understand what the teacher wants. By the time I get home, my brain feels like a phone with 2% battery. There's just nothing left for more thinking."

Creating Nervous System-Friendly Learning Environments

The physical environment where homework occurs can either support or sabotage nervous system regulation. Small environmental modifications can dramatically impact your child's ability to access their learning capacity.

Sensory Environment Considerations

Lighting optimization: Many children learn better with softer, warmer lighting than the harsh overhead fluorescent lights common in schools. Table lamps, natural light, or dimmed overhead lights often support concentration better.

Sound environment: Some children need complete quiet to focus, while others concentrate better with background music or white noise. Identifying your child's optimal auditory environment is crucial for sustained attention.

Visual organization: Cluttered, visually overwhelming spaces can trigger stress responses in children with visual processing sensitivities. Organized, calm visual environments often support better focus and regulation.

Spatial considerations: Some children focus better at traditional desks, while others need alternative seating like exercise balls, standing desks, or floor cushions. The goal is finding what supports your child's nervous system rather than forcing conformity to traditional expectations.

Temperature and air quality: Rooms that are too hot, cold, or stuffy can trigger stress responses that interfere with learning. Optimal temperature and fresh air support nervous system regulation.

Nine-year-old Marcus's homework battles transformed when his parents moved his study space from the brightly lit kitchen table to a quiet corner of the living room with soft lamp lighting and a comfortable chair. His nervous system could regulate in the calmer environment, making learning actually possible.

Creating Regulation Stations

Calm-down corner: A designated space with regulation tools (weighted blankets, fidget items, soft music) where children can go when feeling overwhelmed by homework demands.

Movement options: Many neurodivergent children need movement to maintain focus. This might include exercise balls, standing desks, fidget tools, or permission to take movement breaks.

Sensory supports: Noise-canceling headphones, textured surfaces, essential oils, or other sensory tools that help individual children maintain regulation while learning.

Comfort items: Stuffed animals, favorite blankets, or other comfort objects that help children feel safe enough to engage in challenging cognitive tasks.

The Optimal Arousal Level for Learning and Focus

Understanding your child's optimal arousal level for learning helps you create conditions where homework becomes possible rather than torturous. This optimal level is different for every child and may vary based on factors like time of day, energy level, and recent experiences.

Identifying Your Child's Learning Zone

Under-aroused signs: Your child seems lethargic, unfocused, or "spacey." They might stare blankly at assignments, forget instructions immediately, or seem unable to initiate tasks. These children often need activating activities to reach their learning zone.

Optimal arousal signs: Your child seems alert but calm, can sustain attention on tasks, asks appropriate questions, and can persist through reasonable challenges. This is the state where learning happens most easily.

Over-aroused signs: Your child seems hyperactive, anxious, or emotionally reactive. They might rush through work carelessly, have difficulty sitting still, or become easily frustrated. These children need calming activities to reach their learning zone.

Strategies for Under-Aroused Nervous Systems

Movement activation: Jumping jacks, running in place, dancing, or other physical activities to increase arousal level before homework.

Sensory activation: Crunchy snacks, cold water, upbeat music, or bright lighting to help activate the nervous system.

Interest-based activation: Starting with preferred subjects or incorporating special interests into learning activities.

Social activation: Some children focus better with another person nearby, even if that person isn't directly helping with homework.

Strategies for Over-Aroused Nervous Systems

Calming movement: Gentle stretching, slow walking, or rhythmic activities like swinging to reduce nervous system activation.

Sensory calming: Soft lighting, quiet music, weighted lap pads, or other sensory input that promotes regulation.

Breathing activities: Deep breathing, mindfulness exercises, or other activities that activate the parasympathetic nervous system.

Time and space: Simply providing time for the nervous system to down-regulate before attempting homework.

Movement Breaks and Regulation Activities During Homework

For many neurodivergent children, sustained attention requires regular movement breaks. These aren't rewards for completing work—they're neurobiological necessities that make continued learning possible.

Understanding the Movement-Learning Connection

Dr. John Ratey's research shows that physical activity increases BDNF (brain-derived neurotrophic factor), which supports learning and memory formation (Ratey & Hagerman, 2008). For children with ADHD, movement literally helps their brains function better.

Movement also helps regulate the nervous system by providing proprioceptive and vestibular input that many neurodivergent children need for optimal arousal levels. Rather than being a distraction from learning, movement often enhances the capacity for learning.

Types of Regulation Breaks

Proprioceptive breaks: Heavy work activities like carrying books, doing wall push-ups, or using resistance bands provide deep pressure input that helps regulate the nervous system.

Vestibular breaks: Swinging, spinning in a chair, or other movement activities that stimulate the inner ear can help some children maintain focus.

Bilateral coordination breaks: Activities that cross the body's midline, like cross-lateral exercises or juggling, can support brain integration and focus.

Mindfulness breaks: Brief meditation, breathing exercises, or body awareness activities can help reset nervous system regulation.

Creative breaks: Drawing, coloring, or other creative activities can provide mental rest while maintaining engagement.

Timing and Duration

Individual variation: Some children need 5-minute breaks every 15 minutes, while others can work for 30-45 minutes before needing a break. Understanding your child's attention span helps you plan appropriate breaks.

Quality over quantity: The goal is effective regulation breaks, not just time away from work. A 2-minute movement break that actually resets the nervous system is more valuable than a 10-minute break that doesn't provide regulation.

Proactive vs. reactive: Scheduled breaks work better than waiting until your child is already overwhelmed. Prevention is more effective than crisis intervention.

Natural stopping points: Plan breaks around natural transitions between subjects or after completing specific tasks rather than stopping mid-problem.

Eight-year-old Riley discovered that doing 10 jumping jacks between each math problem helped her maintain focus throughout her homework session. What seemed like it would make homework take longer actually made it more efficient because her brain could stay engaged.

When to Push Through vs. When to Stop

One of the most challenging aspects of homework support is knowing when to encourage persistence and when to recognize that your child's nervous system has reached its limits. This decision requires ongoing assessment of your child's regulation state rather than rigid adherence to homework completion goals.

Signs It's Time to Stop

Nervous system overwhelm: Your child shows signs of fight-or-flight activation (crying, yelling, throwing things) or shutdown (becoming nonresponsive, putting their head down, going silent).

Cognitive capacity exhaustion: Your child cannot access information or skills they clearly possess when regulated. They're making errors on problems they usually find easy.

Escalating emotional distress: The stress of homework is creating negative associations with learning, school, or family relationships that outweigh any potential academic benefit.

Physical symptoms: Headaches, stomachaches, or other stress-related physical symptoms indicate that the nervous system is overwhelmed.

Time vs. benefit analysis: If homework is taking dramatically longer than expected with little learning occurring, the cost may outweigh the benefit.

Signs to Gently Encourage Persistence

Regulated frustration: Your child is appropriately frustrated by challenging material but remains within their window of tolerance and can accept support.

Skill building opportunity: Your child is working on mastering a skill that's within their current developmental zone and the practice is genuinely beneficial.

Confidence building: Your child is close to completing something that will provide a sense of accomplishment and positive association with learning.

External expectations: Your child expresses concern about teacher expectations or consequences, and completing the work supports their social-emotional wellbeing.

Making the Decision

The decision to stop or continue should prioritize your child's relationship with learning over short-term academic completion. A child who develops negative associations with homework may struggle academically for years, while a child who learns to recognize and communicate their limits develops valuable self-advocacy skills.

Consider these questions:

- Is my child learning anything valuable right now, or are we just going through motions?

- What's the cost to our relationship and my child's self-concept if we continue?

- What message am I sending about my child's nervous system needs?

- How will this decision affect tomorrow's homework session and my child's overall relationship with learning?

Collaborating with Teachers on Homework Modifications

Many parents hesitate to request homework modifications, fearing they're making excuses for their children or lowering academic standards. However, research shows that homework modifications based on nervous system understanding often improve rather than impair learning outcomes.

Communicating with Teachers

Focus on learning goals: Frame homework modifications in terms of supporting your child's learning rather than reducing expectations. "Emma learns math concepts well, but her nervous system gets overwhelmed by lengthy worksheets. Could we modify the assignment to focus on demonstrating mastery rather than completing every problem?"

Provide specific suggestions: Rather than just asking for "less homework," suggest specific modifications that maintain learning goals while working with your child's nervous system.

Share what works: When modifications lead to improved learning or engagement, share these successes with teachers to demonstrate the value of nervous system accommodations.

Offer collaboration: Position yourself as a partner in your child's education rather than an adversary requesting special treatment.

Types of Homework Modifications

Quantity modifications: Reducing the number of problems while maintaining the same learning objectives. For example, completing 10 math problems instead of 30 if your child can demonstrate mastery with fewer repetitions.

Time modifications: Setting time limits for homework (such as 20 minutes of math practice) rather than completion requirements, honoring your child's attention capacity.

Format modifications: Allowing alternative ways to demonstrate learning, such as verbal explanations instead of written responses for children with writing difficulties.

Environment modifications: Allowing homework to be completed in alternative environments or with supportive accommodations that aren't available in the classroom.

Timing modifications: Adjusting when homework is due to allow for your child's optimal learning times and nervous system recovery needs.

Sample Teacher Communication

"Dear Mr. Rodriguez,

I wanted to discuss Jake's homework completion with you. Jake is very capable of understanding the math concepts, but after a full day of managing his ADHD at school, his nervous system is often too depleted for lengthy homework sessions.

We've found that Jake can demonstrate his understanding of math concepts with fewer practice problems, and quality work in a shorter time frame is more beneficial for his learning than struggling through entire worksheets when he's dysregulated.

Would it be possible to modify his math homework to focus on 10-15 problems rather than the full worksheet? This would allow him to practice the concepts while maintaining a positive relationship with learning.

I'm happy to discuss this further and work together to support Jake's academic success."

Building Long-Term Relationships

Start early: Don't wait until homework becomes a crisis to begin conversations with teachers about your child's needs.

Provide education: Share resources about how nervous system regulation affects learning, but do so in supportive rather than confrontational ways.

Acknowledge constraints: Recognize that teachers have many students and various pressures, and work within realistic constraints while advocating for your child's needs.

Celebrate successes: When teachers provide accommodations that help your child succeed, acknowledge and appreciate their efforts.

Creating Homework Success Systems

Rather than battling homework every night, many families find success in creating comprehensive systems that support both academic completion and nervous system regulation.

The Homework Routine Structure

Transition time: Allow adequate time for your child to transition from school mode to homework mode, including any needed decompression activities.

Environment setup: Create a consistent homework environment that supports your child's sensory and regulation needs.

Regulation check-in: Assess your child's nervous system state and provide any needed regulation support before beginning academic work.

Flexible pacing: Plan homework sessions around your child's natural energy rhythms and attention capacity rather than arbitrary time requirements.

Success celebration: End homework sessions by acknowledging effort and progress rather than focusing only on completion or perfection.

The Three-Phase Approach

Phase 1 - Regulation: Focus entirely on helping your child's nervous system reach a state where learning is possible. This might take 15 minutes or an hour, depending on their current state.

Phase 2 - Learning: Engage in academic work while continuously monitoring regulation state and providing breaks as needed.

Phase 3 - Recovery: Allow time for nervous system recovery after homework completion, avoiding additional demands or overstimulation.

Backup Plans for Difficult Days

Modified expectations: Have plans for days when your child's nervous system cannot handle typical homework demands.

Alternative activities: Educational activities that maintain learning engagement without the stress of formal homework assignments.

Communication protocols: Systems for communicating with teachers when homework cannot be completed due to nervous system challenges.

Family support: Plans for maintaining family relationships and reducing stress when homework doesn't go as planned.

The Long-Term Benefits of Nervous System-Informed Homework Support

When families shift from homework battles to nervous system support, the benefits extend far beyond improved assignment completion. Children develop healthier relationships with learning, better self-awareness, and stronger family connections.

Academic Benefits

Improved learning retention: Information learned in a regulated state is processed more effectively and remembered longer than information acquired under stress.

Better problem-solving: Children who approach homework from regulated states develop stronger critical thinking and creative problem-solving skills.

Increased motivation: Positive homework experiences create intrinsic motivation for learning rather than compliance-based academic engagement.

Enhanced self-advocacy: Children learn to recognize their learning needs and communicate them effectively to teachers and others.

Emotional and Social Benefits

Stronger family relationships: Families who prioritize connection over homework completion report better relationships and less daily stress.

Improved self-concept: Children develop understanding of their learning style and needs rather than feeling "broken" or inadequate.

Better emotional regulation: The skills children learn for managing homework stress transfer to other challenging situations.

Increased resilience: Children who receive nervous system support during homework challenges develop greater capacity for handling academic difficulties.

Life Skills Development

Self-awareness: Children learn to recognize their own nervous system states and capacity levels.

Self-advocacy: Children develop skills for communicating their needs and requesting appropriate accommodations.

Emotional regulation: Children learn strategies for managing stress and maintaining regulation during challenging tasks.

Realistic goal-setting: Children develop understanding of their capacities and learn to set achievable goals.

Making Homework Work for Your Family

Remember that the goal of homework support isn't perfect assignment completion—it's helping your child develop a healthy relationship with learning while honoring their nervous system needs. This may look different from traditional homework approaches, but it often leads to better long-term academic and emotional outcomes.

Family-Specific Considerations

Individual needs: Each child's homework support needs are unique, even within the same family.

Parent capacity: Homework support must work within the reality of parent work schedules, energy levels, and other family demands.

Resource availability: Effective homework support can be created within any family's resources by focusing on understanding and accommodation rather than expensive interventions.

Long-term perspective: Focus on building sustainable systems rather than perfect daily execution.

The Henderson family from our opening story discovered that Ethan's homework struggles weren't about math ability—they were about nervous system depletion. They implemented a three-part system: 45 minutes of after-school decompression, a 15-minute regulation check-in before homework, and modified homework expectations based on Ethan's daily capacity.

Six months later, homework was no longer a battlefield. Ethan still had challenging days, but he had developed self-awareness about his nervous system needs and could communicate when he needed breaks or support. His math skills actually improved because he was learning from a regulated state rather than a stressed one. Most importantly, the family preserved their relationships while supporting Ethan's academic growth.

Your child's homework struggles aren't laziness, defiance, or lack of ability—they're communications from a nervous system that needs support to access learning capacity. When you approach homework through a polyvagal lens, you can create the conditions your child needs to succeed academically while building self-awareness, regulation skills, and positive family relationships that will benefit them throughout their educational journey and beyond.

Chapter 8: Bedtime Routines for Nervous System Calming

At 9:30 PM, eleven-year-old Maya was wide awake, staring at the ceiling while her mind raced with worries about tomorrow's math test. Her parents had followed every sleep hygiene rule: consistent bedtime, no screens for an hour before sleep, calming activities, comfortable room temperature. But Maya's nervous system was still activated from the day's stresses, and no amount of "trying to sleep" was working.

In the next room, her brother Alex was having a different but equally challenging bedtime experience. The seven-year-old with ADHD was exhausted but couldn't settle his body. He'd been in and out of bed six times in the past hour, asking for water, complaining about his pajamas feeling "wrong," and insisting that every small sound was too scary for sleep.

Both children needed sleep desperately, and both parents were exhausted from lengthy bedtime battles that seemed to get more difficult rather than easier over time. What the family didn't understand was that their children's sleep challenges weren't behavioral choices—they were neurobiological realities that required nervous system support rather than sleep rules.

The Neuroscience of Sleep in Neurodivergent Children

Sleep isn't simply the absence of wakefulness—it's an active neurobiological process that requires specific nervous system conditions to occur successfully. For neurodivergent children, whose nervous systems operate differently from neurotypical norms, sleep often requires more intensive support and different approaches.

The Polyvagal Pathway to Sleep

Dr. Stephen Porges explains that healthy sleep requires activation of the parasympathetic nervous system—specifically, the ventral vagal complex that supports calm, connected states (Porges, 2017). This system must be online and stable for the brain to feel safe enough to let go of consciousness.

For many neurodivergent children, the nervous system remains activated even when the body is tired. Their threat detection systems may be hypervigilant, scanning for dangers that prevent the deep relaxation necessary for sleep. This isn't anxiety in the psychological sense—it's neurobiological activation that interferes with sleep initiation and maintenance.

Signs of nervous system activation at bedtime:

- Physical restlessness despite fatigue

- Racing thoughts or repetitive worries

- Hypervigilance to sounds or environmental changes

- Difficulty with physical settling (tossing, turning, position changes)

- Emotional dysregulation (crying, irritability, fear)

- Somatic complaints (stomachaches, headaches, muscle tension)

Circadian Rhythm Differences

Research shows that many neurodivergent individuals have atypical circadian rhythms—their internal biological clocks operate on different schedules than neurotypical expectations (Coogan & McGowan, 2017). For children with ADHD, natural bedtimes may be 1-2 hours later than their parents expect. For autistic children, melatonin production may be irregular or delayed.

These aren't behavioral choices or poor sleep habits—they're biological realities. Fighting against your child's natural circadian rhythm often creates bedtime battles without actually improving sleep quality or duration.

The Sleep-Regulation Cycle

Poor sleep creates nervous system vulnerability the following day, which leads to more difficulty regulating emotions and behavior, which creates more stress and activation, which interferes with the next night's sleep. Breaking this cycle requires understanding that sleep support is nervous system support.

Dr. Matthew Walker's research demonstrates that sleep deprivation impairs emotional regulation, increases stress reactivity, and decreases cognitive flexibility—all areas where neurodivergent children already face challenges (Walker, 2017). Supporting sleep becomes crucial for daytime regulation and overall nervous system health.

Common Sleep Challenges and Their Nervous System Roots

Understanding the nervous system basis of common sleep challenges helps parents respond with support rather than frustration. Most bedtime difficulties stem from nervous system states rather than behavioral choices.

Sleep Initiation Difficulties (Can't Fall Asleep)

Nervous system perspective: The child's system is still activated and hasn't shifted into the parasympathetic state necessary for sleep onset. Their brain doesn't feel safe enough to let go of consciousness.

Common manifestations:

- Lying awake for hours despite being tired
- Racing thoughts or repetitive worries
- Physical restlessness or uncomfortable sensations
- Hypervigilance to sounds or movements

- Requests for repeated reassurance or comfort

Traditional approach: "Just close your eyes and try to sleep. Stop thinking about things and relax."

Nervous system approach: Provide specific activities and supports that help the nervous system shift from sympathetic (active) to parasympathetic (calm) dominance.

Sleep Maintenance Difficulties (Frequent Waking)

Nervous system perspective: The child's threat detection system remains partially activated during sleep, causing awakening in response to internal or external stimuli that wouldn't wake a deeply sleeping person.

Common manifestations:

- Waking frequently throughout the night
- Difficulty returning to sleep after waking
- Light sleeping with easy arousal to sounds
- Nightmares or anxiety dreams
- Early morning awakening with inability to return to sleep

Bedtime Resistance and Avoidance

Nervous system perspective: The child's system associates bedtime with loss of control, separation from safety figures, or overwhelming internal experiences. Their nervous system activates to avoid the threatening experience of sleep.

Common manifestations:

- Procrastinating bedtime routines
- Repeatedly requesting "one more" story, drink, or bathroom trip
- Emotional meltdowns at bedtime

- Somatic complaints that appear only at bedtime

- Refusing to go to bedroom or bed

Nine-year-old Jordan's bedtime resistance wasn't defiance—it was his nervous system's response to the dark, quiet bedroom that felt overwhelming rather than peaceful. His hypervigilant nervous system interpreted the sensory reduction of bedtime as potentially dangerous, triggering activation rather than relaxation.

Creating Calming Bedtime Sequences

Effective bedtime routines for neurodivergent children focus on gradually shifting the nervous system from daytime activation to sleep-ready calm. This process often takes longer and requires more intensive support than neurotypical bedtime routines.

The Nervous System Bedtime Timeline

2-3 hours before sleep: Begin reducing stimulating activities, bright lights, and high-energy interactions. The nervous system needs time to begin the transition from active to calm states.

1-2 hours before sleep: Implement calming activities that specifically support parasympathetic nervous system activation. This isn't just "quiet time"—it's active nervous system regulation.

30-60 minutes before sleep: Focus on activities that directly prepare the body and brain for sleep, including sensory supports, emotional connection, and environmental preparation.

Sleep transition: The actual process of getting into bed and falling asleep, with ongoing nervous system support as needed.

Calming Activity Categories

Sensory regulation activities:

- Warm baths or showers (the temperature drop after warming helps trigger sleepiness)

- Deep pressure through weighted blankets or firm hugs
- Gentle music or white noise to mask alerting sounds
- Dim, warm lighting to support melatonin production
- Calming scents like lavender (for children who respond positively to olfactory input)

Nervous system down-regulation activities:

- Slow, deep breathing exercises
- Progressive muscle relaxation
- Gentle stretching or yoga poses
- Meditation or mindfulness practices adapted for children
- Rhythmic activities like rocking or gentle swaying

Connection and co-regulation activities:

- Quiet conversation about positive aspects of the day
- Reading together (parent reads to child, not child performing reading)
- Sharing gratitudes or appreciations
- Physical connection through cuddling or back rubbing
- Singing lullabies or listening to calming music together

Cognitive transition activities:

- Journaling about the day (for children who enjoy writing)
- Drawing or other non-stimulating creative activities
- Listening to audiobooks or podcasts designed for bedtime
- Guided imagery or visualization exercises

- Prayer or spiritual practices (for families who find these meaningful)

Environmental Modifications for Better Sleep

The sleep environment can either support or sabotage nervous system regulation for sleep. Many neurodivergent children are more sensitive to environmental factors that interfere with sleep quality.

Lighting Considerations

Blue light exposure: Electronic screens emit blue light that suppresses melatonin production. For sensitive nervous systems, even small amounts of blue light can significantly interfere with sleep preparation.

Bedroom lighting: Complete darkness isn't necessary for everyone—some children feel safer with dim night lights. Red or amber lighting interferes less with sleep chemistry than white or blue light.

Morning light: Exposure to bright light in the morning helps regulate circadian rhythms, making bedtime easier. Many neurodivergent children benefit from light therapy devices or increased morning sunlight exposure.

Sound Environment

Background noise: Some children sleep better with consistent white noise or nature sounds that mask alerting environmental noises. Others need complete quiet.

Household sounds: Consider how family activities, television, or conversations might be affecting your child's ability to settle for sleep.

Neighbor and street noise: External sounds that can't be controlled might require accommodations like sound machines, earplugs, or room location changes.

Temperature and Air Quality

Optimal temperature: Most people sleep best in cooler environments (65-68°F), but individual preferences vary. Some neurodivergent children are particularly sensitive to temperature variations.

Air circulation: Stuffy rooms can trigger activation in sensitive nervous systems. Fans, air purifiers, or simply opening windows can improve sleep environment quality.

Humidity levels: Very dry or humid air can cause physical discomfort that interferes with sleep settling.

Bedroom Organization and Safety

Visual calm: Cluttered or visually stimulating bedrooms can interfere with nervous system down-regulation. Organized, calm visual environments often support better sleep.

Safety and security: Some children need specific safety accommodations—easy access to parents, emergency lights, or comfort objects—to feel secure enough for sleep.

Sensory accommodations: Weighted blankets, specific pillow preferences, favorite stuffed animals, or particular sheet textures can provide sensory support for sleep regulation.

Twelve-year-old Emma discovered that her sleep difficulties dramatically improved when her family made three environmental changes: blackout curtains to eliminate street light, a white noise machine to mask household sounds, and moving her bed away from the wall shared with her younger brother's room. Her sensitive nervous system could finally settle without constant environmental monitoring.

Addressing Bedtime Anxiety and Hypervigilance

Many neurodivergent children experience bedtime anxiety that isn't traditional worry but rather nervous system hypervigilance that makes sleep feel unsafe. Understanding this distinction helps parents provide appropriate support.

Understanding Bedtime Hypervigilance

Hypervigilance is a nervous system state where the threat detection system remains highly activated, constantly scanning for potential dangers. For some children, the quiet, dark, vulnerable state required for sleep triggers this hypervigilant response.

Signs of bedtime hypervigilance:

- Extreme sensitivity to household sounds during bedtime

- Inability to stop "checking" doors, windows, or safety features

- Repetitive questions about family safety or tomorrow's plans

- Physical tension that prevents comfortable settling

- Feeling like they need to "stay alert" even when tired

Nervous system vs. psychological anxiety: While psychological anxiety involves specific worries, hypervigilance is more about the nervous system's general sense that it's not safe to be unconscious and vulnerable.

Supporting the Hypervigilant Nervous System

Environmental safety signals: Provide concrete safety cues that help the nervous system recognize that sleep is safe. This might include night lights, open bedroom doors, or agreed-upon check-in systems.

Predictability and control: Give children some control over their sleep environment and routine. When children feel agency, their nervous systems often feel safer.

Co-regulation presence: Many children with bedtime hypervigilance benefit from gradual parent withdrawal rather than immediate independence. Your regulated presence helps their nervous system feel safe enough to let go.

Somatic supports: Activities that help the body release physical tension—gentle stretching, progressive muscle relaxation, or weighted blankets—can help hypervigilant nervous systems settle.

Gradual Independence Building

For children who need significant parental presence for sleep, independence can be built gradually while honoring nervous system needs:

Week 1-2: Parent stays in child's room until sleep occurs *Week 3-4:* Parent sits by the bed but gradually reduces interaction *Week 5-6:* Parent sits near the doorway *Week 7-8:* Parent checks in every few minutes initially, then less frequently *Week 9+:* Child calls if needed, but parent doesn't need to be present

This timeline should be adjusted based on your child's nervous system responses. Moving too quickly often creates setbacks that take longer to resolve than gradual progress.

Age-Appropriate Sleep Regulation Strategies

Sleep support strategies need to be developmentally appropriate and matched to your child's current capacity for self-regulation. What works for a five-year-old won't necessarily work for a twelve-year-old.

Ages 3-6: Foundation Building

At this age, children are just developing basic self-regulation skills and need intensive co-regulation support for sleep.

Co-regulation focus: Parents provide most of the regulation support through presence, predictable routines, and environmental management.

Sensory supports: Heavy emphasis on sensory accommodations like weighted blankets, soft music, comfortable clothing, and optimal room conditions.

Simple routines: Basic, predictable sequences that help the nervous system prepare for sleep without overwhelming cognitive demands.

Connection emphasis: Bedtime routines should emphasize emotional connection and safety rather than independence or task completion.

Example routine: Warm bath, comfortable pajamas, three stories while cuddling, parent stays until child falls asleep.

Ages 7-11: Skill Development

Children this age can begin learning simple self-regulation strategies while still needing significant support.

Self-awareness building: Help children notice their own nervous system states and what helps them feel calm.

Simple strategies: Teach basic techniques like deep breathing, counting, or visualization that children can use independently.

Graduated independence: Begin building independence gradually while maintaining safety and support.

Problem-solving involvement: Include children in creating solutions for their sleep challenges.

Example routine: Calming activities chosen by child, parent reads while child practices breathing exercises, parent checks in once after lights out.

Ages 12+: Self-Advocacy Development

Adolescents can take increasing responsibility for their sleep regulation while still receiving family support.

Strategy ownership: Teens can learn and implement more sophisticated regulation strategies independently.

Environmental control: Give teenagers more control over their sleep environment and routine timing (within family constraints).

Communication skills: Help teens communicate their sleep needs to family members and advocate for appropriate accommodations.

Natural rhythm respect: Acknowledge that adolescent circadian rhythms naturally shift later while working within family and school constraints.

Example approach: Teen manages own bedtime routine, family provides environmental supports, parents available for support when requested.

Individual Developmental Considerations

Some neurodivergent children may need strategies typically used with younger children, and that's completely appropriate. Developmental age, regulation capacity, and individual needs should guide strategy selection rather than chronological age alone.

Special Considerations for Common Neurodivergent Sleep Challenges

Different neurodivergent profiles often come with specific sleep challenges that benefit from targeted approaches.

ADHD and Sleep

Children with ADHD often have delayed circadian rhythms, medication effects that interfere with sleep, and difficulty with the transition from active to calm states.

Circadian rhythm support: Morning light exposure, consistent sleep schedules, and gradual evening dimming can help regulate delayed biological clocks.

Medication considerations: Work with healthcare providers to understand how ADHD medications affect sleep and adjust timing or dosages if necessary.

Physical energy release: Many children with ADHD need significant physical activity during the day to feel ready for sleep at night.

Transition support: The shift from hyperactive to calm often needs intensive support through movement, sensory input, and nervous system down-regulation activities.

Autism and Sleep

Autistic children often have sensory sensitivities, melatonin production differences, and need for predictability that affect sleep.

Sensory accommodations: Careful attention to lighting, sound, texture, and temperature needs for sleep comfort.

Routine predictability: Highly consistent bedtime routines that reduce uncertainty and support nervous system safety.

Melatonin considerations: Many autistic children benefit from melatonin supplementation under medical supervision.

Social communication: Some autistic children need modified social interaction during bedtime routines—less eye contact, reduced conversation, or alternative connection methods.

Anxiety and Sleep

Children with anxiety disorders often experience bedtime as a particularly vulnerable time when worries feel overwhelming.

Worry time: Designated time earlier in the day for processing concerns so they don't emerge at bedtime.

Safety planning: Concrete plans for handling night fears or anxiety that help the nervous system feel prepared.

Cognitive strategies: Age-appropriate techniques for managing racing thoughts or repetitive worries.

Parent availability: Clear systems for when and how children can access parent support during the night.

Sensory Processing Differences and Sleep

Children with sensory processing challenges may have specific needs related to their sensory systems' impact on sleep regulation.

Proprioceptive needs: Some children need deep pressure input (weighted blankets, firm hugs) to feel settled for sleep.

Vestibular needs: Gentle swaying, rocking, or other movement might help some children transition to sleep.

Tactile accommodations: Specific fabric preferences, temperature needs, or texture sensitivities that must be honored for comfort.

Auditory processing: Careful management of sound environment based on individual sound sensitivities and preferences.

Building Long-Term Sleep Success

Creating sustainable sleep success for neurodivergent children requires understanding that sleep needs may change over time and that flexibility within structure often works better than rigid adherence to rules.

Tracking and Adjusting

Sleep pattern awareness: Keep track of what works and what doesn't, looking for patterns related to daily activities, stress levels, environmental factors, or developmental changes.

Seasonal adjustments: Many families need to adjust sleep routines for daylight changes, school schedule variations, or seasonal activity differences.

Growth and development: Sleep needs and strategies often change as children grow, requiring ongoing adjustment rather than finding one solution that works forever.

Family life integration: Sleep routines must work within the reality of family schedules, sibling needs, and parent capacity.

Building Sleep Confidence

Success building: Focus on progress and improvement rather than perfect sleep every night.

Self-efficacy development: Help children develop confidence in their ability to sleep independently while knowing support is available when needed.

Problem-solving skills: Teach children to identify what's interfering with their sleep and develop their own solutions within family guidelines.

Stress resilience: Help children understand that occasional difficult sleep nights are normal and don't predict ongoing problems.

The Family Sleep Ecosystem

Remember that your child's sleep affects and is affected by the entire family's sleep patterns and stress levels. Creating family approaches that support everyone's sleep needs leads to more sustainable success.

Parent Sleep and Regulation

Your nervous system matters: Parents who are sleep-deprived have more difficulty providing the calm, regulated presence children need for sleep support.

Sustainable support: Create bedtime support systems that don't completely exhaust parents or interfere with parent sleep needs.

Partner coordination: If there are two parents, coordinate sleep support responsibilities so both parents get adequate rest.

Self-care integration: Include parent regulation and self-care in family bedtime routines rather than treating them as separate issues.

Sibling Sleep Considerations

Individual needs: Different children may need different bedtime routines, environmental accommodations, or support levels.

Shared space challenges: When children share rooms, accommodations need to work for all children involved.

Family fairness: Help children understand that fair doesn't mean identical, and different children may need different types of support.

Whole family routines: Create some family bedtime traditions that everyone can participate in while maintaining individual accommodations.

Long-Term Family Benefits

When families successfully support neurodivergent children's sleep needs, the benefits extend far beyond bedtime:

Improved daytime regulation: Children who sleep well have better emotional regulation, attention, and learning capacity during the day.

Reduced family stress: Successful bedtime routines reduce daily family conflict and improve overall family relationships.

Better academic performance: Well-rested children perform better academically and have fewer behavioral challenges at school.

Enhanced family connection: Calm, supportive bedtime routines create positive family memories and strengthen parent-child relationships.

Creating Your Family's Sleep Success Story

The Maya and Alex story from our opening illustrates how different children in the same family can have completely different sleep challenges, both requiring nervous system support but in different ways.

Maya's racing mind needed cognitive and emotional regulation support: a worry journal earlier in the day, calming music, and guided imagery to redirect her thoughts. Her parents learned that trying to stop her thoughts was less effective than giving her mind something calm and predictable to focus on.

Alex's hyperactive body needed physical and sensory regulation support: a warm bath, deep pressure from weighted pajamas, and movement activities before transitioning to bed. His parents discovered that trying to force stillness made his restlessness worse, while providing appropriate sensory input helped his body settle naturally.

Both children benefited from consistent, predictable routines and parent presence that helped their nervous systems feel safe enough for sleep. But the specific strategies needed to be individually tailored to each child's nervous system profile.

Six months after implementing nervous system-informed sleep support, both children were sleeping better, and the family's evening stress had dramatically decreased. More importantly, Maya and Alex had developed understanding of their own sleep needs and could communicate when they needed additional support.

Your child's sleep challenges aren't behavioral problems that need to be fixed—they're nervous system communications that need to be understood and supported. When you approach sleep through a polyvagal lens, you can create the conditions your child's nervous system needs to feel safe enough for restorative sleep, building the foundation for better daytime regulation, learning, and family relationships.

The goal isn't perfect sleep every night—it's creating sleep routines that work with your child's nervous system rather than against it, building their capacity for sleep regulation over time while maintaining the family connections and support that make bedtime a positive experience rather than a nightly battle.

Chapter 9: Preventing Meltdowns

Early Warning Signs and Interventions

At 3:45 PM, ten-year-old Zoe walked through the front door after school, and her mom Lisa immediately knew trouble was brewing. Zoe's shoulders were hunched, her backpack hit the floor with unusual force, and when Lisa cheerfully asked about her day, Zoe's response was a sharp "Fine!" that clearly meant anything but fine.

Lisa's instinct was to probe: "What happened at school? Did something go wrong with your friends?" But instead, she paused. Over the past few months, she'd learned to read the subtle signs of Zoe's nervous system approaching overload. The tight shoulders, the clipped responses, the way Zoe was avoiding eye contact—these weren't attitude problems. They were early warning signals from a nervous system that was running out of regulation capacity.

Instead of pushing for information, Lisa offered what Zoe's nervous system actually needed: "It looks like your nervous system worked really hard today. Want to decompress before we talk about anything?"

Zoe's relief was visible. Her shoulders dropped slightly, and she nodded. Twenty minutes later, after some quiet time in her room with her weighted blanket and favorite playlist, Zoe emerged ready to share about the challenging day she'd had with a substitute teacher who didn't understand her need for processing time.

This story illustrates one of the most powerful tools parents of neurodivergent children can develop: the ability to read early warning signs and intervene before meltdowns occur. Prevention isn't just easier than crisis management—it's often the difference between a regulated family evening and hours of dysregulation that affects everyone.

Reading Your Child's Nervous System Warning Signs

Every child has their own unique pattern of early warning signs that indicate their nervous system is approaching the edge of their window of tolerance. Learning to read these signs is like becoming fluent in your child's nervous system language—it allows you to provide support before crisis occurs.

Physical Early Warning Signs

The body often signals nervous system stress before conscious awareness kicks in. Dr. Bessel van der Kolk's research shows that the body keeps score of stress in ways that the thinking brain might miss (Van der Kolk, 2014).

Muscle tension indicators:

- Shoulders hunching or rising toward the ears
- Jaw clenching or teeth grinding
- Fist clenching or rigid hand postures
- Overall body stiffness or awkward positioning
- Frequent position changes or inability to get comfortable

Breathing and heart rate changes:

- Shallow, rapid breathing
- Holding breath during activities
- Sighing frequently
- Complaints of feeling "stuffy" or needing fresh air
- Visible pulse in neck or temples

Sensory system activation:

- Increased sensitivity to sounds, lights, or touch
- Seeking intense sensory input (crashing, spinning, pressure)

- Covering ears or eyes more frequently

- Complaining about clothing, tags, or textures

- Changes in appetite or food preferences

Twelve-year-old Marcus's parents learned that his first warning sign was always physical—he'd start unconsciously cracking his knuckles repeatedly. This simple gesture, which they'd initially seen as a bad habit, was actually his nervous system's way of seeking proprioceptive input as stress began to build.

Emotional and Behavioral Early Warning Signs

Emotional regulation shifts:

- Increased irritability over small frustrations

- Emotional responses that seem disproportionate to triggers

- Difficulty transitioning between activities

- Increased need for control or rigidity about plans

- Appearing more sensitive or easily hurt

Communication changes:

- Shorter responses to questions

- Speaking more quietly or more loudly than usual

- Increased whining, complaining, or negative comments

- Difficulty finding words or expressing thoughts

- Reverting to younger communication patterns

Behavioral indicators:

- Increased clumsiness or coordination difficulties

- Repetitive behaviors or stimming increases

- Difficulty with tasks that are usually manageable

- Procrastination or avoidance of typical activities
- Changes in sleep or eating patterns

Cognitive Early Warning Signs

Executive function changes:

- Forgetting familiar routines or rules
- Difficulty with decision-making that's usually easy
- Problems with time awareness or time management
- Increased difficulty organizing materials or thoughts
- Appearing confused by instructions they usually understand

Attention and focus shifts:

- Increased distractibility or hyperfocus
- Difficulty shifting attention between tasks
- Appearing "spacey" or disconnected
- Problems with working memory or following multi-step directions
- Increased need for repetition or clarification

Nine-year-old Elena's early warning sign was cognitive—she'd start asking the same questions repeatedly, even after receiving clear answers. Her parents realized this wasn't defiance or not listening; it was her brain's way of seeking certainty and predictability when her nervous system felt threatened by uncertainty.

The Meltdown Cycle: Prevention is Easier Than Intervention

Understanding the meltdown cycle helps parents recognize that there are optimal windows for intervention, and that early intervention is exponentially more effective than crisis response.

The Four Phases of the Meltdown Cycle

Phase 1: The Trigger Phase During this phase, stress begins to accumulate but the child can still access coping strategies with support. Their nervous system is moving toward the edge of their window of tolerance but hasn't crossed it yet.

- Duration: Minutes to hours

- Intervention effectiveness: Very high

- Child's capacity for reasoning: Still available

- Best interventions: Environmental modifications, co-regulation, proactive support

Phase 2: The Escalation Phase The child's nervous system has moved outside their window of tolerance and is activating protective responses. They're beginning to lose access to their thinking brain but haven't reached full crisis yet.

- Duration: Minutes to 30 minutes

- Intervention effectiveness: Moderate

- Child's capacity for reasoning: Diminishing rapidly

- Best interventions: Immediate regulation support, removing demands, providing safety

Phase 3: The Crisis Phase The child is in full fight-or-flight or shutdown mode. Their thinking brain is offline, and they're operating from their survival brain. Traditional interventions are largely ineffective.

- Duration: 20 minutes to 2 hours

- Intervention effectiveness: Very low

- Child's capacity for reasoning: Unavailable

- Best interventions: Safety, patience, minimal stimulation, co-regulation through presence

Phase 4: The Recovery Phase The acute crisis has passed, but the child's nervous system is depleted and vulnerable. They need time and support to fully return to regulation.

- Duration: 30 minutes to 24 hours

- Intervention effectiveness: Moderate for preventing re-escalation

- Child's capacity for reasoning: Gradually returning

- Best interventions: Rest, gentle nurturance, avoiding demands, emotional repair

The Prevention Window

Dr. Ross Greene's research shows that interventions during Phase 1 (the trigger phase) are 80% more effective than interventions during Phase 2, and nearly infinitely more effective than attempts to intervene during Phase 3 (Greene, 2014).

This means that learning to recognize and respond to Phase 1 warning signs can prevent most meltdowns from ever reaching crisis levels. The key is developing the observational skills to notice subtle nervous system changes and the intervention skills to provide what the nervous system needs before it becomes overwhelmed.

Creating Early Intervention Protocols

Once you can recognize your child's early warning signs, the next step is developing specific intervention protocols that address their nervous system needs before crisis occurs.

The STOP-LOOK-LISTEN-RESPOND Protocol

STOP: When you notice early warning signs, stop whatever is happening and shift into nervous system support mode. This might mean pausing homework, changing activities, or postponing planned events.

LOOK: Assess your child's current nervous system state and environmental factors that might be contributing to stress. What's different today? What additional stressors might be present?

LISTEN: Tune in to what your child's nervous system is communicating through their behavior, body language, and responses. What kind of support are they asking for?

RESPOND: Provide targeted nervous system support based on what you've observed. This might be environmental changes, co-regulation, or specific regulation activities.

Individualized Early Intervention Menus

Each child needs their own menu of early intervention strategies based on their unique nervous system profile and what tends to be most effective for them.

For children who tend toward hyperarousal:

- Calming sensory input (weighted blankets, soft music, dim lighting)
- Movement that's organizing rather than activating (slow swinging, gentle stretching)
- Reducing environmental stimulation
- Providing predictability and control
- Co-regulation through calm presence

For children who tend toward hypoarousal:

- Activating sensory input (crunchy snacks, upbeat music, bright lighting)
- Movement that's energizing (jumping, dancing, playground activities)
- Social connection and engagement

- Novel or interesting activities

- Gentle encouragement and support

For children with mixed presentations:

- Offering choices between calming and activating strategies

- Following the child's lead about what they need

- Having multiple intervention options available

- Being flexible about what works in different situations

Eight-year-old David's early intervention menu included three main strategies: proprioceptive input (wall push-ups or carrying heavy items), a brief quiet time in his sensory corner, or a short walk outside. His parents learned to offer these choices when they saw his early warning signs, and David gradually learned to request them himself.

Environmental Scanning and Proactive Adjustments

Prevention often involves identifying and modifying environmental factors that contribute to nervous system stress before they trigger dysregulation.

Daily Environmental Assessment

Morning assessment: Start each day by considering what environmental factors might be challenging for your child's nervous system. Is there a substitute teacher? A schedule change? Unusual weather? Social events planned?

Ongoing monitoring: Throughout the day, stay aware of environmental changes that might affect your child's regulation. Has the noise level increased? Are there unexpected visitors? Have plans changed?

Evening reflection: At the end of each day, consider what environmental factors supported or challenged your child's regulation. This information helps you prepare for future similar situations.

Common Environmental Stressors to Monitor

Sensory environment changes:

- Lighting changes (fluorescent lights, bright sunlight, dim spaces)
- Sound level increases (construction, traffic, crowded spaces)
- Temperature fluctuations
- Strong smells or air quality changes
- Crowded or cluttered spaces

Social environment shifts:

- New people or unfamiliar adults
- Large group situations
- Social conflicts or tension
- Performance or evaluation situations
- Changes in familiar social dynamics

Routine and schedule disruptions:

- Unexpected schedule changes
- Transitions between activities or environments
- Time pressure or rushing
- Competing demands or multitasking expectations
- Uncertainty about future plans

Proactive Environmental Modifications

Immediate modifications: Changes you can make right now to reduce environmental stress. This might include turning down music, opening windows for fresh air, or moving to a quieter space.

Planned modifications: Changes you can implement for known challenging situations. This might include bringing noise-reducing headphones to crowded events, scheduling buffer time around transitions, or providing advance notice of schedule changes.

Advocacy modifications: Changes you can request from schools, family members, or community organizations to create more neurodivergent-friendly environments.

Eleven-year-old Sarah's parents noticed that her regulation challenges always peaked during busy family gatherings. They started implementing proactive modifications: arriving early before crowds gathered, identifying quiet retreat spaces, bringing sensory regulation tools, and planning shorter visit durations. These simple changes allowed Sarah to enjoy family events instead of enduring them.

Teaching Children to Recognize Their Own Early Signs

One of the most powerful prevention strategies is helping children develop self-awareness about their own nervous system states and early warning signs.

Building Body Awareness

Nervous system education: Teach children age-appropriate information about how their nervous system works and why it responds the way it does to different situations.

Body scan activities: Regular practice helping children notice what's happening in their bodies—muscle tension, breathing patterns, energy levels, and sensations.

Feeling identification: Help children develop vocabulary for different nervous system states beyond just "good" or "bad." This might include words like activated, overwhelmed, peaceful, energized, or depleted.

Pattern recognition: Help children notice their own patterns of warning signs and what situations tend to trigger them.

The Traffic Light System

Many families find success with a simple traffic light system for nervous system states:

Green zone: Calm, regulated, able to handle typical challenges and demands. Feeling good, thinking clearly, body feels comfortable.

Yellow zone: Starting to feel stressed or overwhelmed, warning signs appearing, might need extra support soon. Body feels tense, thinking gets harder, emotions stronger.

Red zone: Overwhelmed, dysregulated, thinking brain is offline. Need immediate support and reduced demands.

Blue zone: Shut down, withdrawn, very low energy. Need gentle support and time to recover.

Ten-year-old Jordan learned to identify when he was moving from green to yellow zone by noticing his jaw clenching and his tendency to start arguing about small things. This self-awareness allowed him to request breaks or support before reaching red zone meltdowns.

Self-Advocacy Skill Development

Communication strategies: Help children learn how to communicate their nervous system needs to adults. This might include phrases like "I need a break," "This feels overwhelming," or "My nervous system needs some help."

Self-regulation tools: Teach children specific strategies they can use independently when they notice early warning signs. These should be simple, accessible, and effective for their individual nervous system needs.

Environmental awareness: Help children learn to recognize environmental factors that affect their regulation so they can advocate for modifications or prepare themselves accordingly.

Support seeking: Teach children that asking for help when they need it is a strength, not a weakness, and provide them with clear ways to request support.

Family Meltdown Prevention Plans

Prevention works best when the whole family understands the approach and everyone knows their role in supporting nervous system regulation.

Creating Family Awareness

Education for everyone: Make sure all family members understand basic nervous system concepts and why prevention is important. This includes siblings, extended family, and anyone else who regularly interacts with your child.

Warning sign recognition: Teach family members to recognize your child's early warning signs and know how to respond helpfully rather than escalating the situation.

Intervention protocols: Make sure everyone knows the specific strategies that work for your child and when to implement them.

Communication systems: Develop ways for family members to communicate with each other about your child's regulation state and coordinate support efforts.

Sibling Considerations

Individual needs: If you have multiple children, each may have different warning signs and intervention needs. Family plans need to account for everyone's nervous system needs.

Sibling support: Teach children how to support each other's regulation rather than triggering each other's dysregulation.

Fair vs. equal: Help children understand that everyone gets what they need, even if that looks different for different family members.

Family teamwork: Frame meltdown prevention as a family team effort rather than something that revolves around one child's needs.

Extended Family and Community Education

Grandparents and relatives: Provide education and specific guidance about your child's nervous system needs and how extended family can support rather than inadvertently trigger dysregulation.

Friends and social connections: Help your child's friends and their parents understand basic information about your child's needs so social situations can be more successful.

School communication: Work with teachers and school staff to implement similar prevention approaches in educational settings.

Community preparation: For regular community activities (sports, religious organizations, clubs), provide information about your child's needs and prevention strategies.

Crisis Prevention vs. Crisis Management

Prevention focus: Family plans should emphasize preventing crises rather than managing them after they occur. This means staying proactive rather than reactive.

Early intervention commitment: All family members need to commit to taking early intervention seriously rather than hoping problems will resolve on their own.

Environmental responsibility: Everyone in the family plays a role in creating and maintaining environments that support nervous system regulation.

Long-term perspective: Prevention plans are investments in long-term family wellbeing rather than just short-term crisis avoidance.

Advanced Prevention Strategies

As families become more skilled at reading nervous system signs and providing early intervention, they can develop more sophisticated prevention approaches.

Predictive Prevention

Pattern analysis: Looking at data over time to identify patterns in when and why meltdowns occur, allowing for even more proactive prevention.

Situational preparation: Preparing your child's nervous system in advance for situations that tend to be challenging.

Stress inoculation: Gradually building your child's capacity to handle challenging situations by providing appropriate supports while slowly increasing demands.

Recovery planning: Building recovery time into schedules so that your child's nervous system can recharge before facing additional challenges.

Environmental Design

Home environment optimization: Designing family living spaces to naturally support nervous system regulation for all family members.

Routine optimization: Structuring daily routines to minimize unnecessary stressors and maximize regulation opportunities.

Social environment curation: Being intentional about social situations and relationships that support vs. challenge your child's nervous system.

Activity selection: Choosing activities and commitments based on their impact on your child's overall nervous system health.

Technology Integration

Regulation apps: Using technology tools that help children identify their nervous system states and access appropriate regulation strategies.

Environmental monitoring: Using tools to track environmental factors (noise levels, air quality, etc.) that affect your child's regulation.

Communication systems: Using technology to improve communication between family members, schools, and other support systems about your child's needs.

Data tracking: Using simple apps or systems to track patterns in your child's regulation states and the effectiveness of different interventions.

Building Prevention Into Daily Life

The most effective meltdown prevention happens when nervous system support becomes integrated into daily family life rather than being an add-on during crises.

Daily Rhythm Integration

Morning preparation: Starting each day with nervous system assessment and preparation for potential challenges.

Transition support: Building nervous system support into all daily transitions rather than assuming children can handle them independently.

Evening processing: Ending each day with reflection on what supported or challenged nervous system regulation.

Weekend and holiday planning: Adapting prevention strategies for different schedules and higher-stress periods.

Skill Building Over Time

Gradual responsibility transfer: Slowly helping children take more responsibility for recognizing and responding to their own warning signs.

Capacity building: Gradually expanding your child's window of tolerance by providing appropriate challenges within a supportive framework.

Self-advocacy development: Building your child's ability to communicate their needs and access support independently.

Resilience cultivation: Using prevention experiences to build your child's confidence and sense of capability in managing challenges.

The Long-Term Impact of Prevention

Families who invest in learning prevention strategies report significant improvements not just in the frequency and intensity of meltdowns, but in overall family relationships, child self-esteem, and long-term developmental outcomes.

Immediate Benefits

Reduced family stress: Fewer crises mean less daily stress for all family members and more positive family interactions.

Improved relationships: When parents respond to warning signs with support rather than demands, parent-child relationships strengthen significantly.

Better learning outcomes: Children who receive early nervous system support can access their learning capacity more consistently.

Enhanced family functioning: Families can engage in more activities and experiences when they're not constantly managing crises.

Long-Term Developmental Benefits

Self-awareness development: Children who learn to recognize their own warning signs develop lifelong self-awareness skills.

Self-regulation capacity: Early intervention experiences help build children's internal regulation skills over time.

Self-advocacy abilities: Children learn to communicate their needs effectively and seek appropriate support.

Resilience and confidence: Success with prevention builds children's confidence in their ability to handle challenges.

Family System Benefits

Proactive rather than reactive parenting: Families shift from crisis management mode to proactive support mode.

Improved sibling relationships: Siblings benefit from living in a calmer, more regulated family environment.

Better community integration: Families can participate more fully in community activities when meltdowns are prevented.

Long-term family wellbeing: The skills learned through prevention benefit families for years to come.

Your Family's Prevention Success Story

Learning to prevent meltdowns isn't about eliminating all challenges from your child's life—it's about reading their nervous system needs accurately and providing support before crisis occurs. This approach honors your child's neurobiology while building their capacity for handling life's inevitable stresses.

The story of Zoe and Lisa from our opening illustrates this beautifully. By learning to read Zoe's early warning signs and respond with nervous system support rather than demands for information, Lisa transformed their after-school routine from a daily battle into an opportunity for connection and regulation.

Over time, Zoe internalized this approach. She began recognizing her own warning signs and asking for what she needed: "Mom, I think my nervous system needs some quiet time before I can talk about my day." This self-awareness became a lifelong skill that served her well through adolescence and into adulthood.

Prevention is both an art and a science. It requires careful observation, understanding of your child's unique patterns, and the willingness to prioritize nervous system support over conventional parenting expectations. But the investment pays enormous dividends in family wellbeing, child development, and long-term success.

Your child's early warning signs aren't problems to be eliminated—they're communications from a wise nervous system that's trying to get the support it needs before reaching crisis. When you learn to read and respond to these signs, you become your child's most effective co-regulator and advocate, helping them build the self-awareness and regulation skills they'll need for lifelong success.

Chapter 10: During the Storm: Co-Regulation in Crisis

At 4:30 PM on a Tuesday afternoon, eight-year-old Marcus was in full meltdown mode. What had started as frustration over a broken crayon had escalated into screaming, throwing toys across the room, and kicking the couch. His mom Jennifer stood in the doorway, watching her son completely fall apart, feeling her own heart racing and her palms sweating.

Every parenting instinct told her to do something—to fix it, stop it, control it, or at least make it quieter so the neighbors wouldn't judge her parenting. The rational part of her brain was generating solutions: take away privileges, send him to his room, demand he use his words, or threaten consequences if he didn't calm down immediately.

But Jennifer had been learning about nervous system regulation, and she forced herself to pause. She took three deep breaths, reminded herself that Marcus wasn't giving her a hard time—he was having a hard time—and asked herself the most important question: "What does his nervous system need right now?"

The answer wasn't discipline, consequences, or reasoning. Marcus's nervous system needed safety, patience, and the presence of a regulated adult who could help him through the storm without making it worse.

What's Actually Happening in Your Child's Brain During a Meltdown

Understanding the neurobiology of meltdowns transforms how you respond during crisis. When you know what's happening inside your child's brain and body, you can provide what they actually need rather than what conventional parenting wisdom suggests.

The Hijacked Brain

Dr. Daniel Siegel describes meltdowns as "flipping your lid"—a vivid metaphor for what happens when the emotional brain (limbic system) becomes so activated that it disconnects from the rational brain (prefrontal cortex) (Siegel and Bryson, 2012). During a meltdown, your child literally cannot access the part of their brain responsible for reasoning, language, and self-control.

Imagine your child's brain as a house with multiple floors. The top floor (prefrontal cortex) is where executive function, rational thinking, and emotional regulation happen. The middle floor (limbic system) processes emotions and memories. The basement (brainstem) handles survival functions and threat responses.

During a meltdown, your child is operating entirely from the basement. The elevator to the upper floors is broken, and no amount of reasoning, pleading, or demanding can make it work again. The only thing that can restore the connection is time and nervous system regulation support.

The Stress Response Cascade

When your child's nervous system perceives threat (real or imagined), it triggers a cascade of physiological responses designed for survival:

Immediate response (0-3 seconds):

- Adrenaline floods the system
- Heart rate and breathing accelerate
- Muscles tense for action
- Attention narrows to focus on the threat

Sustained response (30 seconds to several minutes):

- Cortisol is released to maintain high arousal

- Non-essential functions (digestion, immune response, rational thinking) shut down

- Body prepares for prolonged fight or flight

Extended response (if threat persists):

- System may shift into shutdown mode to conserve energy

- Dissociation or "freeze" response may occur

- Recovery becomes more complex and time-consuming

During this cascade, your child's behavior isn't chosen—it's driven by neurochemical processes designed to ensure survival. Understanding this helps you respond with compassion rather than frustration.

The Polyvagal Perspective on Meltdowns

Dr. Stephen Porges's polyvagal theory provides the clearest explanation of what happens during meltdowns (Porges, 2017). Your child moves through three distinct nervous system states:

Social engagement (calm): The ventral vagal complex is active, allowing for connection, communication, and rational thinking. This is where your child usually functions when regulated.

Fight-or-flight (activation): The sympathetic nervous system takes over, preparing for action against perceived threat. Your child may become aggressive, hyperactive, or oppositional.

Shutdown (collapse): If fight-or-flight doesn't resolve the threat, the dorsal vagal complex activates, causing withdrawal, disconnection, or apparent compliance that's actually dissociation.

During meltdowns, children may move rapidly between fight-or-flight and shutdown states, sometimes within the same episode. Your role is to provide safety and co-regulation that helps their nervous system return to social engagement.

Safety First: Protecting Everyone During Dysregulation

The primary goal during any meltdown is safety—physical safety for everyone present, and emotional safety that prevents trauma and preserves relationships.

Physical Safety Considerations

Environmental safety: Remove or secure objects that could be thrown or cause injury. This isn't punishment—it's protection for everyone, including your child who may feel terrible later about any damage caused during dysregulation.

Personal safety: If your child becomes physically aggressive, prioritize everyone's physical safety. This might mean giving them space, removing other children from the area, or in extreme cases, providing gentle physical containment to prevent injury.

Your child's safety: Children in meltdowns sometimes engage in self-injurious behaviors. Stay close enough to intervene if necessary, but avoid restraining unless there's immediate danger.

Sibling and family safety: Other family members, especially other children, should be protected from witnessing or being targeted by aggressive behaviors. This might mean having them go to another room or outside.

Emotional Safety Priorities

Avoiding escalation: Your response during the meltdown should never make it worse. This means avoiding threats, punishment, reasoning, or demands that your child cannot meet in their current state.

Preserving dignity: Your child will remember how you treated them during their most vulnerable moments. Responding with compassion rather than anger protects their self-concept and your relationship.

Preventing trauma: Harsh responses during meltdowns can become traumatic memories that make future regulation more difficult. Your goal is to be a source of safety, not an additional threat.

Maintaining connection: Even during the crisis, you want to preserve the fundamental message that your child is loved and acceptable, even when their behavior is challenging.

Ten-year-old Sofia's parents learned that during her meltdowns, she would sometimes hit herself or bang her head against the wall. Instead of trying to restrain her, they childproofed her meltdown space with soft surfaces and stayed close enough to gently redirect self-injurious behaviors without adding to her distress through physical restraint.

Co-Regulation Techniques for Active Meltdowns

Co-regulation during crisis is different from co-regulation during calm moments. Your child's nervous system is in survival mode, so your co-regulation needs to address their most primitive brain functions rather than their thinking brain.

Your Nervous System is the Tool

The most powerful co-regulation tool you have during a meltdown is your own regulated nervous system. Children's nervous systems naturally attune to the adults around them, especially during stress. Your calm, regulated presence can literally help their nervous system remember how to regulate.

Breathing regulation: Focus on your own breathing, making it slow and deep. Don't try to get your child to breathe with you—just let your regulated breathing be present in the space.

Physical grounding: Keep your body relaxed and grounded. Avoid tense postures, rapid movements, or aggressive gestures that might signal threat to your child's activated nervous system.

Voice regulation: If you speak at all, use a calm, slow, quiet voice. Loud or urgent voices can trigger more activation in an already overwhelmed nervous system.

Emotional regulation: Stay calm and compassionate, even if you're feeling frustrated or scared. Your child's nervous system is monitoring your emotional state and will respond accordingly.

Presence-Based Co-Regulation

Safe proximity: Stay close enough to be available but far enough away that you're not adding to your child's overwhelm. Some children need physical closeness during meltdowns, while others need space.

Non-demanding presence: Simply being present without making any demands can be profoundly regulating. You're communicating safety and availability without adding pressure.

Patient waiting: Resist the urge to rush the process. Meltdowns have their own timeline, and trying to speed them up often makes them last longer.

Consistent availability: Let your child know through your presence that you're not going anywhere and that they're safe with you, even during their most difficult moments.

Environmental Co-Regulation

Sensory management: Reduce overwhelming sensory input by dimming lights, reducing noise, removing crowds, or providing sensory supports like weighted blankets.

Space creation: Make sure your child has adequate physical space to move and express their distress without feeling trapped or crowded.

Comfort items: If your child has comfort objects that help with regulation, make them available without insisting they be used.

Predictable environment: Keep the environment as calm and predictable as possible. This isn't the time for cleaning, cooking, or other household activities that might add stimulation.

Somatic Co-Regulation

Rhythmic activities: If your child tolerates it, gentle rhythmic activities like rocking, swaying, or patting can help regulate the nervous system.

Deep pressure: Some children find firm hugs, weighted blankets, or other deep pressure inputs regulating during meltdowns, but only if they seek this input.

Movement support: If your child is seeking movement (running, jumping, pacing), provide safe spaces for this movement rather than trying to stop it.

Temperature regulation: Cool washcloths, warm blankets, or other temperature supports can sometimes help activate the parasympathetic nervous system.

What Not to Do During a Meltdown (and Why)

Well-meaning parents often make meltdowns worse by responding in ways that seem logical but actually increase nervous system activation. Understanding what not to do is as important as knowing what to do.

Don't Try to Reason or Problem-Solve

Why this doesn't work: Your child's rational brain is offline. Trying to reason with them is like trying to have a conversation with someone who's unconscious—the capacity simply isn't there.

What it looks like: "Let's talk about this," "Why are you so upset?" "This isn't a big deal," or "Let me explain why you're wrong."

Why it makes things worse: Your child experiences reasoning attempts as additional demands when they're already overwhelmed, which can increase their distress.

What to do instead: Save all reasoning and problem-solving for after your child has returned to regulation. Focus on providing safety and support in the moment.

Don't Make Threats or Give Consequences

Why this doesn't work: Threats activate the nervous system's threat detection system even more, making regulation less likely, not more likely.

What it looks like: "If you don't stop this right now, you'll lose your iPad," "You're going to be in big trouble," or "I'm going to tell your father about this."

Why it makes things worse: Consequences during meltdowns teach children that they're not safe when they're struggling, which can make future regulation even more difficult.

What to do instead: Focus on helping your child return to regulation. Address any behavioral concerns after they're calm and can actually learn from the conversation.

Don't Take It Personally or Get Defensive

Why this doesn't work: When you're defensive or hurt, your own nervous system activates, making you less available for co-regulation and more likely to escalate the situation.

What it looks like: "After everything I do for you," "You're being disrespectful," "I don't deserve this treatment," or "You're hurting my feelings."

Why it makes things worse: Making the meltdown about your feelings adds guilt and shame to your child's already overwhelming experience.

What to do instead: Remind yourself that your child isn't giving you a hard time—they're having a hard time. Your hurt feelings can be processed later with other adults.

Don't Try to Stop the Meltdown

Why this doesn't work: Meltdowns are neurobiological processes that need to run their course. Trying to stop them is like trying to stop a sneeze—it often prolongs the process.

What it looks like: "Stop crying," "Calm down right now," "That's enough," or physical attempts to stop the behaviors.

Why it makes things worse: Your child experiences attempts to stop their meltdown as invalidation of their distress, which can increase their need to express it.

What to do instead: Allow the meltdown to happen while providing safety and support. Focus on helping it be as brief and non-traumatic as possible rather than stopping it entirely.

Don't Compare or Shame

Why this doesn't work: Shame triggers additional nervous system activation and creates negative associations with expressing distress.

What it looks like: "Other kids don't act like this," "You're too old for this behavior," "You're embarrassing me," or "What will people think?"

Why it makes things worse: Shame makes regulation more difficult and can lead to children suppressing their distress, which often results in more explosive meltdowns later.

What to do instead: Approach your child's meltdown with curiosity and compassion. Their nervous system is doing exactly what it's designed to do—protect them from perceived threat.

When to Intervene vs. When to Provide Space

One of the most challenging aspects of supporting children during meltdowns is knowing when to move closer and when to give space. This decision depends on your individual child's needs, the type of meltdown, and safety considerations.

Signs Your Child Needs Closer Support

Seeking connection: If your child is reaching for you, calling your name, or moving toward you during the meltdown, they're communicating that they need your physical presence for co-regulation.

Self-injurious behaviors: If your child is engaging in behaviors that could cause physical harm, closer proximity allows you to provide gentle redirection or protection.

Escalating distress: If the meltdown is getting worse rather than better, your regulated presence might help prevent further escalation.

Young developmental age: Younger children or children with developmental delays often need more intensive adult support during dysregulation.

Trauma history: Children who have experienced trauma or abandonment may need consistent presence to feel safe during vulnerable moments.

Signs Your Child Needs More Space

Avoiding contact: If your child is physically pulling away, covering their face, or verbally asking you to leave them alone, they may need space to regulate.

Increased agitation with proximity: If your attempts to move closer result in increased distress or aggression, space might be more regulating.

Sensory overwhelm: Children experiencing sensory overload may find additional human presence overwhelming, even when it's well-intentioned.

Older developmental age: Older children and teens may need more privacy during emotional dysregulation while still knowing support is available.

Individual temperament: Some children are naturally more introverted and need solitude to process overwhelming experiences.

Flexible Proximity Strategies

Available but not intrusive: Position yourself where your child can see you but you're not in their immediate space. This communicates availability without adding pressure.

Following their lead: Let your child indicate through their behavior whether they want you closer or farther away, and be willing to adjust accordingly.

Intermittent check-ins: For children who need space, brief check-ins can communicate ongoing support without overwhelming them with constant presence.

Safe monitoring: Even when giving space, maintain visual or auditory contact to ensure safety and to be ready to intervene if needed.

Twelve-year-old Emma needed very different support depending on the type of meltdown she was having. During sensory overload meltdowns, she needed complete solitude in her dark, quiet bedroom. During emotional overwhelm meltdowns, she needed her mother sitting nearby but not touching or talking. Learning these distinctions allowed her family to provide more effective support.

Managing Your Own Nervous System During Your Child's Crisis

Perhaps the most challenging aspect of supporting a child through a meltdown is managing your own nervous system responses. Your child's dysregulation can trigger your own fight-or-flight responses, making effective co-regulation nearly impossible.

Understanding Your Triggers

Childhood experiences: Your own childhood experiences with big emotions—both your own and others'—influence how you respond to your child's meltdowns.

Cultural and social conditioning: Messages you received about acceptable emotional expression, parental authority, and public behavior affect your comfort level with meltdowns.

Current stress levels: Your overall stress level, sleep deprivation, and other life pressures affect your capacity to stay regulated during your child's crisis.

Perfectionism and control: If you struggle with needing to control situations or appear as a "perfect parent," meltdowns can trigger significant personal distress.

Sensory sensitivities: If you have your own sensory processing differences, your child's loud or intense meltdown might trigger your own nervous system responses.

Strategies for Self-Regulation During Crisis

Breathing regulation: Focus on slow, deep breathing to activate your own parasympathetic nervous system. This benefits both you and your child.

Grounding techniques: Feel your feet on the floor, notice your physical surroundings, or use other grounding strategies to stay present rather than getting lost in your own activation.

Self-talk management: Use phrases like "This is temporary," "My child needs my calm presence," "Their behavior isn't about me," or "I can handle this."

Physical self-care: If possible, drink water, step outside for a moment, or do other brief self-care activities that help maintain your regulation.

Perspective reminders: Remember that meltdowns are neurobiological processes, not character flaws or parenting failures.

When You Become Dysregulated

Recognize it quickly: Learn your own warning signs of activation—increased heart rate, tension, racing thoughts, or emotional reactivity.

Take a brief break: If safety allows, take a few minutes to regulate yourself before returning to support your child.

Get support: If another adult is available, ask them to provide support while you regulate, rather than trying to push through your own dysregulation.

Repair afterwards: If you respond poorly during a meltdown because of your own activation, repair the relationship afterwards by acknowledging your mistake and reconnecting.

Learn from patterns: Notice what tends to trigger your own dysregulation and develop strategies to prevent or manage these triggers in the future.

The Recovery Transition

The end of a meltdown doesn't mean an immediate return to normal functioning. There's typically a recovery period where your child's nervous system is vulnerable and needs continued support.

Recognizing Recovery Signs

Physical indicators: Breathing slows and deepens, muscle tension releases, aggressive movements stop, and your child may appear exhausted or depleted.

Emotional indicators: Crying may shift from angry or panicked to sad or relieved, your child may seek comfort, or they may appear emotionally "empty."

Cognitive indicators: Your child may begin responding to their name or simple questions, though complex thinking may still be limited.

Behavioral indicators: Aggressive or destructive behaviors stop, your child may become still or seek comfort items, or they may fall asleep from exhaustion.

Supporting the Recovery Process

Gentle re-connection: Offer comfort and connection without demands. This might be physical comfort if your child seeks it, or simply calm presence if they need space.

Basic needs attention: Your child may need water, food, bathroom breaks, or other basic needs met after the energy expenditure of a meltdown.

Environmental support: Continue to keep the environment calm and predictable. Avoid returning to normal household activities immediately.

Emotional validation: If your child is able to communicate, validate their experience without trying to process or analyze the meltdown yet.

Protection from demands: Don't expect your child to return to normal activities, responsibilities, or emotional regulation immediately after a meltdown.

Building Your Crisis Support Skills

Supporting your child through meltdowns effectively is a skill that develops over time. Each experience teaches you more about your child's patterns, your own responses, and what strategies work best for your family.

Learning from Each Experience

Post-meltdown reflection: After everyone has recovered, reflect on what worked well and what you might do differently next time.

Pattern identification: Look for patterns in what triggers meltdowns, how they unfold, and what supports recovery most effectively.

Environmental assessment: Consider whether environmental factors contributed to the meltdown and what modifications might prevent similar incidents.

Personal growth: Notice your own growth in staying regulated, providing effective support, and maintaining perspective during difficult moments.

Building Confidence Over Time

Celebrating success: Acknowledge when you provide effective support during meltdowns, even if they're still difficult experiences.

Skill development: Each meltdown you handle well increases your confidence and competence for future challenges.

Relationship strengthening: When you support your child effectively during their most difficult moments, it builds trust and connection that strengthens your relationship.

Family resilience: Families who learn to navigate meltdowns together develop greater overall resilience and capacity to handle life's challenges.

The Transformation That Comes with Understanding

When Jennifer learned to see Marcus's meltdowns as nervous system communications rather than behavioral problems, everything changed. Instead of trying to stop, control, or punish the meltdown, she focused on providing what his nervous system actually needed: safety, patience, and the presence of a regulated adult.

The meltdowns didn't disappear overnight, but they became shorter, less intense, and less traumatic for everyone involved. More importantly, Marcus began to trust that his mom would be there for him during his most difficult moments, which actually helped him feel safer and more regulated overall.

Over time, Marcus internalized his mother's regulated response to his distress. He learned that big feelings were manageable, that he had support during difficult times, and that meltdowns didn't make him bad or unlovable. These lessons became the foundation for lifelong emotional resilience.

Your child's meltdowns aren't failures of parenting or character flaws that need to be eliminated. They're neurobiological processes that communicate your child's need for support, safety, and co-regulation. When you understand what's really happening during these challenging moments and learn to provide what their nervous system actually needs, you become a source of healing and growth rather than additional stress.

The goal isn't to prevent all meltdowns or to handle them perfectly. The goal is to provide safety, support, and connection during your child's most vulnerable moments, helping them learn that they can survive difficult experiences and that they have support when they need it most. This is how resilience is built—not through eliminating all challenges, but through experiencing support and recovery during life's inevitable storms.

Chapter 11: Post-Meltdown Nervous System Reset

The room was finally quiet. Nine-year-old Chloe lay curled on her bed, wrapped in her weighted blanket, breathing still a bit uneven from the 45-minute meltdown that had just ended. Toys were scattered across her bedroom floor where she'd thrown them, her favorite stuffed animal was damp with tears, and the whole house felt emotionally heavy.

Her mom, Rachel, stood in the doorway feeling emotionally drained herself. The immediate crisis was over, but she wasn't sure what came next. Should she clean up the mess? Talk about what happened? Pretend nothing occurred and move on with their evening routine? Give consequences for the thrown toys? Or simply let Chloe rest?

Rachel's instinct was to jump into problem-solving mode—to process what had happened, figure out how to prevent it next time, and get life back to "normal" as quickly as possible. But she'd been learning about nervous system recovery, and she realized that what Chloe needed most right now wasn't analysis or solutions. Her daughter's nervous system had just been through a major storm and needed time, safety, and gentle support to truly reset.

The recovery phase after a meltdown is often overlooked, but it's actually one of the most crucial times for building resilience, maintaining relationships, and preventing future crises. How you handle the hours after a meltdown can determine whether the experience becomes traumatic or healing for your child.

The Recovery Phase: What Your Child Needs Most

Recovery from a meltdown isn't just about stopping the intense behaviors—it's about helping your child's nervous system return to a regulated state and process what happened in a way that builds resilience rather than shame.

The Neurobiological Recovery Process

Dr. Bruce Perry's research shows that recovery from nervous system activation follows predictable stages, but these stages take time and can't be rushed (Perry & Szalavitz, 2007). During a meltdown, your child's brain is flooded with stress hormones like cortisol and adrenaline. These chemicals don't just disappear when the crisis ends—they need to be metabolized and cleared from the system.

Immediate aftermath (0-30 minutes): Your child's brain is still processing the stress response. They may appear calm but are actually in a fragile state where re-activation can happen easily.

Early recovery (30 minutes to 2 hours): Stress hormones begin to clear, but your child's nervous system remains sensitive and depleted. They may seem tired, emotional, or "off."

Extended recovery (2-24 hours): The nervous system gradually returns to baseline, but full recovery may take until the next day, especially after intense or prolonged meltdowns.

Understanding this timeline helps you set appropriate expectations for your child and avoid pushing them to return to normal functioning before their nervous system is ready.

The Vulnerability Window

In the immediate aftermath of a meltdown, your child's nervous system is in what researchers call a "vulnerability window." They're more susceptible to:

- Emotional overwhelm from minor triggers

- Sensory sensitivities that seem worse than usual

- Difficulty with tasks that are normally manageable

- Need for extra support and co-regulation

- Physical exhaustion or hypervigilance

This vulnerability isn't weakness or attention-seeking—it's neurobiology. Just as a person needs time to recover after running a marathon, your child needs time to recover after their nervous system has been in crisis mode.

What Recovery Actually Looks Like

Recovery doesn't mean immediately returning to pre-meltdown functioning. It's a gradual process that might include:

Physical recovery: Your child may need rest, food, water, or other basic needs met. They might appear exhausted or, conversely, hyperalert and unable to settle.

Emotional recovery: Your child might be extra sensitive, weepy, or clingy. They may need comfort and reassurance more than usual.

Cognitive recovery: Your child's thinking may be slower or more concrete than usual. Complex decisions or academic tasks may be particularly challenging.

Social recovery: Your child might need extra space from others, or conversely, might need more connection and support than usual.

Behavioral recovery: Your child might regress to younger behaviors, need more structure, or require modified expectations for responsibilities.

Eleven-year-old Jordan's parents learned that his recovery process was predictable: first he'd sleep for 30-60 minutes, then he'd be quietly clingy for several hours, and finally he'd gradually return to his usual energy and engagement levels. Understanding this pattern helped them support his recovery rather than pushing him to "bounce back" too quickly.

Nervous System Reset Activities and Techniques

Supporting your child's nervous system recovery requires specific activities and approaches that help their system process the stress response and return to regulation.

Somatic Recovery Activities

The body holds the stress of meltdowns in muscle tension, breathing patterns, and nervous system activation. Somatic activities help release this stored stress and signal safety to the nervous system.

Breathing regulation: Gentle breathing exercises can help shift the nervous system from stress response back toward regulation. This might be as simple as breathing with your child or using apps with guided breathing exercises.

Movement release: Gentle movement helps metabolize stress hormones and reset the nervous system. This might include stretching, walking, swinging, or other rhythmic activities.

Temperature regulation: Cool washcloths, warm baths, or other temperature changes can help activate the parasympathetic nervous system and signal safety.

Progressive muscle relaxation: Systematically tensing and releasing muscle groups helps release physical tension and promote relaxation.

Sensory regulation: Providing appropriate sensory input—deep pressure, gentle music, soft lighting, or preferred textures—helps the nervous system reset.

Environmental Recovery Supports

The environment during recovery should support nervous system regulation rather than adding additional stress or stimulation.

Calm sensory environment: Reduce bright lights, loud sounds, strong smells, or other potentially overwhelming sensory input.

Safe physical space: Provide a comfortable, private space where your child can rest and recover without feeling observed or judged.

Minimal demands: Avoid placing any non-essential demands on your child during the recovery period. This isn't the time for chores, homework, or social expectations.

Predictable routine: Maintain familiar, comforting routines that help your child feel safe and supported.

Available comfort items: Make sure your child has access to stuffed animals, blankets, or other comfort objects that help them feel secure.

Co-Regulation During Recovery

Your regulated presence continues to be important during recovery, but the type of co-regulation needed may be different from what's helpful during the actual meltdown.

Calm availability: Be available for support without being intrusive. Your child should know you're there if needed without feeling pressured to interact.

Gentle attunement: Pay attention to your child's cues about what kind of support they need—physical comfort, space, conversation, or simply presence.

Patience with the process: Resist the urge to rush recovery or return to normal activities. Allow your child's nervous system to reset at its own pace.

Non-judgmental presence: Your child may feel embarrassed or ashamed about their meltdown. Your calm, accepting presence helps prevent additional shame from building.

Eight-year-old Maya needed very specific recovery support: a warm bath with lavender Epsom salts, followed by snuggling with her mom while listening to soft music. This routine became a reliable way to help her nervous system reset after difficult experiences.

Repairing Connection After Challenging Moments

Meltdowns can strain family relationships and leave everyone feeling disconnected or emotionally bruised. Repairing these connections is crucial for maintaining trust and preventing shame from building up over time.

The Importance of Relationship Repair

Dr. Dan Siegel's research shows that repair after difficult moments is actually more important for secure attachment than avoiding all conflicts or challenges (Siegel and Bryson, 2012). Children need to learn that relationships can survive difficult moments and that they remain loved and accepted even when their behavior is challenging.

Repair builds resilience: When children experience repair after difficult moments, they learn that mistakes and struggles don't end relationships or make them unlovable.

Repair prevents shame: Without repair, children may develop shame about their struggles, believing that they're "bad" or "broken" when they have meltdowns.

Repair maintains connection: The repair process actually strengthens relationships by demonstrating unconditional love and acceptance.

Repair models healthy relationships: Children learn important skills about how to maintain connections even after difficult experiences.

Elements of Effective Repair

Emotional safety first: Before attempting repair, make sure your child feels emotionally safe and their nervous system has begun to regulate.

Taking responsibility: If you made mistakes during the meltdown (getting activated yourself, saying hurtful things, or responding poorly), acknowledge your part and apologize.

Validating their experience: Help your child understand that their feelings and struggles make sense, even if their behavior was challenging.

Reconnecting: Engage in activities that rebuild emotional connection—physical affection (if welcomed), special time together, or shared positive experiences.

Future planning: Once connection is restored, you can work together on strategies to handle similar situations better in the future.

Age-Appropriate Repair Conversations

Ages 3-6: "I love you even when you have big feelings. Everyone has hard times, and I'm always here to help you."

Ages 7-11: "That was a really hard time for both of us. I love you, and we can figure out how to handle things better next time. What do you think would help?"

Ages 12+: "I know that was difficult for you, and I appreciate that you're working on managing these big feelings. Let's talk about what we both learned and how we can support each other better."

Repair When You've Made Mistakes

Parents aren't perfect, and sometimes you'll respond poorly during your child's meltdown—getting activated yourself, saying things you regret, or handling the situation in ways that aren't helpful. Repairing these mistakes is crucial:

Acknowledge your mistakes: "I got upset too, and I said some things that weren't helpful. That wasn't fair to you."

Apologize sincerely: "I'm sorry for how I handled that. You deserved my support, not my frustration."

Take responsibility: "That was about my stress, not about you. Your feelings were completely understandable."

Commit to doing better: "I'm working on staying calm during hard times so I can be the parent you need."

Processing the Meltdown Without Shame or Blame

Once your child's nervous system has had time to recover, there can be value in processing what happened—but this must be done carefully to avoid creating shame or trauma around the experience.

When to Process

Not immediately: Processing should wait until your child's nervous system has truly recovered, which may be hours or even the next day after an intense meltdown.

When your child is regulated: Only attempt processing when your child is calm, connected, and able to access their thinking brain.

When connection is restored: Make sure your relationship feels secure and connected before attempting to analyze or problem-solve.

When your child is open: Some children never want to talk about their meltdowns, and that's okay. Follow your child's lead about whether processing is helpful.

How to Process Helpfully

Start with validation: "That was a really hard experience for you. Big feelings can be overwhelming."

Normalize the experience: "Everyone has times when their feelings get too big to handle. It's part of being human."

Focus on learning, not blame: "What can we learn from this that might help next time?" rather than "Why did you act that way?"

Identify triggers collaboratively: "It seemed like you were already stressed before the thing with your sister happened. What do you think was making your nervous system work extra hard?"

Problem-solve together: "What could we try differently next time you're feeling overwhelmed?"

What Not to Do During Processing

Don't rehash details: Avoid making your child relive the meltdown by going through every detail of what happened.

Don't assign blame: Focus on understanding and learning rather than determining who was "right" or "wrong."

Don't demand apologies: Forced apologies aren't meaningful and can create shame. If apologies happen naturally, that's different.

Don't make promises about the future: Your child can't promise never to have meltdowns again, and asking them to make such promises sets them up for failure.

Don't turn it into a lecture: Keep processing brief and collaborative rather than lengthy one-sided discussions about behavior.

Twelve-year-old Alex had a helpful processing conversation with his dad the day after a difficult meltdown: "I think my nervous system was already stressed from the math test, and then when my computer froze while I was working on my project, it just felt like too much." This insight helped them plan better support for high-stress days.

Learning from Meltdowns to Prevent Future Occurrences

While you can't prevent all meltdowns, each experience provides valuable information that can help you support your child's nervous system more effectively in the future.

Pattern Recognition

Trigger identification: Look for patterns in what situations, environments, or stressors tend to precede meltdowns.

Early warning signs: Notice the specific signs your child shows when their nervous system is approaching overwhelm.

Time patterns: Pay attention to whether meltdowns happen more frequently at certain times of day, days of the week, or seasons.

Environmental factors: Consider how sensory environments, social situations, or routine changes contribute to meltdowns.

Recovery patterns: Understanding how your child recovers can help you plan support and set appropriate expectations.

System Improvements

Environmental modifications: Based on what you learn, make changes to home, school, or community environments that reduce triggers.

Routine adjustments: Modify daily routines to better support your child's nervous system needs and reduce stress accumulation.

Support system enhancements: Identify where additional support might prevent meltdowns—more co-regulation time, different transitions, or modified expectations.

Communication improvements: Work with your child to develop better ways to communicate their needs before reaching crisis point.

Skill building: Help your child develop age-appropriate regulation skills that they can use when feeling overwhelmed.

Family System Learning

Improved family responses: Each meltdown teaches the whole family how to respond more effectively during crisis.

Better prevention strategies: Families learn to recognize conditions that make meltdowns more likely and adjust accordingly.

Enhanced communication: Family members get better at discussing stress, needs, and support strategies openly.

Stronger relationships: Successfully navigating meltdowns together builds family resilience and connection.

Building Resilience Through Recovery Experiences

The way you handle recovery after meltdowns either builds your child's resilience or contributes to their sense of shame and inadequacy. Recovery experiences can become opportunities for growth and healing.

What Builds Resilience

Unconditional acceptance: Your child learns that they're loved and accepted even during their most difficult moments.

Competence building: Helping your child process and learn from meltdowns builds their sense of capability and self-understanding.

Hope and optimism: Recovery experiences that focus on learning and growth help children feel hopeful about handling future challenges.

Self-compassion: How you treat your child during recovery teaches them how to treat themselves when they struggle.

Connection and support: Children learn that they don't have to face difficult experiences alone and that support is available when needed.

Long-Term Resilience Outcomes

Emotional intelligence: Children who receive support during recovery develop better understanding of their own emotions and needs.

Self-advocacy skills: Children learn to recognize when they need support and how to ask for it appropriately.

Stress tolerance: Positive recovery experiences gradually build children's capacity to handle stress and challenges.

Relationship skills: Children learn how to maintain connections even after difficult moments, which serves them well in all relationships.

Self-acceptance: Children develop a realistic, compassionate view of themselves that includes both strengths and challenges.

The Recovery Investment

Supporting your child's recovery after meltdowns requires time, energy, and patience, but this investment pays enormous dividends in your child's long-term development and your family's overall wellbeing.

Short-Term Benefits

Faster regulation: Children who receive good recovery support typically regulate more quickly after future meltdowns.

Reduced shame: Proper recovery support prevents shame from building up around having meltdowns.

Stronger relationships: Recovery experiences that include repair and connection actually strengthen family bonds.

Better learning: Children who don't feel ashamed about their struggles are more open to learning and growth.

Long-Term Benefits

Emotional resilience: Children develop confidence in their ability to recover from difficult experiences.

Healthy relationship patterns: Children learn that relationships can survive conflict and grow stronger through repair.

Self-compassion: Children internalize the compassionate response they receive and learn to treat themselves kindly during struggles.

Life skills: The recovery process teaches valuable skills for handling stress, relationships, and personal challenges throughout life.

Creating Your Family's Recovery Protocol

Every family needs to develop their own approach to recovery that honors their child's unique needs while fitting within family constraints and values.

Individual Recovery Needs

Sensory preferences: Some children need quiet and calm, while others need gentle activity or sensory input.

Social needs: Some children need solitude to recover, while others need connection and interaction.

Time requirements: Different children need different amounts of time to recover fully.

Environmental needs: Consider what physical environments support your child's recovery best.

Comfort strategies: Identify what specific activities, objects, or routines help your child feel better.

Family Recovery Protocols

Immediate response: What does your family do in the first 30 minutes after a meltdown ends?

Extended support: How do you modify expectations and provide support during the longer recovery period?

Sibling considerations: How do you meet everyone's needs during one child's recovery?

Parent self-care: How do you take care of your own needs so you can provide effective support?

Communication plans: How do you communicate with schools, family members, or others about your child's recovery needs?

The story of Chloe and Rachel from our opening illustrates how understanding recovery can transform the post-meltdown experience. Instead of rushing to clean up and move on, Rachel created space for Chloe's nervous system to reset. She offered gentle comfort, maintained a calm environment, and waited until the next day to have any conversations about what had happened.

This approach helped Chloe learn that meltdowns weren't shameful disasters but rather temporary experiences that she could recover from with support. Over time, Chloe's recovery periods became shorter, and her resilience in handling future challenges grew stronger.

Recovery after meltdowns isn't just about getting back to normal—it's about creating experiences that build resilience, maintain relationships, and teach your child that they can survive difficult moments with their sense of self and family connections intact.

The goal isn't perfect recovery every time, but rather a consistent approach that prioritizes your child's nervous system needs, preserves their dignity, and builds their capacity for handling life's inevitable challenges. When you invest in recovery, you're investing in your child's long-term emotional health and your family's ability to weather future storms together.

.

Chapter 12: Building Resilience Over Time

Fifteen-year-old Sarah sat in her bedroom, laptop open, working on a challenging history essay that would have completely overwhelmed her three years earlier. When she felt her stress levels rising and noticed her jaw clenching—her personal early warning sign—she paused her work, did some deep breathing exercises, and took a ten-minute walk around the block.

"Mom," she called when she returned, "I'm feeling pretty overwhelmed by this essay. Can we talk through my ideas? I think I just need to organize my thoughts with someone."

Sarah's mom, Jennifer, smiled as she put down her book. Three years ago, this same scenario would have ended in a two-hour meltdown, tears, thrown papers, and everyone in the family feeling exhausted and disconnected. Now, Sarah recognized her own nervous system signals, knew what strategies helped her regulate, and could advocate for the support she needed—all while maintaining her emotional equilibrium.

This transformation didn't happen overnight. It was the result of consistent nervous system support, hundreds of co-regulation experiences, and a family commitment to building Sarah's capacity gradually over time. This is what resilience looks like in neurodivergent children: not the absence of challenges, but the growing ability to navigate challenges successfully with appropriate support.

Understanding Resilience in Neurodivergent Children

Resilience for neurodivergent children doesn't mean becoming neurotypical or eliminating all struggles. True resilience is about developing the self-awareness, skills, and support systems needed to thrive within their unique neurobiological design.

168

Redefining Resilience

Traditional definitions of resilience often emphasize independence, emotional control, and the ability to "bounce back" quickly from adversity. For neurodivergent children, these definitions can be problematic because they don't account for nervous system differences and may actually promote masking rather than authentic coping.

Neurodivergent resilience includes:

- Understanding and accepting their own nervous system patterns

- Developing effective strategies for managing their unique challenges

- Building support networks that understand their needs

- Learning to advocate for appropriate accommodations

- Maintaining their authentic self while adapting to environmental demands

- Recognizing that needing support is strength, not weakness

Dr. Brené Brown's research on resilience emphasizes that resilient people aren't those who never fall down, but those who know how to get back up and who have supportive relationships that help them through difficult times (Brown, 2017). This perspective aligns much better with neurodivergent experiences.

The Neurodivergent Resilience Profile

Resilient neurodivergent children typically develop several key characteristics:

Self-awareness: They understand their own nervous system patterns, triggers, and needs. They can recognize when they're approaching overwhelm and know what helps them regulate.

Self-advocacy: They can communicate their needs to others and request appropriate accommodations without shame or apology.

Flexible coping: They have multiple strategies for handling challenges and can adapt their approach based on the situation.

Support utilization: They know how to access and use support systems effectively, understanding that interdependence is healthy and necessary.

Identity integration: They see their neurodivergent traits as part of their identity rather than something to hide or overcome.

Growth mindset: They view challenges as opportunities to learn and develop rather than evidence of personal failure.

Resilience vs. Masking

It's crucial to distinguish between authentic resilience and masking. Masking occurs when neurodivergent individuals suppress their authentic responses and mimic neurotypical behavior to fit in or avoid negative consequences. While masking can look like resilience from the outside, it's actually emotionally and physically exhausting and can lead to burnout and mental health challenges.

Masking behaviors might include:

- Forcing eye contact despite discomfort
- Suppressing stimming behaviors in public
- Pretending to understand social cues when confused
- Hiding sensory overwhelm until reaching private spaces
- Agreeing to activities that are genuinely overwhelming
- Avoiding asking for help even when needed

Authentic resilience includes:

- Using accommodations and supports without shame

- Stimming or self-regulating openly when needed

- Communicating honestly about challenges and needs

- Setting boundaries around overwhelming situations

- Asking for clarification when confused

- Taking breaks or using regulation strategies as needed

The goal is building genuine capacity to handle life's challenges while honoring neurodivergent needs, not teaching children to appear "normal" at the expense of their wellbeing.

Gradual Nervous System Capacity Building

Building resilience in neurodivergent children is like physical fitness training—it requires consistent practice, gradual challenge increases, and adequate recovery time. You can't build capacity by throwing children into overwhelming situations, but you also can't build it by avoiding all challenges.

The Challenge-Support Balance

Dr. Lev Vygotsky's concept of the "zone of proximal development" provides a useful framework for building resilience (Vygotsky, 1978). This is the space between what a child can do independently and what they can do with support. Resilience building happens in this zone—challenging enough to promote growth, but supported enough to prevent overwhelm.

Too little challenge: Children don't develop new skills or confidence if they never encounter difficulties that stretch their current abilities.

Appropriate challenge with support: Children can handle slightly more than their current independent capacity when they have appropriate support and preparation.

Too much challenge: Children become overwhelmed and may develop negative associations with challenging situations if the difficulty exceeds their supported capacity.

The key is gradually expanding the challenge level while maintaining adequate support, then slowly reducing support as the child's independent capacity grows.

Scaffolded Skill Building

Start with regulation foundation: Before building capacity for handling challenges, ensure your child has solid nervous system regulation skills and support.

Identify growth areas: Choose specific areas where you want to build your child's capacity—social situations, academic challenges, sensory environments, or emotional regulation.

Break skills into components: Complex resilience skills need to be broken down into smaller, teachable components.

Practice in safe environments: New skills should be practiced first in low-stakes, supportive environments before being applied in more challenging situations.

Celebrate incremental progress: Acknowledge small improvements rather than waiting for major breakthroughs.

Ten-year-old Marcus was working on building capacity for handling unexpected changes. His parents started by making tiny, positive changes to his routine (ice cream for dessert instead of cookies) and celebrating how well he adapted. Gradually, they introduced slightly larger changes while providing extra support and preparation. Over six months, Marcus's capacity for handling changes grew significantly, and his anxiety around unpredictability decreased.

Recovery and Integration Time

Building capacity isn't just about facing challenges—it's also about having adequate time to recover and integrate new experiences. Neurodivergent nervous systems often need more recovery time than neurotypical systems, and respecting this need is crucial for sustainable growth.

After challenging experiences: Plan recovery time where your child can process and integrate what they've learned without additional demands.

Between challenges: Don't pack too many growth opportunities into a short period. Allow time for consolidation between new experiences.

Seasonal considerations: Some times of year are naturally more demanding (back to school, holidays), requiring modified expectations for capacity building.

Individual rhythms: Each child has their own rhythm for growth and recovery. Some can handle frequent small challenges, while others need longer periods between growth experiences.

The Role of Success Experiences in Building Confidence

Confidence comes from repeated experiences of successfully handling challenges, not from avoiding all difficulties. For neurodivergent children, creating appropriate success experiences requires careful attention to their unique strengths and needs.

Designing Success Experiences

Build on strengths: Use your child's existing strengths as platforms for building confidence in new areas. A child who loves animals might build social skills through pet-related activities.

Set achievable goals: Success experiences should stretch your child's abilities without overwhelming their capacity. The goal is growth, not perfection.

Provide appropriate support: Success doesn't mean independent achievement—it means accomplishing goals with whatever support is needed.

Celebrate effort, not just outcomes: Acknowledge the courage it takes to try new things and the effort your child puts into challenges, regardless of the results.

Document progress: Keep records of your child's successes, big and small, so you can remind them of their growth during difficult times.

Types of Success Experiences

Academic successes: Completing challenging assignments with appropriate supports, mastering new concepts, or receiving recognition for effort and improvement.

Social successes: Having positive interactions with peers, successfully navigating social situations, or building meaningful friendships.

Emotional regulation successes: Using coping strategies effectively, recovering from setbacks more quickly, or recognizing and communicating needs appropriately.

Independence successes: Taking on new responsibilities, solving problems independently, or advocating for their needs in new situations.

Creative and personal successes: Pursuing special interests, developing talents, or expressing themselves authentically in various contexts.

Eight-year-old Emma built confidence through a series of carefully planned success experiences around her love of reading. Starting with reading to stuffed animals, she progressed to reading to her little brother, then to volunteering at the library's story time for younger children. Each success built her confidence and communication skills while honoring her introverted nature and need for predictable social interactions.

Learning from Setbacks

Not every experience will be successful, and that's actually important for building resilience. Children need to learn that setbacks are part of growth, not evidence of failure.

Normalize struggle: Help your child understand that everyone faces challenges and that struggling doesn't mean they're doing something wrong.

Process disappointments: When things don't go as planned, help your child process the experience without shame while identifying what they learned.

Adjust strategies: Use setbacks as opportunities to refine approaches, modify supports, or try different strategies.

Maintain perspective: Help your child see individual setbacks in the context of their overall growth and progress.

Plan next steps: After processing a setback, work together to plan how to approach similar situations in the future.

Supporting Your Child's Growing Self-Awareness

Self-awareness is perhaps the most important component of neurodivergent resilience. Children who understand their own patterns, needs, and responses can advocate for themselves and make choices that support their wellbeing.

Building Nervous System Awareness

Body awareness activities: Regular practices that help children notice physical sensations, tension patterns, breathing, and other bodily experiences.

Emotional vocabulary: Helping children develop rich language for describing their internal experiences beyond basic happy/sad/mad categories.

Pattern recognition: Supporting children in noticing their own patterns—what situations are challenging, what helps them feel better, what time of day they function best.

Trigger identification: Helping children recognize what environmental, social, or internal factors tend to trigger stress responses.

Strength recognition: Supporting children in identifying and celebrating their unique strengths, talents, and positive qualities.

Self-Monitoring Skills

Check-in practices: Teaching children to regularly assess their own nervous system state and needs throughout the day.

Early warning recognition: Helping children identify their personal early warning signs of overwhelm or dysregulation.

Strategy effectiveness tracking: Supporting children in noticing which coping strategies work best for them in different situations.

Environmental awareness: Helping children recognize how different environments affect their regulation and performance.

Social dynamics awareness: Supporting children in understanding how different social situations and relationships impact their wellbeing.

Thirteen-year-old David developed a personal "regulation checklist" that he used several times throughout the day: Am I hungry/thirsty? How's my energy level? Do I need movement or rest? What's my stress level? Do I need to use any coping strategies? This self-monitoring practice helped him catch problems early and maintain better regulation throughout the day.

Identity Integration

Neurodivergent identity: Helping children understand and accept their neurodivergent traits as part of their identity rather than something to hide or fix.

Strength-based perspective: Focusing on how neurodivergent traits can be advantages in certain contexts while acknowledging areas that need support.

Community connection: Connecting children with other neurodivergent individuals who can serve as positive role models and provide community.

Advocacy skills: Teaching children how to explain their needs to others and request appropriate accommodations without shame.

Future planning: Helping children envision how their unique traits and strengths might contribute to future educational and career goals.

Celebrating Progress and Small Wins

Building resilience is a long-term process with many small steps rather than dramatic breakthroughs. Learning to notice and celebrate incremental progress is crucial for maintaining motivation and building confidence.

What to Celebrate

Effort over outcome: Acknowledge when your child tries something difficult, regardless of how well it goes.

Strategy use: Celebrate when your child remembers to use coping strategies, even if they don't work perfectly.

Self-awareness moments: Acknowledge when your child recognizes their own needs or emotional states.

Problem-solving attempts: Celebrate creative problem-solving, even when the solutions aren't perfect.

Recovery improvements: Notice when your child bounces back from setbacks more quickly than before.

Self-advocacy instances: Acknowledge when your child communicates their needs or asks for help appropriately.

Growth in challenging areas: Celebrate progress in areas that are particularly difficult for your child.

How to Celebrate Meaningfully

Specific acknowledgment: Instead of generic praise, specifically acknowledge what your child did well. "I noticed how you took deep breaths when you started feeling overwhelmed. That helped you stay regulated."

Process focus: Celebrate the process of growth rather than just achievements. "You've been working so hard on recognizing your feelings. I can see how much more aware you're becoming."

Individual relevance: Celebrate progress that's meaningful for your specific child rather than comparing to external standards.

Connection building: Use celebration as an opportunity for positive connection rather than just performance recognition.

Future orientation: Help your child see how their current progress connects to future goals and capabilities.

Creating Progress Documentation

Growth journals: Keep records of your child's progress, challenges overcome, and skills developed over time.

Photo documentation: Take pictures of your child engaged in challenging activities or celebrating achievements.

Skill checklists: Create visual representations of skills your child has developed and is working on.

Success stories: Write down specific examples of times your child handled challenges well or showed growth.

Video messages: Record your child talking about their experiences and growth to watch during difficult times.

Nine-year-old Jordan's family created a "resilience scrapbook" with photos and stories of challenging things he'd accomplished, strategies he'd learned, and growth he'd experienced. During difficult periods, they'd look through the book together to remind Jordan of his capabilities and progress.

Long-Term Nervous System Health Strategies

Building resilience isn't just about handling current challenges—it's about creating sustainable practices that support nervous system health throughout life.

Daily Nervous System Maintenance

Consistent sleep routines: Prioritizing sleep hygiene and adequate rest as foundation for nervous system health.

Nutritional support: Eating patterns that support stable blood sugar and provide nutrients needed for neurotransmitter production.

Movement integration: Regular physical activity that supports nervous system regulation and overall health.

Stress management: Daily practices that help process and release accumulated stress.

Connection and community: Regular positive social interactions that provide co-regulation and emotional support.

Environmental Optimization

Home environment: Creating living spaces that support rather than stress the nervous system.

School collaboration: Working with educational teams to ensure school environments and expectations honor neurodivergent needs.

Community engagement: Finding community activities and organizations that appreciate neurodivergent contributions.

Technology use: Developing healthy relationships with technology that support rather than overwhelm the nervous system.

Seasonal adjustments: Modifying routines and expectations to account for seasonal changes and their impact on nervous system functioning.

Preventive Strategies

Stress inoculation: Gradually building capacity to handle stress through appropriately challenging experiences with support.

Skill building: Continuously developing new coping strategies and regulation techniques.

Support network development: Building relationships with family, friends, professionals, and community members who understand and support neurodivergent needs.

Self-advocacy advancement: Continuously improving ability to communicate needs and access appropriate supports.

Identity development: Ongoing work to integrate neurodivergent identity in positive, strength-based ways.

The Family System and Resilience

Building resilience in neurodivergent children affects and requires support from the entire family system. When families approach resilience building as a team effort, everyone benefits.

Family Resilience Practices

Shared understanding: Ensuring all family members understand neurodivergent nervous systems and the approaches being used to build resilience.

Collective celebration: Making resilience building a family celebration rather than focusing only on one child's progress.

Sibling support: Helping all children in the family develop understanding and support for each other's growth processes.

Parent modeling: Demonstrating healthy stress management, self-advocacy, and growth mindset for children to observe.

Family traditions: Creating family traditions around growth, challenge, and support that reinforce resilience values.

Addressing Family Stress

Parent self-care: Ensuring parents get the support they need to maintain their own resilience and ability to support their children.

Sibling needs: Making sure neurotypical siblings don't feel neglected or resentful of the attention given to neurodivergent family members.

Extended family education: Helping extended family members understand and support the family's approach to building resilience.

Community resources: Accessing community resources, support groups, and services that reduce family stress and increase available support.

Professional support: Working with therapists, coaches, or other professionals who can provide additional expertise and support.

The Long-Term Vision

Building resilience in neurodivergent children is an investment in their future capacity to live fulfilling, authentic lives while navigating a world that often doesn't understand their needs.

Adult Outcomes of Childhood Resilience Building

Self-acceptance: Adults who received resilience support as children tend to have positive relationships with their neurodivergent identity.

Effective self-advocacy: They can communicate their needs in work, relationships, and community settings.

Appropriate support utilization: They know how to access and use support systems without shame.

Stress management: They have effective strategies for managing the ongoing stresses of living in a neurotypical world.

Relationship skills: They can form and maintain meaningful relationships while honoring their neurodivergent needs.

Career success: They can find and succeed in work environments that utilize their strengths and accommodate their needs.

Community contribution: They can contribute meaningfully to their communities while maintaining their authentic selves.

The Ripple Effects

When neurodivergent children develop genuine resilience, the benefits extend far beyond the individual:

Family relationships: Stronger, more connected family relationships based on understanding and acceptance.

Community awareness: Increased community understanding and acceptance of neurodivergent individuals.

Next generation preparation: Parents who understand nervous system differences are better equipped to support future children.

Professional impact: Adults who've experienced effective support often become advocates and professionals who support other neurodivergent individuals.

Cultural change: Each resilient neurodivergent adult contributes to broader cultural shifts toward acceptance and accommodation.

Your Family's Resilience Journey

The story of Sarah from our opening illustrates what's possible when families commit to building genuine resilience over time. Her transformation from frequent meltdowns to effective self-regulation and self-advocacy didn't happen through forcing compliance or eliminating challenges. It happened through consistent nervous system support, gradual capacity building, and a family commitment to honoring her neurodivergent needs while helping her develop skills for navigating the world.

Building resilience in your neurodivergent child is both a marathon and a series of daily sprints. It requires patience with the long-term process while maintaining consistency in daily support. It means celebrating small victories while keeping sight of larger goals. It involves accepting your child's neurodivergent traits while helping them build capacity to handle life's challenges.

Most importantly, it requires understanding that resilience for neurodivergent children doesn't mean becoming indistinguishable from their neurotypical peers. True resilience is about developing the self-awareness, skills, and support systems needed to thrive as their authentic neurodivergent selves in a world that often demands conformity.

Your child's resilience journey is unique, and there's no perfect timeline or guaranteed outcome. But with consistent support, understanding, and celebration of their authentic self, you can help them develop the confidence and capacity to handle whatever challenges life brings while maintaining their essential sense of self and connection to others.

The goal isn't to eliminate all struggles or create a perfect child. The goal is to support your child in developing genuine resilience—the kind that lasts a lifetime and enables them to contribute their unique gifts to the world while getting their own needs met along the way.

Chapter 13: Creating a Sensory-Smart Home Environment

The Martinez family had tried everything. Behavioral charts, reward systems, consequences, even family therapy. But their ten-year-old daughter Sophia continued to have daily meltdowns, their eight-year-old son Diego refused to eat meals with the family, and everyone walked on eggshells wondering when the next explosion would occur.

Then Maria Martinez attended a workshop on sensory processing and had a revelation. The problem wasn't her children's behavior—it was their home environment. The open-concept kitchen and living room that looked so beautiful in magazines created a sensory nightmare for her children's nervous systems. The fluorescent lights, echoing sounds, competing smells from cooking, and constant visual stimulation were triggering fight-or-flight responses multiple times every day.

Six months later, the same family had transformed their home into a sensory-supportive haven. Strategic lighting changes, sound-absorbing materials, organized visual spaces, and designated quiet zones had dramatically reduced daily meltdowns. More importantly, the children were happier, more regulated, and actually enjoyed spending time in family spaces.

The Martinez family discovered what many families learn: your physical environment is either supporting or sabotaging your neurodivergent child's nervous system every single day. Creating a sensory-smart home isn't about expensive renovations or perfect spaces—it's about understanding how environmental factors affect nervous system regulation and making targeted modifications that help your child thrive.

Understanding Your Home's Sensory Impact

Most families don't realize how much their home environment affects everyone's nervous system, especially sensitive neurodivergent nervous systems. Every aspect of your physical space—from lighting and sound to visual organization and spatial flow—either supports regulation or triggers stress responses.

The Sensory Environment Assessment

Dr. Lucy Jane Miller's research shows that environmental factors can be as powerful as medication in affecting children's behavior and regulation (Miller et al., 2007). But unlike medication, environmental modifications are within every family's control and can benefit everyone in the household.

Think of your home as having a sensory "signature"—a unique combination of visual, auditory, tactile, olfactory, and spatial elements that create either nervous system safety or activation. For neurotypical individuals, a wide range of sensory environments feel comfortable. For neurodivergent individuals, the comfort zone is often much narrower, and environments that seem fine to others can trigger significant stress responses.

Signs your home environment may be triggering stress responses:

- Frequent meltdowns or behavioral challenges that seem to come "out of nowhere"
- Children avoiding certain rooms or areas of the house
- Difficulty with transitions between different areas of the home
- Family members seeming constantly on edge or irritable at home
- Sleep difficulties despite good sleep routines
- Homework battles that seem disproportionate to the actual academic demands

The Eight Sensory Systems in Your Home

Visual system impacts: Lighting quality and quantity, visual clutter, color choices, contrast levels, and the amount of visual information competing for attention in each space.

Auditory system impacts: Background noise levels, echo and reverberation, competing sounds, sudden or unpredictable noises, and the acoustic qualities of different materials and room shapes.

Tactile system impacts: Textures of furniture, flooring, and fabrics, temperature variations, air circulation, humidity levels, and the availability of different tactile experiences.

Olfactory system impacts: Cooking smells, cleaning products, air fresheners, pet odors, and the general scent profile of different spaces.

Gustatory system impacts: Kitchen organization, food storage and presentation, dining space setup, and the sensory experience of family meals.

Proprioceptive system impacts: Furniture that provides deep pressure, spaces for heavy work activities, and opportunities for resistive movement throughout the home.

Vestibular system impacts: Opportunities for safe movement, swinging or rocking options, stairs and elevation changes, and spatial relationships that either support or challenge balance systems.

Interoceptive system impacts: Temperature regulation, air quality, and environmental cues that help or hinder body awareness and internal regulation.

Room-by-Room Sensory Considerations

Each room in your home has its own sensory profile and serves different functions for family life. Understanding how to optimize each space can create a more supportive overall environment.

Living Rooms and Family Spaces

186

Family rooms are often the hub of daily life, which means they need to support a wide range of activities and nervous system states throughout the day.

Lighting optimization: Multiple lighting sources allow you to adjust the environment based on time of day and family needs. Table lamps, floor lamps, and dimmers create more regulation-supportive lighting than bright overhead fixtures. Natural light from windows should be manageable—blinds or curtains can reduce overwhelming brightness when needed.

Sound management: Hard surfaces like hardwood floors and bare walls can create echoing that's overwhelming for auditory-sensitive nervous systems. Area rugs, furniture with soft fabrics, wall hangings, and bookshelves can absorb sound and reduce acoustic overwhelm.

Visual organization: While some visual stimulation is interesting and engaging, too much can trigger hypervigilance in sensitive nervous systems. Organized toy storage, designated spaces for different activities, and periodic decluttering help create visual calm.

Seating variety: Different family members may need different types of seating for optimal regulation. Some children focus better in bean bags or on exercise balls, while others need the support of traditional furniture. Having options allows everyone to find what works for their nervous system.

Twelve-year-old Emma's family discovered that she could only tolerate family movie nights when they dimmed the overhead lights and she could sit in a specific corner of the couch with her weighted blanket. These simple accommodations transformed family time from triggering to connecting.

Kitchens and Dining Areas

Kitchens are sensory-intense environments with sounds, smells, textures, and visual complexity that can be overwhelming for sensitive nervous systems.

Sensory intensity management: During meal preparation, kitchens can become overwhelming with competing smells, sounds from appliances, steam and temperature changes, and visual complexity. Having strategies for reducing intensity during peak cooking times helps everyone stay regulated.

Dining space setup: Consider the sensory experience of family meals. Is the dining table in a high-traffic area with lots of visual distractions? Are there competing sounds from appliances or other family activities? Is the lighting harsh or gentle? Simple changes can make mealtimes more enjoyable for everyone.

Food-related sensory supports: How you store, present, and serve food can significantly impact children with gustatory and tactile sensitivities. Having systems that honor food preferences while encouraging nutritional variety reduces mealtime battles.

Kitchen work spaces: If children help with cooking or food preparation, consider how counter heights, tool accessibility, and work flow support or challenge their sensory systems.

Bedrooms and Sleep Spaces

Bedrooms need to support both active play during the day and nervous system down-regulation for sleep at night.

Sleep environment optimization: Temperature control, lighting that can be gradually reduced, sound management for both internal house sounds and external noise, and tactile comfort through bedding choices all impact sleep quality.

Personal space organization: Bedrooms often serve as retreat spaces where children can decompress from daily stressors. Having organized systems for belongings, comfortable seating or floor space, and sensory regulation tools makes bedrooms more effective as safe havens.

Transition support: The bedroom environment should support the transition from daytime alertness to nighttime calm. This might mean different lighting options, sound management, and environmental cues that signal bedtime preparation.

Individual sensory preferences: Each child's bedroom can be customized to their specific sensory needs—some need minimal visual stimulation while others feel more regulated with favorite posters or decorations. Some need complete darkness while others feel safer with night lights.

Bathrooms and Personal Care Spaces

Bathrooms present unique sensory challenges with their hard surfaces, bright lighting, water sounds, and personal care demands.

Acoustic considerations: Bathroom tiles and hard surfaces create echo that can be overwhelming. Simple additions like bath mats, shower curtains, and towels can soften the acoustic environment.

Lighting adjustments: Bright bathroom lighting can be jarring, especially during nighttime bathroom visits. Consider softer lighting options or dimmer switches that allow for gentler illumination.

Personal care accommodations: Many personal care tasks involve challenging sensory experiences—tooth brushing, hair washing, face washing. Having accommodations like different toothbrush textures, adjustable water temperature, or alternative hair care methods can reduce daily battles.

Privacy and safety: Bathrooms should feel safe and private, with good ventilation, appropriate temperature control, and organization that reduces stress around finding needed items.

Lighting and Visual Environment

Lighting has a profound impact on nervous system regulation, yet it's often overlooked as a source of daily stress or support. The quality, quantity, and timing of light exposure affects mood, attention, sleep patterns, and overall nervous system function.

Understanding Light's Impact on Regulation

Research by Dr. Russell Foster shows that light exposure directly affects circadian rhythms, mood regulation, and cognitive function (Foster & Kreitzman, 2017). For neurodivergent individuals, these effects can be more pronounced, making lighting choices crucial for daily regulation.

Fluorescent lighting challenges: Many schools and public buildings use fluorescent lighting, which flickers at frequencies that can trigger sensory overwhelm, headaches, and attention difficulties in sensitive individuals. At home, avoiding fluorescent lights and choosing alternatives can significantly improve daily regulation.

Blue light considerations: Electronic screens emit blue light that can interfere with sleep preparation and overstimulate already sensitive nervous systems. Managing blue light exposure, especially in evening hours, supports better regulation and sleep.

Natural light benefits: Exposure to natural light, particularly in the morning, helps regulate circadian rhythms and supports overall nervous system health. However, some children are sensitive to bright natural light and need ways to manage intensity.

Practical Lighting Strategies

Multiple light sources: Instead of relying on single overhead fixtures, use multiple smaller light sources that can be adjusted based on activity and time of day. This allows for customization based on current nervous system needs.

Dimmer switches: Installing dimmer switches on major light fixtures allows you to adjust brightness based on time of day, activity, and individual sensory needs.

Warm vs. cool lighting: Warmer light (yellow/orange tones) tends to be more calming and regulation-supportive, while cooler light (blue/white tones) is more alerting. Choose based on the function of each space and time of day usage.

Task-specific lighting: Different activities need different lighting. Reading requires focused task lighting, while relaxation benefits from softer ambient lighting. Having options allows you to match lighting to nervous system needs.

Light filtering options: Blinds, curtains, and window films can help manage natural light intensity throughout the day, allowing you to optimize lighting conditions based on weather, season, and individual sensitivity.

Sound and Acoustic Environment

Sound environments significantly impact nervous system regulation, but acoustic considerations are often invisible until they become problematic. Understanding and managing your home's sound profile can dramatically improve daily family life.

The Neuroscience of Sound and Regulation

Dr. Stephen Porges's research demonstrates that certain sound frequencies directly activate the social engagement system, while others can trigger defensive responses (Porges, 2017). For neurodivergent individuals, sound environments that seem normal to others can constantly activate stress responses.

Background noise accumulation: Many homes have multiple sources of background noise—HVAC systems, appliances, electronics, traffic, neighbors—that create a constant low-level stress on sensitive nervous systems.

Sudden sound reactivity: Unpredictable sounds like doorbells, phone notifications, appliance beeps, and sudden loud noises can trigger startle responses that take time to recover from.

Echoing and reverberation: Hard surfaces create sound reflection that can make spaces feel chaotic and overwhelming, even when actual sound levels aren't particularly high.

Competing sounds: When multiple sound sources compete for attention—TV, conversation, kitchen appliances, music—sensitive nervous systems can become overwhelmed trying to process all the auditory information.

Creating Sound-Supportive Environments

Sound absorption: Adding soft materials throughout your home reduces echo and creates calmer acoustic environments. Area rugs, curtains, upholstered furniture, wall hangings, and even strategically placed blankets can significantly improve room acoustics.

Background noise management: Identify and address sources of unnecessary background noise. This might mean moving humming appliances, fixing squeaky hinges, or creating barriers between noisy and quiet areas.

White noise and sound masking: For some families, consistent background sounds like fans, white noise machines, or soft music can mask sudden noises and create more predictable sound environments.

Quiet zones: Designating certain areas of your home as quiet zones gives family members places to retreat when auditory overwhelm occurs.

Sound awareness: Help family members become aware of how their sound choices affect others. This isn't about complete silence, but about being mindful of cumulative sound effects.

Nine-year-old Marcus couldn't concentrate on homework at the kitchen table until his parents realized that the refrigerator's cycling, the dishwasher's operation, and the neighbor's dog created a combination of sounds that kept his nervous system activated. Moving his homework space to a quieter room solved the problem immediately.

Organization and Visual Calm

Visual environments can either support calm focus or trigger hypervigilance and overwhelm. The goal isn't minimalism for its own sake, but rather creating visual environments that support nervous system regulation.

Visual Processing and Regulation

Dr. Temple Grandin's work highlights how visual environments affect autistic individuals, but these principles apply to many neurodivergent nervous systems (Grandin, 2006). Visual overwhelm can trigger stress responses, while organized, predictable visual environments support calm and focus.

Visual clutter impact: Too much visual information competing for attention can trigger hypervigilance in sensitive nervous systems. This doesn't mean empty rooms, but rather organized, purposeful visual environments.

Color and contrast considerations: High contrast or very bright colors can be overstimulating for some individuals, while others find them focusing. Understanding your child's visual preferences helps create supportive environments.

Organizational systems: Clear organizational systems reduce the cognitive load of finding items and create predictable visual environments that feel safer to sensitive nervous systems.

Practical Organization Strategies

Designated spaces for items: When everything has a specific place, visual environments feel more predictable and manageable. This doesn't require perfect organization, but rather consistent systems that make sense to your family.

Storage solutions: Closed storage can reduce visual clutter while still keeping necessary items accessible. Clear containers allow you to see contents without creating visual overwhelm.

Activity zones: Designating specific areas for different activities—homework, art projects, reading, sensory breaks—helps organize visual environments and supports transitions between activities.

Rotation systems: Instead of having all toys, books, and materials available simultaneously, rotating items keeps visual environments manageable while maintaining variety and interest.

Personal space respect: Each family member may have different visual organization needs. Some children feel regulated by seeing their belongings displayed, while others need minimal visual input to focus.

Temperature and Air Quality

Physical comfort factors like temperature and air quality have significant impacts on nervous system regulation, yet they're often overlooked as sources of daily stress or support.

Environmental Comfort and Regulation

Research shows that temperature extremes and poor air quality can trigger stress responses and interfere with cognitive function (Wargocki & Wyon, 2017). For individuals with sensory processing differences, these effects can be more pronounced.

Temperature sensitivity: Many neurodivergent individuals have heightened sensitivity to temperature variations. Rooms that feel comfortable to some family members might be triggering for others.

Air circulation importance: Stuffy or stagnant air can trigger feelings of overwhelm and difficulty concentrating. Good air circulation supports alertness and regulation.

Humidity considerations: Both very dry and very humid environments can affect comfort and regulation. Finding the right balance for your family's needs may require attention and adjustment.

Air quality factors: Dust, pet dander, cleaning product residues, and other air quality issues can affect sensitive individuals' ability to regulate and focus.

Creating Comfortable Environmental Conditions

Individual temperature zones: Using fans, space heaters, and layered clothing options allows family members to customize their temperature comfort within shared spaces.

Air circulation improvements: Fans, air purifiers, and opening windows when weather permits can improve air quality and circulation throughout your home.

Humidity management: Humidifiers in dry climates or dehumidifiers in humid climates can help create more comfortable environmental conditions.

Air quality attention: Using natural cleaning products, managing dust and allergens, and being mindful of air fresheners and scented products can improve the air quality for sensitive family members.

Creating Sensory Regulation Zones

Every neurodivergent child benefits from having designated spaces where they can retreat when overwhelmed and access tools for nervous system regulation.

The Importance of Retreat Spaces

Dr. Mona Delahooke emphasizes that children need access to regulation spaces where they can decompress without judgment or demands (Delahooke, 2019). These spaces don't have to be entire rooms—they can be corners, closets, or even portable setups that can be used anywhere.

Calming spaces: Areas designed to support nervous system down-regulation when children are feeling overwhelmed or overstimulated.

Alerting spaces: Areas designed to support nervous system activation when children are feeling sluggish or under-aroused.

Neutral spaces: Areas that provide sensory input without being specifically calming or alerting, allowing children to find their own regulation level.

Calming Zone Elements

Lighting: Soft, dim, warm lighting that reduces visual stimulation and supports parasympathetic nervous system activation.

Seating: Comfortable seating options that provide support and security. This might include bean bags, floor cushions, rocking chairs, or cocoon-like spaces.

Sensory tools: Weighted blankets, soft textures, fidget items, noise-reducing headphones, and other tools that provide regulating sensory input.

Visual environment: Minimal visual clutter with perhaps a few preferred calming images or colors. The goal is reducing rather than increasing visual input.

Sound options: Access to calming sounds, music, or white noise, as well as the option for silence.

Alerting Zone Elements

Lighting: Brighter, cooler lighting that supports alertness and activation.

Movement options: Space and equipment for safe movement—mini trampolines, exercise balls, resistance bands, or simply open floor space for stretching and moving.

Sensory input: Items that provide organizing sensory input like crunchy snacks, textured materials, or aromatherapy options that support alertness.

Visual stimulation: Interesting but not overwhelming visual elements that support engagement and focus.

Interactive elements: Art supplies, building materials, or other items that support active, engaging activities.

Eight-year-old Lily's regulation zone was a corner of the living room with a small tent, weighted lap pad, basket of fidget toys, and noise-reducing headphones. When she felt overwhelmed, she could retreat to her space without needing to leave the family area entirely.

Budget-Friendly Environmental Modifications

Creating a sensory-supportive home environment doesn't require expensive renovations or specialized products. Many effective modifications can be implemented with creativity and modest budgets.

Low-Cost High-Impact Changes

Lighting modifications: Switching light bulbs to warmer tones, adding inexpensive table lamps, or installing simple dimmer switches can dramatically improve lighting environments without major expense.

Sound improvements: Area rugs, curtains, blankets, and rearranging furniture can significantly improve room acoustics at minimal cost.

Organization systems: Cardboard boxes, baskets from discount stores, and simple storage solutions can create visual organization without expensive built-ins.

DIY sensory tools: Weighted lap pads can be made with rice in pillowcases, fidget tools can be created from household items, and calming spaces can be made with blankets and pillows.

Natural elements: Plants, stones, shells, and other natural elements can provide calming sensory input and improve air quality at low cost.

Creative Problem-Solving

Repurposing existing items: Look at your current furniture and belongings with new eyes. Can bookshelves be rearranged to create cozy reading nooks? Can blankets be used as wall hangings to improve acoustics?

Community resources: Thrift stores, community groups, and online marketplaces can provide affordable furniture and materials for environmental modifications.

DIY projects: Simple projects like painting walls in calming colors, creating sensory bins, or building simple furniture can be cost-effective ways to improve your environment.

Gradual implementation: You don't need to change everything at once. Implementing modifications gradually allows you to see what works and spread costs over time.

Family involvement: Including children in environmental modifications helps them understand their sensory needs and creates ownership of their spaces.

Family-Wide Benefits of Sensory-Smart Environments

When you create environments that support neurodivergent nervous systems, the benefits extend to all family members. Most people feel calmer and more focused in well-designed sensory environments.

Universal Design Principles

Benefits for neurotypical family members: Reduced visual clutter, good lighting, comfortable acoustics, and organized spaces support everyone's nervous system regulation and daily functioning.

Improved family relationships: When everyone feels more regulated in home environments, family interactions become more positive and connected.

Reduced daily stress: Environmental modifications can prevent many daily challenges before they occur, reducing overall family stress levels.

Enhanced learning and productivity: Family members of all ages can focus and learn better in sensory-supportive environments.

Better sleep for everyone: Bedroom modifications that support one child's sleep often improve sleep quality for the whole family.

Long-Term Investment Value

Sustainable changes: Environmental modifications are one-time investments that continue providing benefits over years.

Adaptable solutions: Most sensory-smart modifications can be adapted as children grow and needs change.

Transferable skills: Children who grow up in sensory-supportive environments develop awareness of their environmental needs that serves them throughout life.

Community impact: Families who understand environmental impacts often become advocates for better design in schools and community spaces.

Your Home as a Nervous System Sanctuary

The Martinez family's transformation illustrates the powerful impact that environmental modifications can have on family life. By understanding how their home's sensory profile affected their children's nervous systems, they were able to make targeted changes that dramatically improved daily regulation and family relationships.

Creating a sensory-smart home isn't about perfection or expensive renovations. It's about understanding how environmental factors affect nervous system regulation and making thoughtful modifications that support your family's unique needs. The goal is creating a home environment that functions as a nervous system sanctuary—a place where everyone can regulate, recharge, and connect.

Your home environment is working for or against your child's nervous system twenty-four hours a day. Small changes in lighting, sound, organization, and comfort can have profound impacts on daily regulation, family relationships, and long-term development. Most importantly, when children grow up in environments designed to support their nervous systems, they develop lifelong awareness of their environmental needs and the confidence to create supportive spaces wherever they go.

The investment you make in creating a sensory-smart home pays dividends not just in reduced daily struggles, but in your child's developing understanding of their own needs and their growing capacity to thrive in a world that often doesn't understand the importance of sensory-supportive environments.

Chapter 14: Supporting Digital Nervous System Health

At 7 PM on a school night, the Chen household erupted into chaos. When mom Linda asked eleven-year-old Kevin to turn off his tablet for dinner, he flew into a rage unlike anything she'd seen during his younger years. Screaming, throwing pillows, and declaring that she was "ruining his life," Kevin seemed completely unable to regulate his emotions around this simple transition.

Linda found herself in a familiar modern parenting dilemma: technology was clearly affecting her son's nervous system, but she couldn't figure out if screens were helping or hurting his regulation. During school, Kevin used his tablet for assignments and seemed more focused with digital tools. But transitions away from screens had become increasingly difficult, and his sleep had gotten worse since getting his own device.

What Linda didn't understand was that technology's impact on neurodivergent nervous systems is complex—screens can be both powerful regulation tools and significant sources of dysregulation, sometimes simultaneously. The key isn't eliminating technology or giving unlimited access, but rather understanding how different types of screen activities affect your child's nervous system and creating intentional approaches that support rather than sabotage regulation.

How Screens Affect the Neurodivergent Nervous System

Technology interacts with neurodivergent nervous systems in ways that can be dramatically different from neurotypical experiences. Understanding these interactions helps you make informed decisions about screen time that support rather than undermine your child's overall regulation and development.

The Neurobiological Impact of Screen Time

Dr. Victoria Dunckley's research reveals that excessive or inappropriate screen time can trigger what she terms "Electronic Screen Syndrome"—a pattern of symptoms including irritability, mood swings, difficulty with transitions, and sleep disruption (Dunckley, 2015). For neurodivergent children, these effects can be more pronounced because their nervous systems are already more sensitive to stimulation and change.

Dopamine and reward system effects: Many digital activities trigger dopamine release through variable reward schedules—likes on social media, points in games, or new content recommendations. For children with ADHD, whose brains already have differences in dopamine processing, this can create particularly strong attractions to screen activities and difficulty transitioning away.

Visual system overstimulation: The rapid visual changes, bright colors, and constant motion in many digital media can overwhelm visual processing systems that are already sensitive. This is particularly relevant for autistic children who may have differences in visual processing.

Attention regulation impacts: While some screen activities can help focus and regulate attention, others fragment attention in ways that make sustained focus more difficult. The key is understanding which types of digital activities support vs. scatter your child's attention.

Sleep cycle disruption: Blue light from screens interferes with melatonin production, which is already often irregular in neurodivergent children. Additionally, the stimulating content of many screen activities can keep nervous systems activated when they need to be winding down.

Positive Screen Time Effects for Neurodivergent Children

Predictable social interaction: For children who find face-to-face social interaction overwhelming, online interactions can provide social connection with more predictable rules and fewer simultaneous social cues to process.

Special interest exploration: Digital platforms can provide unlimited access to information about special interests, which can be highly regulating and motivating for many neurodivergent children.

Sensory regulation tools: Apps for breathing, meditation, music, or visual stimming can provide portable regulation tools that children can access when needed.

Communication support: For children who struggle with verbal communication, digital communication tools can provide alternative ways to express thoughts and connect with others.

Executive function support: Calendar apps, reminder systems, and organization tools can provide external support for executive function challenges.

Twelve-year-old Sarah with autism found that watching videos about marine biology—her special interest—was deeply regulating when she felt overwhelmed. Her parents learned to distinguish between this regulation-supportive screen time and the dysregulating effects of social media or fast-paced games.

Setting Up Technology for Regulation Rather Than Dysregulation

The goal isn't to eliminate technology but to set it up intentionally so it supports your child's nervous system regulation rather than creating additional stress or dysregulation.

Creating Regulation-Supportive Digital Environments

Screen brightness and color temperature: Adjusting screen brightness to match room lighting and using blue light filters, especially in evening hours, can reduce visual strain and support better sleep preparation.

Audio environment: Using headphones can help children control their auditory environment and prevent sound from screens from affecting other family members. However, some children need to be able to hear environmental sounds for safety and regulation.

Physical positioning: How children position their bodies during screen time affects their overall regulation. Comfortable seating, appropriate screen distance, and opportunities for movement can make screen time more regulation-supportive.

Time of day considerations: The same screen activity can have different effects on the nervous system depending on time of day. Stimulating content that's energizing in the morning might be overwhelming in the evening.

Content curation: Being intentional about what content your child accesses helps ensure screen time supports rather than challenges their nervous system.

App and Platform Selection

Regulation-supportive apps: Apps for breathing exercises, meditation, calming music, or sensory stimulation can provide portable regulation tools.

Educational content aligned with interests: Content that matches your child's special interests or learning style can be both educational and regulating.

Creative platforms: Digital art, music creation, writing, or building apps can provide positive outlets for creativity and expression.

Communication tools: Platforms that support positive social connection while avoiding the comparison and drama common in many social media environments.

Avoiding dysregulating content: Content with rapid scene changes, loud sudden sounds, violence, or social comparison elements often triggers stress responses in sensitive nervous systems.

Creating Healthy Digital Boundaries

Physical boundaries: Designating screen-free zones in your home helps ensure that some spaces remain available for non-digital regulation and family connection.

Time boundaries: Setting limits on daily screen time that honor your child's individual needs while ensuring balance with other important activities.

Content boundaries: Having clear guidelines about what types of digital content are appropriate for your child's developmental level and sensory sensitivities.

Social boundaries: Monitoring and supporting your child's online social interactions to ensure they're positive and developmentally appropriate.

Screen Time Boundaries That Honor Nervous System Needs

Traditional screen time rules often fail with neurodivergent children because they don't account for how differently various screen activities affect nervous system regulation. Creating effective boundaries requires understanding these individual differences.

Moving Beyond Time-Based Rules

Quality over quantity focus: Two hours of educational content about your child's special interests affects their nervous system differently than two hours of fast-paced gaming or social media.

Regulation-based boundaries: Instead of arbitrary time limits, consider how different screen activities affect your child's ability to sleep, transition, focus on other activities, and regulate emotions.

Individual capacity recognition: Some children can handle more screen time without negative effects, while others become dysregulated quickly. Boundaries should be based on your specific child's responses.

Activity-specific rules: Different types of screen activities may need different boundaries. Educational videos might have different limits than games or social media.

Flexible implementation: Boundaries may need to be different on weekends vs. school days, during illness, or during particularly stressful periods.

Understanding Your Child's Screen Time Patterns

Energy level impacts: Notice how different screen activities affect your child's energy levels. Some content is energizing, some is calming, and some is depleting.

Transition difficulties: Pay attention to which screen activities make transitions most difficult and plan accordingly.

Sleep impacts: Track how different types and timing of screen use affect your child's ability to fall asleep and sleep quality.

Attention effects: Notice whether screen time helps or hinders your child's ability to focus on other activities like homework, chores, or family interactions.

Emotional regulation changes: Observe how different screen experiences affect your child's mood, emotional regulation, and stress responses.

Ten-year-old Marcus's parents discovered that while he could watch nature documentaries for hours without negative effects, just 30 minutes of action-packed cartoons would leave him hyperactive and unable to focus on anything else. This led them to create content-specific rather than time-specific boundaries.

Using Technology as a Regulation Tool

When used intentionally, technology can provide powerful tools for nervous system regulation, especially for children who struggle with traditional regulation strategies.

Regulation Apps and Tools

Breathing and meditation apps: Guided breathing exercises, progressive muscle relaxation, and mindfulness activities designed for children can provide accessible regulation tools.

Sensory regulation apps: Apps that provide visual stimming, calming sounds, or tactile input through device vibration can offer regulation support when other tools aren't available.

Music and sound tools: Streaming services, playlist creation, and sound apps can provide personalized auditory regulation support.

Visual regulation tools: Apps with calming visual patterns, nature scenes, or customizable visual experiences can help some children regulate when overwhelmed.

Organization and planning tools: Digital calendars, reminder systems, and task management apps can provide external support for executive function challenges.

Creating Personal Regulation Toolkits

Customized app collections: Help your child create a folder of apps specifically designed to support their regulation needs.

Personalized content playlists: Work with your child to create playlists of videos, music, or other content that they find regulating.

Digital sensory breaks: Teach your child to use technology for planned regulation breaks rather than just entertainment or distraction.

Portable regulation support: Help your child understand how to use technology for regulation support in different environments—school, community activities, or social situations.

Self-monitoring tools: Apps that help children track their mood, energy levels, or regulation state can build self-awareness and help with regulation planning.

Teaching Technology Self-Regulation

Awareness building: Help your child notice how different screen activities affect their nervous system and overall regulation.

Choice-making skills: Teach your child to choose screen activities based on their current regulation needs rather than just immediate preferences.

Transition strategies: Work with your child to develop strategies for transitioning away from screens without dysregulation.

Balance recognition: Help your child understand the importance of balancing screen time with other activities that support nervous system health.

Problem-solving skills: When technology use becomes problematic, involve your child in identifying solutions rather than just imposing restrictions.

Managing the Transition Away from Screens

For many neurodivergent children, transitioning away from screens can be more challenging than the screen time itself. Understanding and supporting these transitions is crucial for family harmony and your child's regulation.

Why Screen Transitions Are Particularly Difficult

Attention absorption: Many digital activities capture attention so completely that children lose awareness of time, surroundings, and internal body signals. Transitioning requires reorienting to the physical world.

Dopamine crash: When engaging digital activities end, there can be a drop in dopamine levels that feels uncomfortable, leading to attempts to return to the stimulating activity.

Executive function demands: Transitions require executive function skills—stopping one activity, remembering what comes next, organizing materials, and initiating new behaviors—that may be challenging for neurodivergent children.

Sensory adjustment: Moving from the controlled sensory environment of screens to the unpredictable sensory environment of real-world activities can trigger overwhelm.

Social demands: Screen activities often involve fewer social demands than family or peer interactions, making transitions to social environments particularly challenging.

Transition Support Strategies

Advance warnings: Give multiple warnings before screen time ends, allowing your child's nervous system to prepare for the transition.

Visual timers: Visual representations of remaining screen time help children prepare mentally for transitions without constant time monitoring from parents.

Transition activities: Plan specific activities that help bridge from screen engagement to other activities. This might be movement, sensory input, or quiet processing time.

Choice and control: When possible, give children some control over their transitions—choosing when to save their progress, selecting what activity comes next, or deciding on the transition timing within reasonable boundaries.

Regulation support: Be available to provide co-regulation support during difficult transitions rather than expecting children to manage independently.

Creating Transition Rituals

Consistent routines: Develop predictable routines around screen transitions that help your child's nervous system prepare for the change.

Sensory bridges: Use sensory activities to help your child transition from the digital world to physical world activities.

Connection time: Plan for brief connection with parents or family members after screen time to help with social re-engagement.

Processing time: Some children need a few minutes to process and decompress after intense screen engagement before being ready for new activities.

Positive associations: Help your child develop positive associations with post-screen activities rather than seeing them as punishments for screen time ending.

Nine-year-old Emma needed a specific transition routine when ending tablet time: a 10-minute warning, then a 5-minute warning, then time to save her progress and close the apps herself. This was followed by 15 minutes of quiet time in her room with her weighted blanket before rejoining family activities.

Digital Wellness for Neurodivergent Families

Creating healthy relationships with technology requires a family approach that honors everyone's needs while building awareness of how digital activities affect nervous system health.

Family Digital Agreements

Collaborative rule-making: Involve children in creating family agreements about technology use rather than imposing top-down restrictions.

Individual accommodations: Recognition that different family members may need different technology boundaries based on their neurological differences.

Regular review and adjustment: Family technology agreements should be reviewed and adjusted regularly as children grow and family circumstances change.

Modeling healthy use: Parents need to model the kind of technology relationship they want their children to develop.

Balance emphasis: Focus on creating balance between screen activities and other important activities rather than just limiting screen time.

Building Digital Literacy and Self-Awareness

Media literacy education: Help children understand how digital media is designed to capture attention and trigger responses.

Self-monitoring skills: Teach children to notice how different digital activities affect their mood, energy, sleep, and relationships.

Critical thinking development: Help children evaluate digital content for accuracy, bias, and appropriateness.

Privacy and safety education: Teach children about digital privacy, online safety, and appropriate digital citizenship.

Technology problem-solving: Help children learn to troubleshoot technology problems independently and know when to ask for help.

Balancing Digital and Non-Digital Activities

Ensuring diverse experiences: Make sure children have regular access to non-digital activities that support nervous system development— outdoor play, creative activities, physical exercise, and face-to-face social interaction.

Nature connection: Regular time in natural environments provides important nervous system regulation that can't be replicated digitally.

Physical activity integration: Ensure that screen time is balanced with adequate physical movement and exercise.

Creative expression opportunities: While digital creativity tools are valuable, children also benefit from non-digital creative experiences.

Social skill development: Face-to-face social interactions provide important learning opportunities that digital communication can't fully replace.

Age-Appropriate Digital Boundaries and Expectations

Different developmental stages require different approaches to technology use, and neurodivergent children may need modified expectations based on their individual development rather than chronological age.

Early Elementary (Ages 5-8)

Limited independent access: Most screen time should be co-viewed or supervised, with parents helping children understand what they're seeing and experiencing.

Content curation: Carefully selected educational content that matches your child's interests and developmental level.

Short time periods: Brief periods of screen engagement with frequent breaks and transitions to other activities.

Family media time: Emphasizing screen time as a family activity rather than solitary entertainment.

Basic digital literacy: Beginning to teach about how technology works and making good digital choices.

Late Elementary (Ages 8-12)

Increased independence with supervision: Children can begin making some choices about digital content within parent-established boundaries.

Skill-building focus: Using technology to develop specific skills—typing, research, creative expression, or learning about interests.

Social media preparation: Beginning conversations about online social interaction, digital citizenship, and internet safety.

Self-monitoring introduction: Helping children begin to notice how different digital activities affect their mood and behavior.

Balance emphasis: Ensuring that screen time is balanced with other important activities and interests.

Middle School (Ages 12-14)

Greater autonomy with accountability: Children can have more independence in digital choices while being accountable for the effects of those choices.

Social media introduction: If appropriate, beginning supervised introduction to age-appropriate social media platforms.

Digital creation emphasis: Moving beyond consumption to creating digital content—videos, blogs, artwork, or other creative expression.

Critical thinking development: Helping children evaluate digital content for accuracy, bias, and appropriateness.

Problem-solving skill building: Supporting children in solving their own technology problems and conflicts.

Supporting Your Child's Relationship with Technology

The goal isn't to eliminate technology from your child's life but to help them develop a healthy, intentional relationship with digital tools that enhances rather than detracts from their overall wellbeing and development.

Building Positive Associations

Technology as a tool: Help your child see technology as one of many tools available for learning, creativity, communication, and regulation rather than as entertainment or escape.

Skill development focus: Emphasize how technology can help your child develop skills, pursue interests, and express creativity.

Connection facilitation: Use technology to facilitate positive connections with family, friends, and communities rather than as a substitute for in-person relationships.

Problem-solving support: Help your child use technology to solve problems, organize their life, and support their learning rather than just for passive entertainment.

Regulation tool integration: Teach your child to use technology intentionally for nervous system regulation when appropriate.

Long-Term Digital Health Goals

Self-regulation development: The ultimate goal is helping your child develop internal regulation around technology use rather than relying entirely on external controls.

Critical thinking skills: Building your child's ability to evaluate digital content and make good choices about technology use.

Balance awareness: Helping your child understand the importance of balancing screen time with other activities that support their development.

Social skill integration: Using technology to enhance rather than replace face-to-face social skills and relationships.

Future preparation: Helping your child develop the digital literacy and self-regulation skills they'll need as they gain more independence with technology.

The Technology Integration Success Story

Kevin's family learned that the key to managing his relationship with technology wasn't elimination or unlimited access—it was understanding how different digital activities affected his ADHD nervous system and creating boundaries that supported rather than undermined his overall regulation.

They discovered that educational videos about his special interest in space were actually regulating for Kevin and helped him focus better on homework afterwards. However, fast-paced games and social media triggered hyperactivity and made transitions extremely difficult. By creating content-specific rather than time-specific boundaries, they were able to support Kevin's interests while preventing technology use from sabotaging his nervous system regulation.

Most importantly, they involved Kevin in understanding how different screen activities affected his mood, sleep, and ability to focus. This self-awareness helped him make better choices about technology use and developed his capacity for self-regulation around digital media.

Creating a healthy relationship with technology for your neurodivergent child requires understanding how screens affect their unique nervous system, setting boundaries that honor their individual needs, and teaching them to use technology intentionally as a tool for learning, creativity, and regulation rather than just entertainment or escape.

The goal isn't perfect technology use but rather building your child's awareness and self-regulation skills so they can navigate our increasingly digital world while maintaining their nervous system health and overall wellbeing. When technology is integrated thoughtfully into your child's life, it can become a powerful tool for supporting their unique strengths and addressing their challenges.

Chapter 15: Preparing the Nervous System for Connection

Ten-year-old Maya loved her friend Isabella dearly, but birthday parties were becoming impossible. The last three invitations had ended the same way: Maya excited and looking forward to the party, arriving and initially having fun, then becoming overwhelmed and needing to leave early with tears, frustration, and disappointment for everyone involved.

Maya's mom, Jennifer, felt caught between supporting her daughter's social needs and protecting her from repeated overwhelming experiences. She could see that Maya desperately wanted to connect with friends, but traditional social situations seemed designed to trigger rather than support neurodivergent nervous systems.

What Jennifer didn't understand was that social success for neurodivergent children requires the same approach as any other challenging activity: nervous system preparation, environmental awareness, support strategies, and recovery planning. Maya wasn't failing at social situations—she was trying to navigate complex social environments without the nervous system support she needed to be successful.

The key to social success for neurodivergent children isn't avoiding all challenging social situations or forcing them to endure overwhelming experiences. It's understanding how social environments affect nervous system regulation and providing the preparation, support, and recovery that allows your child to connect authentically while honoring their neurobiological needs.

Why Social Situations Are Uniquely Challenging for Neurodivergent Children

Social interactions involve multiple complex systems simultaneously—communication, sensory processing, emotional regulation, attention, and executive function. For neurodivergent children, social situations can quickly become overwhelming even when they genuinely want to connect with others.

The Multisystem Load of Social Interaction

Dr. Michelle Garcia Winner's research on social thinking demonstrates that successful social interaction requires simultaneous processing of verbal communication, nonverbal cues, environmental context, social rules, and personal regulation—all while maintaining appropriate behavior and emotional responses (Winner, 2007).

Communication processing demands: Following conversations, understanding implied meanings, processing rapid verbal exchanges, and formulating appropriate responses requires significant cognitive resources.

Nonverbal information overload: Facial expressions, body language, tone of voice, personal space, and gesture interpretation happen simultaneously and often unconsciously for neurotypical individuals but may require conscious effort for neurodivergent children.

Environmental complexity: Social situations often occur in sensory-rich environments with competing sounds, visual information, crowded spaces, and unpredictable sensory experiences.

Social rule navigation: Understanding unwritten social rules that change based on context, relationship, and situation requires constant social cognitive processing.

Emotional regulation under pressure: Managing personal emotions while responding appropriately to others' emotional states is particularly challenging when nervous systems are already working hard to process social information.

The Hidden Energy Cost of Social Interaction

Dr. Ari Ne'eman's research on autistic experiences highlights that social interaction often requires what he terms "social performance energy"—the additional cognitive and emotional resources needed to navigate neurotypical social expectations (Ne'eman, 2010). This energy cost can be significant and cumulative.

Masking and camouflaging: Many neurodivergent children learn to suppress their natural responses and mimic neurotypical social behaviors, which requires enormous energy and can lead to exhaustion and eventual breakdown.

Hypervigilance in social settings: Sensitive nervous systems may constantly scan social environments for threats, signs of rejection, or evidence that they're not fitting in correctly.

Executive function overload: Social situations require constant decision-making, flexibility, and problem-solving while managing multiple simultaneous demands.

Recovery time needs: After intense social experiences, many neurodivergent children need significant downtime to process the experience and restore their nervous system resources.

Twelve-year-old David described social situations this way: "It's like trying to follow five different conversations while solving math problems in my head and making sure I don't do anything weird. By the end, my brain feels like it's going to explode."

Pre-Social Preparation Strategies

Just as athletes prepare for competition, neurodivergent children benefit from specific preparation strategies that help their nervous systems get ready for social challenges.

Nervous System State Assessment

Before any social activity, it's helpful to assess your child's current nervous system state and capacity for social challenges.

Regulation check-in: How regulated does your child seem today? Are they in their green zone, yellow zone, or already showing signs of activation or withdrawal?

Energy level assessment: How much energy does your child have available for social challenges? Have they already used significant regulation resources earlier in the day?

Environmental readiness: What has your child's sensory environment been like today? Have they had opportunities for regulation and decompression?

Emotional state consideration: What's your child's emotional baseline today? Are they excited, anxious, tired, or dealing with other stressors?

Recent experience factor: How have recent social experiences gone? Is your child approaching this situation with confidence or trepidation based on past experiences?

Information and Expectation Setting

Uncertainty and unpredictability are particularly challenging for neurodivergent nervous systems. Providing information about upcoming social situations helps reduce anxiety and allows for mental preparation.

Event details: When and where will the social activity occur? How long is it expected to last? What activities are planned?

Social composition: Who will be there? Will your child know the other attendees? Will there be new people to meet?

Environmental preparation: What will the physical environment be like? Indoor or outdoor? Loud or quiet? Crowded or spacious?

Activity structure: Will the social situation be structured with planned activities, or will it be free-form socializing? What are the expectations for participation?

Exit planning: What's the plan if your child becomes overwhelmed? How can they communicate their needs, and what support will be available?

Skills and Strategy Preparation

Social skills review: If your child has been working on specific social skills, briefly review strategies that might be helpful in the upcoming situation.

Communication support planning: For children who struggle with verbal communication under stress, plan alternative ways they can communicate their needs.

Regulation strategy identification: Help your child identify which regulation strategies they can use in the social environment if they become overwhelmed.

Conversation starter preparation: For children who struggle with conversation initiation, prepare a few topics or questions they can use to engage with others.

Problem-solving preview: Discuss potential challenges that might arise and brainstorm solutions in advance.

During-Event Support and Check-Ins

Supporting your child during social events requires a delicate balance of providing help when needed while encouraging independence and authentic social connection.

Monitoring Without Hovering

Subtle check-ins: Find ways to assess how your child is doing without calling attention to them or interrupting their social interactions.

Environmental awareness: Stay aware of changes in the social environment that might affect your child—increasing noise levels, growing crowds, or shifts in activity structure.

Early warning sign recognition: Watch for your child's personal early warning signs of overwhelm so you can provide support before crisis occurs.

Peer relationship monitoring: Be aware of how social interactions are progressing. Are other children being inclusive and kind, or are there signs of social conflict or exclusion?

Timing awareness: Consider how long your child has been socially engaged and whether they might be approaching their social capacity limits.

Providing Regulation Support

Environmental modifications: When possible, help create sensory breaks or quieter spaces where your child can decompress without leaving the social situation entirely.

Co-regulation availability: Be available to provide brief co-regulation support when your child needs it, without making it obvious or embarrassing.

Activity facilitation: Sometimes children benefit from adult support in joining activities or navigating social challenges, but this should be done carefully to preserve peer relationships.

Communication support: For children who struggle with communication under stress, provide subtle support in expressing their needs or participating in conversations.

Transition assistance: Help your child navigate transitions between different activities or social groupings within the event.

Recognizing When to Intervene vs. When to Allow Independence

Safety considerations: Always intervene if there are safety concerns—bullying, exclusion, or situations that could cause physical or emotional harm.

Overwhelm prevention: Intervene when you recognize that your child is approaching overwhelm, even if they haven't explicitly asked for help.

Learning opportunities: Allow your child to navigate manageable social challenges independently, as these experiences build confidence and skills.

Peer relationship preservation: Be mindful of how your interventions might affect your child's peer relationships and reputation.

Individual communication: Know your child's preferences about intervention and respect their developing autonomy while providing necessary support.

Eight-year-old Sophia's parents developed a subtle check-in system where they would make eye contact across the room, and Sophia could give a thumbs up if she was doing well or point to the door if she needed a break. This allowed her to maintain social independence while knowing support was available.

Post-Social Recovery Protocols

The period immediately following social activities is crucial for helping your child's nervous system recover from the demands of social interaction and process the experience positively.

Understanding Post-Social Exhaustion

Normal recovery needs: It's completely normal for neurodivergent children to be tired after social activities, even ones they enjoyed. This doesn't mean the experience was negative—just that it required significant energy.

Delayed reaction patterns: Some children don't show signs of social overwhelm until hours after the event ends, when they finally feel safe enough to release the stress they've been managing.

Emotional processing time: Children often need time to process social experiences emotionally before they can talk about them or analyze what happened.

Sensory system reset needs: After managing complex social environments, many children need quiet, predictable sensory environments to help their systems reset.

Executive function recovery: The cognitive demands of social interaction can leave executive function systems depleted, making routine tasks more difficult immediately after social events.

Creating Recovery-Supportive Environments

Sensory calm: Provide low-stimulation environments with comfortable lighting, minimal noise, and preferred sensory supports.

Routine predictability: Return to familiar, comforting routines that don't require additional decision-making or social performance.

Connection without demands: Be available for connection if your child seeks it, but don't demand processing or conversation about the social event immediately.

Basic needs attention: Ensure your child's basic needs are met—food, water, bathroom, rest—without requiring them to ask or remember independently.

Space and time: Allow adequate recovery time before expecting your child to engage in additional challenging activities.

Processing Social Experiences

Timing considerations: Wait until your child's nervous system has recovered before attempting to process or analyze the social experience.

Child-led processing: Let your child determine how much they want to discuss about the social event rather than conducting detailed debriefings.

Positive focus: Start with what went well or what your child enjoyed about the social experience before addressing any challenges.

Learning opportunity identification: Help your child identify any social learning that occurred, but frame it as growth rather than correction of mistakes.

Future planning: If the social experience was challenging, work together to identify strategies for similar situations in the future.

Building Social Stamina Gradually

Like physical fitness, social capacity can be built gradually over time through appropriate challenges with adequate support and recovery.

Understanding Social Capacity Development

Individual variation: Every child has their own baseline social capacity and rate of development. Comparisons to neurotypical peers or even other neurodivergent children aren't helpful.

Capacity building vs. masking: The goal is building genuine capacity for social interaction, not teaching children to suppress their needs and appear more neurotypical.

Recovery time needs: As social capacity builds, children may still need significant recovery time after social challenges, and that's completely normal.

Skill integration: Social skills learned in structured settings need time and practice to become integrated into natural social interactions.

Confidence and competence cycle: Success experiences build confidence, which supports future social risk-taking, which builds competence, creating a positive cycle.

Graduated Social Challenges

Start with strengths: Begin social capacity building in areas where your child already has some success or comfort.

Controlled environments first: Practice social skills in predictable, supportive environments before applying them in more challenging settings.

Short duration building: Gradually increase the length of social interactions as your child's capacity grows.

Small group progression: Start with one-on-one interactions, then small groups, then larger social situations.

Interest-based connections: Use your child's special interests or preferred activities as platforms for social connection.

Celebrating Social Growth

Effort recognition: Acknowledge the courage it takes for your child to engage in social challenges, regardless of outcomes.

Process celebration: Celebrate improvements in social skills, regulation during social events, or recovery from social challenges.

Individual progress focus: Compare your child's social development to their own past performance rather than to external standards.

Strength identification: Help your child recognize their unique social strengths and contributions to social interactions.

Confidence building: Use positive social experiences to build your child's confidence in their ability to connect with others.

Helping Your Child Develop Social Nervous System Awareness

One of the most valuable skills you can teach your neurodivergent child is awareness of how social situations affect their nervous system and what they can do to support themselves during social challenges.

Building Social Self-Awareness

Energy monitoring: Help your child learn to recognize their social energy levels and understand when they need breaks or recovery time.

Social environment assessment: Teach your child to notice environmental factors that make social situations easier or harder for them.

Personal pattern recognition: Help your child identify their own patterns of social success and challenge.

Regulation strategy identification: Work with your child to identify which regulation strategies work best for them in social environments.

Communication skill development: Help your child learn to communicate their social needs without shame or apology.

Teaching Social Self-Advocacy

Need identification: Help your child recognize and articulate their social support needs.

Request strategies: Teach your child how to ask for breaks, changes in activity, or other accommodations in social settings.

Boundary setting: Help your child understand that it's okay to set boundaries around social interaction when they need to.

Problem-solving skills: Teach your child strategies for handling common social challenges independently.

Recovery planning: Help your child learn to plan for recovery time after social events.

Building Social Confidence

Strength focus: Help your child identify and celebrate their unique social strengths and contributions.

Success memory bank: Keep records of positive social experiences your child can remember during challenging times.

Growth mindset: Help your child understand that social skills can be learned and improved over time.

Authenticity support: Encourage your child to be authentic in social interactions rather than trying to be someone they're not.

Community building: Help your child find social communities where their neurodivergent traits are understood and appreciated.

Creating Neurodivergent-Friendly Social Opportunities

While it's important for children to learn to navigate neurotypical social environments, it's equally important to create social opportunities specifically designed to support neurodivergent nervous systems.

Structured Social Activities

Interest-based groups: Activities organized around special interests provide natural conversation topics and shared passions that facilitate connection.

Skill-based activities: Sports, arts, music, or other structured activities provide social interaction with clear rules and expectations.

Educational programs: Classes, workshops, or camps that include social interaction as part of learning provide structured social opportunities.

Therapeutic social groups: Groups specifically designed to support social skills development in understanding environments.

Family friend networks: Cultivating friendships with other families who understand neurodivergent needs creates more supportive social opportunities.

Environmental Modifications for Social Success

Sensory-friendly venues: Choose social activities in environments that support rather than challenge sensory processing.

Predictable structures: Look for social opportunities with clear expectations, planned activities, and predictable routines.

Smaller group sizes: Seek social opportunities with fewer participants to reduce complexity and overwhelm.

Shorter duration events: Choose social activities that match your child's current social capacity rather than pushing endurance limits.

Adult supervision: Select social opportunities with understanding adult supervision who can provide support if needed.

Ten-year-old Jordan found his social confidence through a Lego robotics club where his engineering interests and attention to detail were seen as assets rather than quirks. The structured nature of the activities and shared interests made social connection feel natural rather than forced.

The Long-Term Social Development Vision

Supporting your neurodivergent child's social development isn't about making them indistinguishable from neurotypical peers—it's about helping them develop authentic connections while honoring their neurobiological needs and celebrating their unique contributions to social interactions.

Authentic Social Connection Goals

Meaningful relationships: The goal is helping your child develop deep, meaningful relationships rather than superficial social popularity.

Self-acceptance in relationships: Supporting your child in finding friends and communities where they can be authentically themselves.

Reciprocal relationships: Helping your child develop social skills that allow for give-and-take in friendships.

Advocacy and communication: Building your child's ability to communicate their needs and advocate for accommodations in social settings.

Community contribution: Helping your child recognize how their unique traits and perspectives can contribute positively to social groups.

Lifelong Social Skills

Nervous system awareness: Understanding how social situations affect their regulation and what they need to be successful.

Environment evaluation: The ability to assess social environments and identify what supports or challenges their social success.

Self-advocacy: Skills for communicating their needs and requesting accommodations in social settings.

Relationship maintenance: Understanding how to maintain friendships and connections over time.

Community finding: Ability to seek out and participate in communities that appreciate their authentic selves.

Your Child's Social Success Story

Maya's social transformation didn't happen by forcing her to endure overwhelming birthday parties or avoiding social situations entirely. It happened through understanding how social environments affected her nervous system and providing the preparation, support, and recovery she needed to connect successfully with friends.

Her family learned to prepare Maya for social events by discussing what to expect, helping her identify regulation strategies she could use, and planning for recovery time afterwards. During events, they stayed available for support while encouraging independence. After social activities, they provided the quiet recovery time Maya's nervous system needed.

Most importantly, they helped Maya understand her own social patterns and needs. She learned to recognize when she was getting overwhelmed at social events and developed strategies for taking breaks or asking for help. This self-awareness allowed her to participate more successfully in social activities while maintaining her authentic self.

Maya still finds large birthday parties challenging, but she now has alternative ways to maintain friendships—smaller playdates, shared interest activities, and family gatherings that honor her social needs while supporting meaningful connections.

Creating social success for your neurodivergent child requires understanding that social interaction is a complex neurobiological challenge that requires the same kind of support and accommodation as any other area of difference. When you provide appropriate preparation, support, and recovery, you help your child build genuine social capacity while maintaining their authentic self.

The goal isn't eliminating all social challenges or making your child appear neurotypical in social situations. The goal is supporting your child in developing meaningful connections, social confidence, and the self-awareness to navigate social environments successfully throughout their life. When social experiences are supported appropriately, they become opportunities for growth, connection, and joy rather than sources of stress and failure.

Chapter 16: Parent Self-Care: Your Nervous System Matters Too

Rachel stood in her kitchen at 11 PM, dishes still piled in the sink from dinner, laundry overflowing from baskets in three different rooms, and her phone buzzing with emails from her son's teacher about another difficult day at school. Her ten-year-old with ADHD had had two meltdowns, her eight-year-old daughter was struggling with friendship drama, and her husband was working late again.

As she finally collapsed onto the couch, Rachel felt the familiar tightness in her chest and the overwhelming sense that she was failing everyone. She'd spent the entire day focused on regulating everyone else's nervous systems—co-regulating meltdowns, providing sensory breaks, managing transitions, and advocating with teachers. But her own nervous system was running on empty, and she couldn't shake the feeling that she was barely keeping her head above water.

Sound familiar? Parents of neurodivergent children often become so focused on supporting their child's nervous system that they completely neglect their own. But here's what Rachel didn't understand: her nervous system state directly affects her children's regulation. When she's chronically stressed, overwhelmed, or depleted, her children feel it and respond accordingly.

Taking care of your own nervous system isn't selfish—it's one of the most important things you can do for your neurodivergent child. Your regulated presence is the foundation that makes everything else possible.

The Impact of Parenting a Neurodivergent Child on Your Nervous System

Parenting any child is demanding, but parenting a neurodivergent child involves unique stressors that can significantly impact your nervous system over time. Understanding these impacts helps normalize your experiences and motivates the self-care that's essential for sustainable parenting.

Chronic Hypervigilance and Stress

Dr. Bruce Perry's research shows that chronic stress fundamentally changes how our nervous systems function (Perry & Szalavitz, 2007). Parents of neurodivergent children often live in a state of hypervigilance—constantly scanning for early warning signs, potential triggers, and environmental factors that might affect their child's regulation.

Hypervigilance signs in parents:

- Constantly monitoring your child's emotional state and behavior
- Feeling anxious when away from your child
- Difficulty relaxing or "turning off" parental awareness
- Physical tension that you carry throughout the day
- Sleep difficulties due to worry or planning for the next day
- Startled responses to normal household sounds

The accumulation effect: Daily stressors that might be manageable individually can accumulate over months and years, creating chronic nervous system activation that affects your health, relationships, and capacity to support your family.

Anticipatory stress: Many parents develop anxiety about future challenges—upcoming school meetings, social events, or transitions—that keeps their nervous system activated even during calm periods.

Secondary Trauma and Emotional Overwhelm

232

Watching your child struggle with meltdowns, social rejection, academic challenges, or emotional dysregulation can create what psychologists call "secondary trauma"—the emotional impact of witnessing someone you love experience distress.

Empathic distress: Parents often absorb their children's emotional states, feeling anxious when their child is anxious, overwhelmed when their child is overwhelmed, or heartbroken when their child faces rejection or failure.

Helplessness and grief: Many parents experience grief over the challenges their child faces and frustration at their inability to "fix" everything for them.

Identity challenges: Parenting a neurodivergent child can challenge assumptions about parenthood and create identity confusion about your role and effectiveness as a parent.

Isolation and Lack of Understanding

Social isolation: Many families find that their social circles narrow as friends and extended family struggle to understand neurodivergent behaviors or accommodate different family needs.

Professional frustration: Dealing with schools, healthcare providers, and other professionals who don't understand neurodivergent needs can create chronic stress and advocacy fatigue.

Partner relationship strain: The demands of parenting a neurodivergent child can strain marriages and partnerships, especially when partners have different approaches or understanding levels.

Community judgment: Many parents experience judgment from others about their child's behavior or their parenting choices, creating additional stress and self-doubt.

Thirty-eight-year-old Maria described her experience: "I realized I hadn't had a relaxed moment in three years. Even when things were going well, I was bracing for the next challenge. My shoulders were permanently hunched, and I'd forgotten what it felt like to just breathe normally."

Recognizing Your Own Dysregulation Patterns

Just as you've learned to recognize your child's warning signs of nervous system overwhelm, it's crucial to identify your own patterns of dysregulation so you can provide yourself with appropriate support.

Physical Signs of Parental Nervous System Overwhelm

Muscle tension and pain: Chronic stress often manifests as tension headaches, neck and shoulder tightness, back pain, or jaw clenching.

Sleep disruption: Difficulty falling asleep due to racing thoughts, waking frequently to check on children, or early morning awakening with anxiety.

Digestive issues: Stress can cause stomach problems, changes in appetite, or digestive sensitivities that weren't present before.

Immune system impacts: Getting sick more frequently, slower healing from injuries, or increased susceptibility to infections.

Energy fluctuations: Feeling exhausted but wired, experiencing afternoon crashes, or needing caffeine to function.

Emotional and Mental Signs

Emotional reactivity: Finding yourself more easily frustrated, quick to anger, or emotionally overwhelmed by minor stressors.

Cognitive overload: Difficulty concentrating, memory problems, or feeling mentally "foggy."

Anxiety and worry: Persistent worry about your child's future, ruminating about past challenges, or anticipating future problems.

Mood changes: Feeling sad, hopeless, or experiencing mood swings that aren't typical for you.

Decision fatigue: Feeling overwhelmed by even simple decisions or avoiding decision-making altogether.

Behavioral and Social Signs

Social withdrawal: Avoiding social activities, declining invitations, or isolating from friends and family.

Neglecting personal needs: Skipping meals, avoiding medical appointments, or neglecting personal hygiene and self-care.

Relationship difficulties: Increased conflict with partners, friends, or family members.

Work or household struggles: Difficulty maintaining work performance or keeping up with household responsibilities.

Coping mechanism changes: Increased use of caffeine, alcohol, food, or other substances to manage stress.

Daily Nervous System Maintenance for Parents

Just as your child needs daily nervous system support, you need consistent practices that help maintain your own regulation and resilience.

Morning Regulation Practices

Mindful awakening: Instead of immediately checking your phone or jumping into action, spend a few minutes noticing your body, breathing, and mental state upon waking.

Intention setting: Briefly consider what you hope to prioritize that day and what support you might need to maintain your regulation.

Physical preparation: Simple stretching, deep breathing, or brief meditation can help start your day from a more regulated state.

Nutritional support: Eating protein-rich breakfasts and staying hydrated supports stable energy throughout the day.

Realistic planning: Set realistic expectations for the day that include buffer time and self-care rather than overpacking schedules.

Throughout-the-Day Regulation

Micro-breaks: Brief moments of conscious breathing, stretching, or mindfulness throughout the day can prevent stress accumulation.

Body awareness check-ins: Regularly noticing physical tension, breathing patterns, and energy levels allows for proactive self-care.

Boundary maintenance: Saying no to additional commitments when you're already stretched thin, setting limits on advocacy activities, and protecting your energy for priority areas.

Support utilization: Actually using the support systems you have available rather than trying to handle everything independently.

Hydration and nutrition: Maintaining stable blood sugar and adequate hydration supports nervous system regulation throughout the day.

Evening Regulation and Recovery

Transition rituals: Creating clear transitions from "parent mode" to personal time, even if that time is brief.

Physical tension release: Hot baths, stretching, massage, or other activities that help release the physical stress accumulated during the day.

Mental processing: Journaling, talking with supportive friends, or other ways of processing daily experiences.

Technology boundaries: Limiting evening screen time and avoiding stimulating content before bed.

Sleep preparation: Creating bedtime routines that support your own nervous system's transition to rest.

Building Your Own Support Network

Parenting a neurodivergent child can be isolating, but building connections with others who understand your experiences is crucial for maintaining your own nervous system health.

Finding Your Tribe

Parent support groups: Both in-person and online groups for parents of neurodivergent children provide understanding, practical advice, and emotional support.

Special interest communities: Connecting with families through your child's interests—sports teams, hobby groups, or activity clubs—can provide natural social opportunities.

Neighborhood networks: Building relationships with neighbors who can provide occasional support or simply understand your family's unique needs.

Professional relationships: Developing positive relationships with therapists, teachers, or other professionals who work with your child can provide ongoing support and guidance.

Extended family education: When possible, educating extended family members about neurodivergent needs can expand your support network.

Online and Digital Support

Social media groups: Facebook groups, Reddit communities, or other online spaces where parents share experiences and support each other.

Educational resources: Podcasts, blogs, or online courses that provide ongoing learning and connection with experts and other parents.

Virtual meetups: Online gatherings, webinars, or virtual support groups that don't require childcare arrangements or travel.

Resource sharing: Online platforms where parents share recommendations for professionals, products, or strategies.

Professional Support Systems

Therapeutic support: Individual therapy can provide personalized support for the unique challenges of parenting a neurodivergent child.

Family therapy: Working with therapists who understand neurodivergent families can strengthen family relationships and communication.

Respite services: Professional or volunteer services that provide breaks so you can rest and recharge.

Parent coaching: Specialized coaches who work with parents of neurodivergent children can provide practical strategies and emotional support.

Forty-two-year-old Jennifer found that joining an online support group for parents of autistic children was transformational: "For the first time in years, I felt understood. These parents got it—the daily challenges, the advocacy exhaustion, the worry about the future. I wasn't alone anymore."

Managing Caregiver Burnout and Compassion Fatigue

Caregiver burnout is a real risk for parents of neurodivergent children. Recognizing the signs early and having intervention strategies can prevent more serious mental health impacts.

Understanding Caregiver Burnout

Dr. Christina Maslach's research on burnout identifies three key components: emotional exhaustion, depersonalization, and reduced sense of personal accomplishment (Maslach et al., 2001). For parents, this might manifest as:

Emotional exhaustion: Feeling drained, overwhelmed, and emotionally depleted even after rest periods.

Detachment or resentment: Beginning to feel emotionally distant from your child or resentful about the demands of parenting.

Reduced effectiveness: Feeling like nothing you do helps, that you're failing as a parent, or that your efforts don't make a difference.

Physical symptoms: Chronic fatigue, frequent illness, sleep problems, or other physical manifestations of chronic stress.

Loss of enjoyment: No longer finding joy in activities you used to enjoy, including spending time with your child.

Compassion Fatigue Specifically

Secondary traumatic stress: Absorbing your child's distress to the point that it affects your own emotional regulation and mental health.

Hyperempathy exhaustion: Feeling so attuned to your child's emotional state that you lose awareness of your own needs and feelings.

Advocacy burnout: Feeling exhausted by the constant need to advocate, educate, and fight for your child's needs in various systems.

Decision overload: Feeling overwhelmed by the constant need to make decisions about therapies, schools, accommodations, and interventions.

Prevention and Intervention Strategies

Regular self-assessment: Honestly evaluating your emotional and physical state regularly rather than waiting until you're in crisis.

Professional support: Seeking therapy or counseling before burnout reaches crisis levels rather than waiting until you're overwhelmed.

Respite planning: Scheduling regular breaks from caregiving responsibilities, even if they're brief.

Expectation adjustment: Regularly evaluating and adjusting expectations about what you can realistically handle.

Boundary setting: Learning to say no to additional commitments and setting limits on how much you take on.

Modeling Healthy Nervous System Habits

One of the most powerful ways to support your child's nervous system development is to model healthy regulation habits yourself. Children learn more from what they observe than from what they're told.

Demonstrating Self-Awareness

Emotional labeling: When you're feeling stressed or overwhelmed, naming those emotions helps your child understand that all feelings are normal and manageable.

Need identification: Modeling how to recognize and communicate your own needs: "I'm feeling overwhelmed right now, so I need a few minutes to breathe and gather myself."

Strategy use: Openly using regulation strategies—taking deep breaths, going for walks, or taking breaks—shows your child that self-care is normal and necessary.

Mistake acknowledgment: When you handle situations poorly due to your own dysregulation, acknowledging it and making repairs models healthy relationship skills.

Growth mindset: Demonstrating that adults continue learning and growing, especially in challenging areas.

Creating Family Regulation Culture

Regulation time for everyone: Making self-care and regulation a family value rather than something only children need.

Stress normalization: Talking openly about stress as a normal part of life that everyone experiences and manages.

Support seeking: Modeling how to ask for help and use support systems when needed.

Balance demonstration: Showing how to balance demanding responsibilities with rest, play, and connection.

Resilience building: Demonstrating how to recover from difficult days and maintain hope during challenging periods.

Teaching Through Example

Boundary setting: Showing your child how to set appropriate boundaries by setting your own boundaries respectfully but firmly.

Self-advocacy: Modeling how to communicate needs and advocate for accommodations in various settings.

Problem-solving: Demonstrating how to approach challenges with curiosity and persistence rather than panic or avoidance.

Relationship maintenance: Showing how to maintain connections with others even during stressful periods.

Joy and playfulness: Demonstrating that adults can still find joy, humor, and playfulness even while managing serious responsibilities.

Ten-year-old Marcus learned about regulation by watching his mom: "When Mom gets stressed, she takes three deep breaths and goes outside for a minute. Then she comes back and handles whatever the problem is. I started doing that too when I feel overwhelmed."

Creating Sustainable Family Systems

Building family systems that support everyone's nervous system needs prevents burnout and creates more resilient family functioning over time.

Distributing Responsibility

Age-appropriate contributions: All family members, including neurodivergent children, can contribute to family functioning in ways that match their capabilities.

Strength utilization: Using each family member's strengths rather than expecting everyone to contribute in identical ways.

Task sharing: Dividing household and family management tasks among capable family members rather than having one person handle everything.

Advocacy distribution: When possible, sharing advocacy responsibilities between parents or with other family members.

Support coordination: Having systems for coordinating support rather than relying on one person to manage all appointments, communication, and interventions.

Building Family Resilience

Flexible expectations: Creating family systems that can adapt to changing needs, difficult periods, or unexpected challenges.

Communication systems: Regular family meetings or check-ins where everyone can share needs, concerns, and appreciations.

Celebration practices: Intentional celebration of successes, progress, and positive family moments.

Conflict resolution: Healthy ways of handling disagreements and repairing relationships after conflicts.

Shared values: Clear family values that guide decision-making and help prioritize what's most important.

Resource Management

Financial planning: Realistic budgeting for the additional costs often associated with neurodivergent support needs.

Time management: Protecting family time and individual time within busy schedules of appointments and activities.

Energy conservation: Choosing battles wisely and focusing energy on the most important priorities.

Professional relationship management: Building positive relationships with key professionals while maintaining appropriate boundaries.

Community resource utilization: Knowing what resources are available in your community and how to access them when needed.

The Oxygen Mask Principle

Airlines instruct passengers to put on their own oxygen masks before helping others because you can't help anyone else if you're unconscious. The same principle applies to nervous system regulation in families—you must maintain your own regulation to effectively support your child's development.

Why Parent Self-Care Isn't Selfish

Co-regulation foundation: Your regulated nervous system is what allows you to provide co-regulation support to your child during difficult moments.

Modeling importance: Children learn more about self-care from watching you practice it than from being told it's important.

Relationship preservation: Taking care of your own needs prevents resentment and burnout that can damage family relationships.

Long-term sustainability: Parenting a neurodivergent child is a marathon, not a sprint. Sustainable practices prevent long-term physical and mental health problems.

Family stability: When parents are regulated and healthy, the entire family system functions more effectively.

Making Self-Care Practical

Micro-practices: Self-care doesn't have to mean spa days or extended retreats. Brief moments of mindfulness, short walks, or five minutes of deep breathing can be effective.

Integration rather than addition: Finding ways to incorporate self-care into existing routines rather than adding more items to your to-do list.

Support utilization: Using available help—whether from family, friends, or professionals—to create space for self-care.

Guilt release: Understanding that caring for yourself is part of caring for your family, not separate from it.

Flexibility: Adapting self-care practices based on current circumstances rather than having rigid expectations.

Building Your Personal Regulation Toolkit

Every parent needs their own personalized collection of regulation strategies that work within their lifestyle, preferences, and circumstances.

Physical Regulation Strategies

Movement options: Finding forms of physical activity that you enjoy and can fit into your schedule—walking, dancing, yoga, or simple stretching.

Breathing practices: Learning breathing techniques that you can use anywhere—during car rides, waiting for appointments, or before difficult conversations.

Sensory supports: Identifying what sensory experiences help you regulate—music, nature sounds, essential oils, or specific textures.

Rest and recovery: Creating opportunities for physical rest that work within your family's schedule and needs.

Nutrition support: Eating in ways that support stable energy and mood rather than adding to physical stress.

Emotional Regulation Strategies

Processing methods: Finding ways to process daily experiences—journaling, talking with friends, or creative expression.

Mindfulness practices: Developing present-moment awareness that can help interrupt worry spirals and stress accumulation.

Gratitude practices: Intentionally noticing positive aspects of your life and parenting journey.

Emotional boundaries: Learning to support your child without absorbing all their emotions as your own.

Joy cultivation: Intentionally seeking experiences that bring you joy and connection to your authentic self.

Mental and Cognitive Strategies

Perspective practices: Developing ways to maintain broader perspective during difficult moments or periods.

Problem-solving approaches: Having systematic ways to approach challenges rather than feeling overwhelmed by them.

Learning and growth: Continuing to learn about neurodivergent development and parenting strategies.

Future focus: Maintaining hope and vision for your child's future while staying present to current needs.

Meaning-making: Finding ways to understand your parenting journey as meaningful and valuable.

Your Self-Care Success Story

Rachel's transformation didn't happen overnight, but it began when she realized that her chronic stress was actually making it harder for her to support her children effectively. She started with tiny changes—taking three deep breaths before responding to challenging behaviors, drinking water throughout the day, and taking a brief walk after her kids went to bed.

As these small practices became habits, Rachel began to feel more like herself again. She had more patience with her children, more energy for the daily challenges, and more joy in the positive moments. Most importantly, her children began to regulate more easily because she was providing more consistent co-regulation from her own stable nervous system.

Rachel learned that taking care of herself wasn't separate from taking care of her family—it was the foundation that made everything else possible. When she honored her own nervous system needs, she became a more effective parent, a better partner, and a happier person.

Your nervous system matters too. Not just because you deserve care and support, but because your regulated presence is one of the most powerful tools you have for supporting your neurodivergent child's development. When you invest in your own nervous system health, you're investing in your entire family's wellbeing.

The goal isn't perfect self-care or eliminating all stress from your life. The goal is recognizing that your regulation matters, developing sustainable practices that support your nervous system health, and modeling for your child that taking care of yourself is a normal, necessary part of being human.

Your child needs you to be healthy, regulated, and present for the long haul. Taking care of your nervous system isn't selfish—it's one of the most important gifts you can give to your family.

Chapter 17: Sibling Support and Family Co-Regulation

At the dinner table, the Johnson family's evening unfolded in a familiar pattern. Eight-year-old Tyler with autism was having difficulty with the texture of the mashed potatoes, beginning to show signs of distress that his parents recognized as potential meltdown territory. His twelve-year-old sister Emma immediately tensed up, pushing food around her plate and glancing anxiously between Tyler and the door.

"Here we go again," Emma muttered under her breath, just loud enough for her parents to hear but quiet enough to avoid escalating Tyler's distress.

Their parents, Mark and Lisa, found themselves in the impossible position of needing to support Tyler's nervous system while also recognizing Emma's legitimate frustration. Emma loved her brother deeply, but she was tired of family life revolving around Tyler's needs. She felt like she had to be perfect all the time because her parents were already dealing with "enough" from Tyler.

This scenario plays out in millions of families where one child has significant nervous system support needs while siblings struggle with their own complex feelings about family dynamics, attention, and their role in supporting their neurodivergent brother or sister.

Creating family co-regulation that supports everyone— neurodivergent children, their siblings, and parents—is one of the most challenging aspects of raising neurodivergent children. It requires understanding how nervous system regulation works not just individually, but as a family system where everyone's emotional states affect everyone else.

How Neurodivergent Siblings Affect the Whole Family System

Families function as interconnected nervous system networks where each person's regulation state influences everyone else. When one family member has significant nervous system challenges, it creates ripple effects that impact the entire family's emotional climate.

The Nervous System Contagion Effect

Dr. Stephen Porges's research demonstrates that nervous system states are "contagious"—we unconsciously mirror the autonomic nervous system states of people around us, especially family members (Porges, 2017). In families with neurodivergent children, this contagion effect can create complex patterns.

Hypervigilance spreading: When parents are chronically vigilant about their neurodivergent child's regulation, siblings often develop their own hypervigilance, constantly monitoring family emotional temperature.

Stress amplification: One person's dysregulation can trigger dysregulation in others, creating escalation cycles that affect everyone in the household.

Emotional suppression: Siblings may learn to suppress their own emotional expressions to avoid "adding" to family stress.

Regulation responsibility: Siblings may feel responsible for maintaining family calm by managing their own needs and emotions perfectly.

Sibling Roles and Identity Development

The "perfect" child: Many siblings of neurodivergent children develop identities as the "easy" child who doesn't cause problems, which can limit authentic emotional expression.

The "helper" child: Some siblings take on premature caregiving responsibilities, feeling like co-parents rather than children with their own developmental needs.

The "invisible" child: When family energy is consistently focused on the neurodivergent child's crises, siblings may feel overlooked or forgotten.

The "acting out" child: Some siblings develop behavioral challenges as a way of getting attention or expressing their unmet needs.

The "advocate" child: Siblings may develop strong advocacy skills and protective instincts toward their neurodivergent sibling, sometimes at the expense of their own social relationships.

Fourteen-year-old Sarah described her experience: "I love my brother, but sometimes I feel like I'm not allowed to have problems because his problems are always bigger. I've gotten really good at handling everything myself, but sometimes I wish someone would notice that I need help too."

Supporting Neurotypical Siblings' Nervous System Needs

Neurotypical siblings have their own legitimate nervous system needs that deserve attention and support, even when their neurodivergent sibling requires intensive intervention.

Understanding Sibling Stress Responses

Chronic stress exposure: Living with frequent family crises, disrupted routines, and high emotional intensity can create chronic stress responses in neurotypical siblings.

Anticipatory anxiety: Siblings often develop anxiety about when the next meltdown will occur, making it difficult to relax even during calm periods.

Social anxiety: Siblings may worry about friends' reactions to their neurodivergent sibling's behavior or feel embarrassed about family differences.

Future concerns: Older siblings may worry about their role in their neurodivergent sibling's future care and support.

Identity confusion: Growing up in a family focused on neurodivergent needs can make it challenging for siblings to identify and express their own authentic needs and interests.

Providing Individual Attention and Support

One-on-one time: Regular individual time with each parent helps siblings feel seen and valued for their unique qualities and interests.

Interest validation: Supporting siblings' individual interests and activities, even when they're different from or competing with the neurodivergent child's needs.

Emotional validation: Acknowledging that siblings' feelings about family dynamics are legitimate and understandable.

Age-appropriate responsibilities: Ensuring that siblings have age-appropriate responsibilities rather than taking on adult caregiving roles.

Personal space and boundaries: Protecting siblings' personal belongings, space, and activities from disruption when possible.

Creating Sibling-Specific Support

Individual therapy or counseling: Professional support for siblings to process their experiences and develop their own coping strategies.

Sibling support groups: Connecting with other children who have neurodivergent siblings to share experiences and strategies.

Educational support: Helping siblings understand their neurodivergent sibling's needs while maintaining focus on their own development.

Advocacy skills: Teaching siblings how to communicate their needs and advocate for their interests within the family system.

Future planning: Age-appropriate discussions about future family dynamics and siblings' choices about their role in their neurodivergent sibling's life.

Family Co-Regulation Activities and Rituals

Creating family activities that support everyone's nervous system regulation helps build connection while honoring individual differences and needs.

Understanding Family Nervous System Patterns

Family regulation rhythms: Every family develops patterns around when regulation is typically high or low, and what triggers family-wide stress or calm.

Individual contribution recognition: Understanding how each family member's regulation state affects the overall family emotional climate.

Trigger identification: Recognizing environmental, timing, or situational factors that tend to trigger family-wide dysregulation.

Strength utilization: Identifying each family member's natural regulation strengths and using them to support family stability.

Recovery pattern awareness: Understanding how long different family members need to recover from stressful events and planning accordingly.

Daily Family Regulation Practices

Morning connection rituals: Brief family check-ins or connection activities that start the day with positive family energy.

Transition support: Family practices that help everyone handle transitions—coming home from school/work, bedtime routines, or weekend schedule changes.

Mealtime regulation: Creating mealtime environments and practices that support rather than stress family nervous systems.

Evening decompression: Family rituals that help everyone process the day and transition to rest mode.

Weekly family meetings: Regular times for family members to share needs, plan for challenges, and celebrate successes together.

Inclusive Activities That Support Different Nervous Systems

Nature-based activities: Outdoor time that provides regulation support for various nervous system needs while allowing for different participation levels.

Creative projects: Art, music, or building activities that can accommodate different sensory preferences and skill levels.

Movement activities: Family physical activities that can be modified for different abilities and provide nervous system regulation.

Quiet activities: Reading together, puzzles, or other calm activities that support nervous systems that need less stimulation.

Service activities: Family volunteer activities that build connection while contributing to community, giving everyone a sense of purpose.

The Martinez family found that Sunday evening "family regulation time" worked well for them. Each family member could choose a regulation activity—Mom might do yoga, Dad would listen to music, their neurodivergent son would use his sensory swing, and their neurotypical daughter would draw. They stayed in the same room but each did their own thing, creating calm family energy without forcing interaction.

Managing Different Nervous System Needs Within One Family

Every family member has unique nervous system needs, and successful families learn to honor these differences while maintaining family cohesion.

Accommodating Sensory Differences

Environmental flexibility: Creating family spaces that can be adjusted for different sensory needs—lighting options, sound levels, seating choices.

Individual accommodations: Allowing family members to use personal regulation tools—headphones, fidget items, comfort objects—during family activities.

Activity modifications: Adapting family activities so that everyone can participate in ways that work for their nervous system.

Compromise strategies: Finding middle ground when family members have conflicting sensory needs.

Respect for boundaries: Understanding when family members need to opt out of activities due to sensory overwhelm.

Balancing Individual and Family Needs

Separate space provisions: Ensuring that each family member has access to space where they can regulate individually when needed.

Schedule considerations: Planning family activities around individual family members' regulation patterns and capacity.

Expectation flexibility: Adjusting expectations based on each family member's current nervous system state and capacity.

Support resource allocation: Ensuring that support resources are distributed fairly rather than only going to the family member with the most obvious needs.

Individual growth support: Supporting each family member's personal development and interests, not just family functioning.

Communication About Different Needs

Family nervous system education: Teaching all family members age-appropriate information about how nervous systems work and why people have different needs.

Difference celebration: Framing individual differences as family strengths rather than problems to be solved.

Need expression skills: Teaching all family members how to communicate their nervous system needs clearly and respectfully.

Conflict resolution: Having systems for handling conflicts that arise from different nervous system needs.

Empathy development: Helping family members understand and appreciate each other's perspectives and challenges.

Building Empathy and Understanding Between Siblings

Creating sibling relationships based on understanding rather than resentment requires intentional effort to help children understand each other's experiences and develop mutual support.

Age-Appropriate Neurodivergent Education

Basic nervous system concepts: Teaching neurotypical siblings age-appropriate information about how their neurodivergent sibling's brain and nervous system work differently.

Strength recognition: Helping siblings recognize and appreciate their neurodivergent sibling's unique strengths and contributions.

Challenge understanding: Explaining why certain situations are difficult for their neurodivergent sibling without creating pity or condescension.

Behavior interpretation: Helping siblings understand that challenging behaviors are communications about nervous system needs rather than character flaws.

Individual uniqueness: Emphasizing that everyone has unique needs and challenges, not just neurodivergent family members.

Developing Sibling Support Skills

Co-regulation support: Teaching siblings how to provide calm presence during their neurodivergent sibling's difficult moments without taking responsibility for fixing everything.

Environmental awareness: Helping siblings recognize and modify environmental factors that might trigger their neurodivergent sibling's stress responses.

Communication strategies: Teaching siblings how to communicate effectively with their neurodivergent sibling, including when and how to give space.

Advocacy skills: Helping siblings learn how to support their neurodivergent sibling in social or educational settings when appropriate.

Boundary maintenance: Teaching siblings how to support their neurodivergent sibling while maintaining their own boundaries and needs.

Creating Positive Sibling Experiences

Shared interest activities: Finding activities that both siblings genuinely enjoy rather than forcing interaction.

Individual relationship building: Supporting the unique relationship between siblings rather than comparing it to typical sibling relationships.

Success celebration: Acknowledging positive sibling interactions and mutual support when they occur naturally.

Conflict resolution: Teaching siblings how to handle conflicts respectfully while accommodating different communication styles and needs.

Future planning: Age-appropriate discussions about the sibling relationship as everyone grows and changes.

Ten-year-old Marcus learned to be his autistic brother's "regulation detective," noticing when family environments were getting overwhelming and suggesting family dance parties or quiet time before meltdowns occurred. This gave him a positive, helpful role while building his empathy and observation skills.

Creating Family Safety and Connection

The foundation of successful family co-regulation is creating an emotional and physical environment where every family member feels safe, valued, and connected.

Physical Safety for Everyone

Crisis management plans: Having clear plans for keeping everyone safe during meltdowns or behavioral crises that protect all family members.

Personal space protection: Ensuring that each family member has access to private space where they can retreat when overwhelmed.

Property boundaries: Clear guidelines about personal belongings and consequences for destroying or damaging others' property.

Sibling protection: Strategies for protecting neurotypical siblings from physical aggression while supporting the dysregulated child.

Professional support: Knowing when and how to access professional help if family safety becomes a concern.

Emotional Safety and Connection

Unconditional love expression: Ensuring that all family members know they're loved regardless of their challenges or contributions to family stress.

Individual value recognition: Regular acknowledgment of each family member's unique qualities, strengths, and contributions.

Mistake acceptance: Creating family cultures where mistakes are learning opportunities rather than sources of shame or punishment.

Feeling validation: Accepting and validating all family members' emotions, even when behaviors need to be addressed.

Future security: Helping all family members feel secure about their place in the family and their future relationships with each other.

Building Family Resilience

Challenge reframing: Helping the family see difficult periods as temporary challenges that they can handle together rather than permanent problems.

Strength identification: Regularly acknowledging how the family's experiences with neurodivergent challenges have built unique strengths and capabilities.

Growth celebration: Celebrating family growth, learning, and improved functioning over time.

Community connection: Building connections with other families who understand neurodivergent challenges and can provide support and perspective.

Meaning-making: Helping family members find meaning and purpose in their unique family experiences.

Long-Term Family Relationship Building

Supporting sibling relationships and family co-regulation isn't just about managing current challenges—it's about building family connections that will last throughout life.

Preparing for Developmental Changes

Adolescent considerations: Understanding how teenage development affects both neurodivergent and neurotypical siblings and adjusting family approaches accordingly.

Adult relationship preparation: Helping siblings develop skills and perspectives that will support positive adult relationships with each other.

Independence planning: Supporting all children's movement toward independence while maintaining family connections.

Life transition support: Preparing the family for major transitions like graduation, moving out, marriage, or career changes.

Ongoing relationship maintenance: Teaching skills for maintaining close relationships despite different life paths and responsibilities.

Building Sibling Advocacy and Support

Natural support development: Allowing siblings to develop their own supportive relationships rather than forcing particular dynamics.

Advocacy skill building: Teaching siblings how to advocate for their neurodivergent sibling in various contexts while maintaining their own boundaries.

Professional collaboration: Including siblings appropriately in professional discussions and planning for their neurodivergent sibling's future.

Decision-making preparation: Age-appropriate discussions about future decision-making regarding their neurodivergent sibling's care and support.

Relationship choice respect: Understanding that siblings get to choose their level of involvement in their neurodivergent sibling's adult life.

Creating Family Legacy

Value transmission: Helping family members identify and maintain the positive values that have developed through their neurodivergent parenting journey.

Story creation: Building positive family narratives about resilience, growth, and love that overcome challenges.

Tradition development: Creating family traditions that can continue throughout life transitions and changes.

Wisdom sharing: Preparing family members to share their experiences and insights with others who face similar challenges.

Love multiplication: Understanding how the deep love and acceptance developed in neurodivergent families can positively impact extended relationships and communities.

Your Family Co-Regulation Success Story

The Johnson family's transformation began when Mark and Lisa realized that supporting Tyler's autism couldn't come at Emma's expense. They started scheduling weekly one-on-one time with Emma, got her connected with a support group for siblings of autistic children, and began family meetings where everyone could share their needs and feelings.

Most importantly, they helped Emma understand that Tyler's behaviors weren't personal choices but nervous system communications, while also validating her feelings about the challenges of family life. Emma learned strategies for staying regulated during Tyler's difficult moments while also developing confidence in advocating for her own needs.

Two years later, Emma described her relationship with Tyler this way: "He's still autistic, and our family is still different from other families. But now I know how to take care of myself, and I actually like being Tyler's sister. He sees the world in ways that help me notice things I would miss. We're a good team."

Creating family co-regulation that works for everyone requires understanding that each family member's nervous system matters and contributes to the overall family emotional climate. When you support all family members' regulation needs, you create stronger, more resilient family relationships that can weather any challenge.

The goal isn't perfect family harmony or eliminating all sibling conflict. The goal is creating family systems where everyone feels seen, valued, and supported in their individual development while maintaining strong family connections based on understanding, empathy, and love.

Your neurodivergent child needs sibling relationships that will support them throughout life, and their siblings deserve to grow up feeling valued for their own unique contributions to the family. When you invest in family co-regulation, you're building relationships and skills that will strengthen your family for generations.

Chapter 18: Working with Schools and Therapists

At 2:30 PM, Jennifer's phone rang with the familiar number from Lincoln Elementary. Her heart sank as she recognized the pattern—it was the third call this week about her son Alex's behavior at school.

"Mrs. Chen, we need you to come pick up Alex. He had another outburst in math class and is refusing to do his work. We think he might benefit from some consequences at home to help him understand that this behavior isn't acceptable."

Jennifer felt the familiar frustration building. At home, Alex was a curious, creative eight-year-old who loved building with Legos and could focus for hours on projects that interested him. But at school, he was labeled as defiant, disruptive, and unmotivated. His teachers saw behavioral problems that needed managing, while Jennifer saw a child whose nervous system was overwhelmed by an environment that didn't understand his sensory and attention needs.

The disconnect between home and school experiences is one of the most challenging aspects of supporting neurodivergent children. Well-meaning educators and therapists often approach behavior through traditional behavior management models that can actually make regulation worse for neurodivergent nervous systems.

Building collaborative relationships with professionals who understand nervous system regulation—and educating those who don't yet understand—is crucial for creating consistent support that helps your child thrive across all environments.

Educating Your Child's Team About Nervous System Needs

Most educators and therapists receive limited training in neurodivergent nervous system differences, often focusing instead on behavior modification techniques that don't address underlying regulation challenges.

Understanding Professional Perspectives

Traditional behavior models: Many professionals were trained in approaches that view behavior as choices that can be changed through consequences and rewards, rather than as communications about nervous system states.

Compliance expectations: School environments often prioritize compliance and conformity, which can conflict with nervous system accommodations that support authentic learning.

Resource limitations: Professionals may understand nervous system needs but feel constrained by time, funding, or institutional expectations that prevent them from providing optimal support.

Training gaps: Many professionals want to help but lack specific knowledge about polyvagal theory, sensory processing, or nervous system regulation approaches.

Systemic pressures: Schools and therapy practices often have requirements for documentation, progress measurement, and standardized approaches that don't align well with individualized nervous system support.

Effective Communication Strategies

Collaborative language: Approaching professionals as partners in supporting your child rather than adversaries who need to be convinced or corrected.

Concrete examples: Providing specific examples of what your child looks like when regulated vs. dysregulated, and what strategies have been effective at home.

Educational sharing: Offering to share articles, books, or resources about nervous system regulation without overwhelming or insulting their professional knowledge.

Strength focus: Starting conversations by acknowledging what the professional is doing well and what's working before addressing areas that need adjustment.

Solution orientation: Coming to meetings with specific suggestions and strategies rather than just complaints about current approaches.

Building Professional Understanding

Nervous system basics: Sharing age-appropriate explanations of polyvagal theory and how nervous system states affect learning and behavior.

Individual patterns: Helping professionals understand your child's specific patterns, triggers, and regulation needs.

Environmental factors: Educating about how classroom or therapy environments might be supporting or hindering your child's nervous system regulation.

Intervention timing: Explaining why traditional interventions often fail during dysregulation and when your child can actually access learning and behavior change.

Progress measurement: Helping professionals understand what progress looks like for neurodivergent children and how to measure meaningful change.

Dr. Sarah Johnson, a school psychologist who shifted to nervous system approaches, described her experience: "Once I understood that the behaviors I was seeing were nervous system communications rather than compliance issues, everything changed. Instead of asking 'How do I stop this behavior?' I started asking 'What is this child's nervous system trying to tell me?' The interventions became so much more effective."

Effective Communication with Professionals

Building productive relationships with your child's educational and therapeutic team requires strategic communication that honors their expertise while advocating for your child's needs.

Preparation for Professional Meetings

Documentation: Keep records of your child's patterns, successful strategies, and specific examples of how nervous system approaches have helped at home.

Goal clarity: Know what specific outcomes you want from meetings and what accommodations or changes would most benefit your child.

Team understanding: Learn about each professional's role, constraints, and perspective so you can tailor your communication accordingly.

Resource preparation: Have articles, books, or other materials ready to share if professionals are interested in learning more about nervous system approaches.

Advocacy balance: Prepare to advocate firmly for your child's needs while maintaining collaborative relationships with team members.

During Professional Meetings

Relationship building: Spend time building rapport and understanding each team member's perspective before jumping into problem-solving.

Child-centered focus: Keep conversations focused on your child's individual needs rather than general theories or approaches.

Specific examples: Use concrete examples of how nervous system understanding has improved your child's functioning rather than abstract explanations.

Collaborative problem-solving: Involve professionals in developing solutions rather than telling them what they should do differently.

Follow-up planning: End meetings with clear action steps, timelines, and plans for ongoing communication.

Ongoing Communication

Regular check-ins: Maintain regular communication with key team members to monitor progress and adjust strategies as needed.

Success sharing: Share successes and positive developments to build team confidence in nervous system approaches.

Challenge discussion: Address problems early and collaboratively rather than letting frustrations build.

Information updates: Keep team members informed about changes in your child's development, family circumstances, or other factors that might affect functioning.

Appreciation expression: Acknowledge team members' efforts and contributions to your child's success.

IEP/504 Plan Accommodations from a Polyvagal Perspective

Traditional special education accommodations often focus on academic modifications or behavioral interventions without addressing the underlying nervous system needs that drive both learning and behavior challenges.

Reframing Accommodation Language

Instead of: "Student will remain in seat during instruction." Nervous system approach: "Student will have access to movement breaks and alternative seating options to support optimal arousal for learning."

Instead of: "Student will complete assignments without disrupting others." Nervous system approach: "Student will receive sensory supports and environmental modifications to maintain regulation during independent work."

Instead of: "Student will ask for help appropriately." Nervous system approach: "Student will have multiple ways to communicate overwhelm and request regulation support, including non-verbal options."

Instead of: "Student will transition between activities within expected timeframes." Nervous system approach: "Student will receive advance warning and transition supports to help their nervous system prepare for environmental changes."

Essential Nervous System Accommodations

Environmental supports:

- Preferential seating away from high-traffic areas and sensory distractions

- Access to noise-reducing headphones or other sensory accommodations

- Alternative lighting options when available

- Quiet space access for regulation breaks

Regulation supports:

- Scheduled movement breaks based on individual needs rather than predetermined intervals

- Access to fidget tools, weighted items, or other sensory supports

- Permission to take regulation breaks when early warning signs appear

- Adult check-ins during transitions or challenging activities

Communication accommodations:

- Recognition that behavior communicates nervous system needs

- Alternative ways to request help or breaks when verbal communication is difficult

- Modified expectations during periods of dysregulation

- Use of visual or written communication when verbal processing is overwhelmed

Academic adjustments:

- Modified workload during periods of nervous system stress

- Alternative assessment methods that don't rely solely on traditional testing

- Extended time or alternative environments for assignments and tests

- Priority focus on learning objectives rather than compliance behaviors

Implementation and Monitoring

Team training: Ensuring that all team members understand the nervous system basis for accommodations and how to implement them effectively.

Data collection: Measuring progress through nervous system regulation indicators rather than just compliance behaviors.

Regular review: Frequent assessment of accommodation effectiveness and adjustment based on your child's changing needs.

Generalization support: Helping your child understand and advocate for their accommodations across different environments and activities.

Transition planning: Ensuring that nervous system accommodations are maintained and adjusted as your child moves through different grades and schools.

Advocating for Nervous System-Informed Supports

Sometimes you need to advocate more assertively for approaches that honor your child's nervous system needs, especially in systems that are resistant to change or unfamiliar with regulation-based interventions.

Building Your Advocacy Skills

Legal knowledge: Understanding your rights under IDEA, Section 504, and other relevant laws that protect neurodivergent students.

Documentation skills: Keeping detailed records of your child's needs, current interventions, and the effectiveness of different approaches.

Professional language: Learning to communicate in ways that professionals find credible and compelling.

Research backing: Having access to research and evidence that supports nervous system approaches to learning and behavior.

Network building: Connecting with other parents and advocates who can provide support and shared experiences.

When to Advocate More Assertively

Safety concerns: If current approaches are creating trauma, increasing behavioral challenges, or compromising your child's emotional safety.

Lack of progress: When traditional interventions aren't producing meaningful improvements in learning or behavior after reasonable trial periods.

Regression indicators: If your child is showing increased anxiety, behavioral challenges, or academic struggles despite interventions.

Professional resistance: When team members are unwilling to consider nervous system perspectives or continue using approaches that aren't working.

System limitations: When school or therapy policies prevent implementation of accommodations your child needs to succeed.

Advocacy Strategies

Independent evaluations: Seeking assessments from professionals who understand nervous system approaches to provide additional documentation of your child's needs.

Parent training documentation: Showing that you've educated yourself about your child's needs and evidence-based approaches.

Professional consultation: Bringing nervous system-informed professionals to meetings to provide expert perspective and recommendations.

Legal support: Consulting with special education attorneys when necessary to ensure your child's rights are protected.

Community building: Working with other parents to advocate for system-wide changes that benefit all neurodivergent students.

Twelve-year-old Emma's parents had to advocate assertively when her middle school wanted to use a behavior chart system that was actually increasing her anxiety and shutdown behaviors. They brought in an independent evaluation that documented her nervous system needs and worked with the team to develop regulation-based supports that helped Emma succeed both academically and socially.

Monitoring and Adjusting Accommodations

Effective accommodations require ongoing monitoring and adjustment as your child develops and their needs change over time.

Data Collection That Matters

Regulation indicators: Tracking your child's nervous system regulation throughout the school day rather than just compliance behaviors.

Learning engagement: Measuring authentic learning engagement rather than just task completion.

Social connection: Monitoring your child's peer relationships and social integration, not just absence of behavioral problems.

Self-advocacy development: Tracking your child's growing awareness of their needs and ability to communicate them.

Stress indicators: Monitoring signs of chronic stress that might indicate accommodations need adjustment.

Regular Review and Adjustment

Quarterly assessments: Regular meetings to review accommodation effectiveness and make necessary adjustments.

Developmental considerations: Adjusting accommodations as your child grows and their needs change.

Environmental changes: Modifying supports when classroom environments, teachers, or school situations change.

Skill development: Reducing supports gradually as your child develops internal regulation skills while maintaining safety nets.

Crisis prevention: Adjusting accommodations proactively when you notice patterns that suggest increased stress or regulation challenges.

Collaborative Problem-Solving

Team input: Involving all team members in identifying what's working, what isn't, and what adjustments might be helpful.

Child input: Including your child in accommodation reviews appropriate to their developmental level and communication abilities.

Family context: Considering how school accommodations interact with home life and whether adjustments are needed for consistency.

Future planning: Anticipating upcoming challenges or transitions that might require accommodation modifications.

Success building: Using successful accommodations as foundations for expanding your child's capacity and independence.

Building Collaborative Relationships

The most effective support for neurodivergent children happens when families and professionals work as true partners with shared goals and mutual respect.

Creating Partnership Dynamics

Shared expertise recognition: Acknowledging that parents are experts on their individual child while professionals bring expertise about child development and educational strategies.

Common goal identification: Focusing on shared goals for your child's success rather than disagreements about methods.

Communication preferences: Establishing how team members prefer to communicate and how often check-ins should occur.

Conflict resolution: Having agreed-upon processes for handling disagreements or challenges that arise.

Celebration practices: Regularly acknowledging successes and positive developments as a team.

Professional Development Support

Resource sharing: Offering to share books, articles, or training opportunities about nervous system approaches.

Conference attendance: Attending professional development events together when possible.

Peer connection: Connecting professionals with others who are already using nervous system approaches successfully.

Gradual implementation: Supporting professionals in gradually implementing new approaches rather than expecting immediate wholesale changes.

Success documentation: Helping document the effectiveness of nervous system approaches to build professional confidence and institutional support.

Long-Term Relationship Building

Consistency maintenance: Working to maintain relationships with key professionals across school years when possible.

Transition support: Helping new team members understand your child's needs and successful approaches.

System influence: Using positive relationships to influence broader system changes that benefit all neurodivergent students.

Professional networking: Building connections with professionals who understand nervous system approaches for future reference and support.

Community building: Working with professionals to build community awareness and support for neurodivergent students and families.

Working with Resistant Professionals

Not every professional will immediately embrace nervous system approaches, and some may be actively resistant to changing established practices.

Understanding Professional Resistance

Training investment: Professionals may be reluctant to abandon approaches they've invested significant time learning.

Institutional pressure: Schools and agencies may have policies or expectations that make nervous system approaches seem difficult to implement.

Liability concerns: Some professionals worry about departing from established practices due to concerns about accountability or legal issues.

Resource limitations: Professionals may believe nervous system approaches require resources they don't have available.

Previous experiences: Negative experiences with pushy parents or ineffective interventions may make professionals cautious about new approaches.

Strategies for Working with Resistance

Patience and persistence: Understanding that change takes time and maintaining relationships even when progress is slow.

Small steps: Asking for minor accommodations that demonstrate effectiveness before requesting larger changes.

Evidence provision: Sharing research and documentation that supports nervous system approaches without being overwhelming or condescending.

Success stories: Providing examples of how nervous system approaches have helped other children with similar profiles.

Professional language: Communicating in ways that respect professional expertise while introducing new perspectives.

When to Consider Alternatives

Safety concerns: If professionals are using approaches that are harmful to your child's nervous system or emotional wellbeing.

Entrenched resistance: When professionals consistently refuse to consider your child's documented needs or evidence-based approaches.

Lack of progress: If your child continues to struggle despite your advocacy efforts and accommodation requests.

Professional competence: When professionals lack basic understanding of neurodivergent needs and are unwilling to learn.

System limitations: When institutional constraints prevent implementation of necessary supports.

Your Professional Partnership Success Story

Jennifer's relationship with Alex's school transformed when she shifted her approach from demanding changes to offering partnership. Instead of criticizing the school's behavior management system, she shared specific examples of what helped Alex regulate at home and offered to work with teachers to adapt these strategies for the classroom.

She brought research articles about ADHD and nervous system regulation to share, not as criticism of current approaches but as additional tools that might be helpful. She volunteered to help create sensory regulation tools for the classroom and offered to provide training for staff about Alex's specific needs and triggers.

Most importantly, she consistently acknowledged and appreciated the efforts that teachers and staff made to support Alex, building relationships based on mutual respect and shared commitment to his success.

Six months later, Alex's teacher commented: "Working with Jennifer taught me so much about how different kids' brains work. The strategies we developed for Alex ended up helping several other students in my classroom too. Now I look at behavior differently— instead of asking 'How do I stop this?' I ask 'What is this child's nervous system trying to tell me?'"

Building collaborative relationships with your child's professional team requires patience, persistence, and the willingness to educate while honoring professional expertise. When you approach professionals as partners rather than adversaries, you're more likely to create the consistent, comprehensive support your child needs to thrive.

The goal isn't to convert every professional to polyvagal theory, but rather to build understanding and support for your child's individual nervous system needs. When professionals understand that behavior is communication about regulation needs, they can provide more effective support that addresses root causes rather than just managing symptoms.

Your advocacy and partnership with professionals not only benefits your child but often helps other neurodivergent students whose families may not have the knowledge or resources to advocate as effectively. When you build collaborative relationships that honor nervous system differences, you're creating positive change that extends far beyond your individual child.

Chapter 19: Teen Years: Autonomy and Nervous System Support

Fifteen-year-old Maya slammed her bedroom door and threw herself onto her bed, tears of frustration streaming down her face. The argument with her parents had started over something small—whether she could go to a friend's house on a school night—but had escalated into a bigger conflict about independence, trust, and expectations.

"You don't understand!" Maya had shouted. "I'm not a little kid anymore! I can handle my own problems!"

Her parents, David and Lisa, stood in the hallway feeling defeated. They'd been supporting Maya's autism and anxiety for years, providing the co-regulation and environmental supports that helped her succeed in elementary and middle school. But now that she was a teenager, Maya wanted more independence while still needing significant nervous system support.

The challenge felt impossible: how do you support a teenager's growing need for autonomy while still providing the regulation support their neurodivergent nervous system requires? How do you balance independence with safety, growth with support, and teenage desires with neurobiological realities?

The teen years are complex for all families, but for neurodivergent teens and their parents, this developmental period requires careful navigation of competing needs: the universal adolescent drive toward independence and the ongoing reality of nervous system differences that require support and accommodation.

How Nervous System Needs Change During Adolescence

Adolescence brings significant neurobiological changes that affect all teenagers, but these changes can be particularly complex for neurodivergent teens whose nervous systems already function differently from typical expectations.

The Adolescent Brain and Nervous System Development

Dr. Laurence Steinberg's research reveals that adolescent brains undergo significant reorganization, with emotional centers developing faster than regulatory centers, creating a period of increased emotional intensity and decreased regulation capacity (Steinberg, 2013). For neurodivergent teens, this normal developmental process can create additional challenges.

Increased emotional intensity: The hormonal and neurological changes of adolescence can make emotional experiences more intense for all teens, but neurodivergent teens may find this intensity particularly overwhelming given their existing regulation challenges.

Social pressure amplification: The increased importance of peer relationships during adolescence can create additional stress for teens who already struggle with social communication and connection.

Identity development complexity: All teens work on developing their identity, but neurodivergent teens must integrate their neurological differences into their sense of self during this critical period.

Executive function demands: High school academic and social expectations require more sophisticated executive function skills at a time when the adolescent brain's regulatory systems are still developing.

Independence-support tension: The normal adolescent drive toward independence can conflict with ongoing needs for nervous system support and accommodation.

Unique Challenges for Neurodivergent Teens

Masking exhaustion: Many neurodivergent teens have been masking their differences to fit in, and the energy required for this becomes increasingly unsustainable during adolescence.

Sensory sensitivity changes: Hormonal changes can affect sensory processing, making previously manageable environments suddenly overwhelming.

Social complexity increases: Teenage social dynamics become more complex and subtle, challenging teens who already struggle with social communication.

Academic pressure intensification: High school academic demands can overwhelm executive function systems that are already challenged.

Future planning anxiety: Questions about college, career, and independence can create significant anxiety for teens who already worry about their ability to navigate the world.

Seventeen-year-old Jordan with ADHD described his experience: "It's like everyone expects me to suddenly be able to handle everything on my own, but my brain still works the same way it always has. I want to be independent, but I also know I still need help with some things. It's confusing and frustrating."

Supporting Growing Independence While Providing Safety

The key to supporting neurodivergent teens is finding ways to honor their need for autonomy while still providing the nervous system support they require for success and safety.

Scaffolded Independence Development

Gradual responsibility increase: Slowly transferring responsibilities from parents to teens while maintaining safety nets and support systems.

Skill-building focus: Teaching specific skills that will support independence rather than just removing supports and hoping teens figure it out.

Mistake tolerance: Allowing teens to make manageable mistakes while protecting them from consequences that could be harmful or traumatic.

Success building: Creating opportunities for teens to experience success with increasing levels of independence.

Support modification: Changing the type of support provided rather than eliminating support entirely.

Autonomy in Supported Environments

Choice within structure: Providing teens with meaningful choices within frameworks that support their nervous system needs.

Self-advocacy development: Teaching teens to identify and communicate their own needs rather than having parents always advocate for them.

Environmental control: Helping teens learn to modify their environments to support their nervous system needs independently.

Relationship management: Supporting teens in building their own relationships with teachers, employers, and other adults.

Problem-solving partnership: Moving from solving problems for teens to solving problems with teens.

Safety Net Maintenance

Crisis support systems: Ensuring that teens know how to access help when their regulation strategies aren't sufficient.

Professional relationship continuity: Maintaining relationships with therapists, doctors, and other professionals while gradually increasing teen involvement in their own care.

Family support availability: Making it clear that family support remains available even as independence increases.

Environmental safety: Ensuring that teens' expanding environments (jobs, social activities, driving) include appropriate safety considerations.

Communication systems: Developing ways for teens to stay connected with family support while maintaining privacy and independence.

Helping Teens Understand Their Own Nervous System

One of the most important developmental tasks for neurodivergent teens is developing sophisticated understanding of their own nervous system patterns, triggers, and support needs.

Building Self-Awareness

Personal pattern recognition: Helping teens identify their individual patterns of regulation and dysregulation across different environments and situations.

Trigger identification: Supporting teens in recognizing what environmental, social, or internal factors tend to challenge their nervous system regulation.

Strength recognition: Helping teens understand their unique strengths and how their neurodivergent traits can be assets in appropriate contexts.

Strategy effectiveness evaluation: Teaching teens to assess which regulation strategies work best for them in different situations.

Body awareness development: Supporting teens in developing sophisticated awareness of physical sensations, energy levels, and internal states.

Nervous System Education

Adolescent development understanding: Helping teens understand how typical adolescent development interacts with their neurodivergent patterns.

Neurobiological literacy: Teaching teens age-appropriate information about how their brains and nervous systems work.

Individual difference appreciation: Helping teens understand that their nervous system differences are variations rather than deficits.

Accommodation rationale: Explaining why certain accommodations or supports help their nervous system function optimally.

Future planning integration: Helping teens understand how their nervous system needs might affect future educational and career planning.

Identity Integration

Neurodivergent identity acceptance: Supporting teens in developing positive relationships with their neurodivergent identity rather than seeing it as something to hide or overcome.

Strength-based perspective: Helping teens recognize how their neurodivergent traits contribute positively to their identity and potential contributions.

Community connection: Connecting teens with neurodivergent role models and communities where they can see positive examples of neurodivergent adults.

Self-advocacy skills: Teaching teens how to communicate their needs and advocate for accommodations in various settings.

Future visioning: Helping teens envision positive futures that honor their authentic selves rather than requiring them to become neurotypical.

Sixteen-year-old Sarah with autism learned to describe her needs this way: "I know that parties can be overwhelming for my nervous system, so I usually go for an hour or two and then leave when I start feeling overwhelmed. My friends understand that it's not about them—it's just how my brain works."

Managing Increased Academic and Social Pressures

High school brings intensified academic expectations and more complex social dynamics that can be particularly challenging for neurodivergent teens whose nervous systems are already managing significant demands.

Academic Pressure Management

Course load balancing: Helping teens choose course loads that challenge them appropriately without overwhelming their regulation capacity.

Study strategy development: Teaching teens study methods that work with their learning styles and attention patterns.

Time management skills: Developing systems for managing complex schedules and multiple deadlines.

Accommodation advocacy: Teaching teens to advocate for their own accommodations and communicate with teachers about their needs.

Stress monitoring: Helping teens recognize when academic stress is affecting their nervous system regulation and adjust accordingly.

Social Pressure Navigation

Peer relationship skills: Teaching teens how to build and maintain friendships while honoring their nervous system needs.

Social energy management: Helping teens understand how much social interaction they can handle and how to take breaks when needed.

Boundary setting: Teaching teens how to set appropriate boundaries in relationships and social situations.

Conflict resolution: Developing skills for handling social conflicts and misunderstandings respectfully.

Authentic relationship building: Supporting teens in finding friends and communities where they can be authentically themselves.

Pressure Response Strategies

Perfectionism management: Helping teens develop realistic expectations and self-compassion when facing challenges.

Anxiety coping: Teaching teens specific strategies for managing anxiety about academic performance and social acceptance.

Support seeking: Developing teens' ability to recognize when they need help and how to access appropriate support.

Resilience building: Helping teens develop confidence in their ability to handle challenges and recover from setbacks.

Value clarification: Supporting teens in identifying what's truly important to them rather than just meeting external expectations.

Preparing for Adulthood Transitions

The ultimate goal of supporting neurodivergent teens is preparing them for successful transitions to adult life while honoring their ongoing nervous system needs.

Post-High School Planning

College preparation: If college is appropriate, helping teens understand how to access disability services and advocate for their needs in higher education.

Career exploration: Identifying career paths that utilize teens' strengths while providing environments that support their nervous system needs.

Independent living skills: Teaching practical skills needed for independent living while considering ongoing support needs.

Financial planning: Helping teens understand budgeting, financial management, and the costs associated with their support needs.

Legal considerations: Understanding legal rights and protections that continue into adulthood.

Support System Development

Adult service connections: Helping teens connect with adult mental health services, vocational rehabilitation, or other adult support systems.

Mentorship relationships: Connecting teens with neurodivergent adults who can provide guidance and role modeling.

Community integration: Helping teens find communities and activities where they can continue to grow and contribute.

Professional relationships: Supporting teens in developing their own relationships with healthcare providers, therapists, and other professionals.

Family relationship evolution: Helping family relationships evolve from caregiver-dependent to adult interdependent relationships.

Skill Consolidation

Self-advocacy mastery: Ensuring teens can effectively communicate their needs and advocate for accommodations independently.

Regulation independence: Building teens' capacity to recognize and respond to their own nervous system needs without constant external support.

Problem-solving confidence: Developing teens' confidence in their ability to handle challenges and find solutions.

Relationship skills: Preparing teens for adult relationships including friendships, romantic relationships, and professional relationships.

Life management: Building skills for managing all aspects of adult life while honoring neurodivergent needs.

Eighteen-year-old Marcus described his preparation for college: "I know I'll need some accommodations in college, and I've learned how to ask for what I need. I also know which environments help me study best and what to do when I'm feeling overwhelmed. I'm nervous about being on my own, but I think I'm ready."

Maintaining Connection During the Teen Years

The adolescent drive toward independence can strain parent-child relationships, but maintaining connection is particularly important for neurodivergent teens who may need ongoing support even as they assert their autonomy.

Evolving Parent-Child Relationships

Role transitions: Moving from primary caregiver to consultant and supporter as teens develop more independence.

Communication adaptation: Adjusting communication styles to honor teens' growing autonomy while maintaining emotional connection.

Conflict navigation: Learning to handle disagreements about independence and support needs respectfully.

Trust building: Developing mutual trust as teens demonstrate increasing capacity for self-management.

Boundary respect: Honoring teens' need for privacy and space while maintaining safety and support availability.

Connection Maintenance Strategies

Shared interests: Continuing to connect around topics and activities that both teen and parent enjoy.

Regular check-ins: Maintaining regular communication about how things are going without being intrusive.

Support availability: Making it clear that support is available when needed without being overwhelming about offering help.

Celebration practices: Continuing to celebrate successes and milestones as teens grow and change.

Future planning together: Involving teens in planning for their future while providing guidance and perspective.

Crisis Support Systems

Emergency protocols: Having clear plans for when teens' regulation strategies aren't sufficient and additional support is needed.

Professional backup: Maintaining relationships with therapists and other professionals who can provide support during difficult periods.

Extended support networks: Ensuring that teens have multiple adults they can turn to for support, including family members, mentors, and trusted professionals.

Family adaptability: Building family systems that can adapt to teens' changing needs while maintaining core support and connection.

Community resources: Connecting teens with community resources and support systems that can provide ongoing assistance as they transition to adulthood.

Long-Term Success Strategies

Supporting neurodivergent teens effectively requires a long-term perspective that focuses on building sustainable skills and systems rather than just managing immediate challenges.

Building Intrinsic Motivation

Value-based decision making: Helping teens identify their personal values and make decisions based on these values rather than external pressures.

Interest cultivation: Supporting teens in pursuing their genuine interests and passions as sources of motivation and potential career paths.

Autonomy support: Providing choices and control in areas where teens can handle increased responsibility.

Competence building: Creating opportunities for teens to develop skills and experience success in areas that matter to them.

Purpose development: Helping teens identify how their unique traits and interests can contribute positively to their communities and the world.

Resilience and Adaptability

Growth mindset cultivation: Teaching teens that abilities can be developed through effort and practice, including regulation skills.

Challenge reframing: Helping teens see difficulties as opportunities for growth rather than evidence of personal failure.

Failure recovery: Teaching teens how to recover from setbacks and learn from mistakes without developing shame or learned helplessness.

Adaptability skills: Building teens' ability to adjust to new situations and environments while maintaining their core support needs.

Stress tolerance building: Gradually expanding teens' capacity to handle stress and challenges with appropriate support.

Life Skills Integration

Practical skills development: Teaching teens the practical skills they'll need for adult life, from basic cooking and cleaning to complex problem-solving.

287

Relationship skills: Building teens' capacity for healthy relationships in all areas of life.

Self-care mastery: Helping teens develop sustainable self-care practices that support their long-term wellbeing.

Financial literacy: Teaching teens about money management, including the costs and benefits of various support services.

Career preparation: Helping teens develop skills and knowledge needed for their chosen career paths while honoring their nervous system needs.

Your Teen's Success Story

Maya's family learned that supporting her growing independence didn't mean eliminating all supports—it meant changing the type and delivery of support to honor her developmental needs. Instead of making decisions for Maya, her parents began involving her in understanding her own patterns and needs.

They worked together to identify which social situations energized Maya and which ones depleted her. They practiced role-playing how Maya could advocate for her needs with teachers and friends. Most importantly, they maintained connection and support availability while respecting Maya's need for increased autonomy.

By graduation, Maya could articulate her own needs clearly: "I know that I need quieter environments to focus, and I've learned how to ask for accommodations without feeling embarrassed about it. I also know which friends understand me and which social activities I enjoy versus the ones that stress me out."

Maya went on to college with a clear understanding of her nervous system needs, well-developed self-advocacy skills, and the confidence that her family would continue to support her even as she became increasingly independent. She found a college with strong disability services, connected with other neurodivergent students, and built a life that honored both her need for independence and her ongoing nervous system support needs.

Supporting neurodivergent teens through the complex balance of autonomy and support requires patience, flexibility, and a long-term perspective that honors both their universal developmental needs and their unique neurobiological differences. The goal isn't to eliminate all challenges or create perfect independence, but rather to build teens' capacity to navigate the world authentically while accessing the support they need to thrive.

When you invest in building your teen's self-awareness, self-advocacy skills, and nervous system understanding, you're preparing them for lifelong success that honors their authentic selves rather than requiring them to mask or minimize their differences. The adolescent years may be challenging, but they're also opportunities to build the foundation for fulfilling, authentic adult lives.

Chapter 20: Age-Specific Regulation Activities and Games

The Murphy family's regulation toolkit had evolved dramatically over the years. What started as a desperate search for anything that would help four-year-old Connor during his daily meltdowns had grown into a comprehensive collection of age-appropriate activities that supported the whole family's nervous system needs.

Now, at age twelve, Connor no longer needed the sensory bin that had been his lifeline during preschool, but he still used modified versions of some early regulation activities. His nine-year-old sister Lily had different needs entirely, gravitating toward movement-based regulation activities that helped her ADHD brain focus. Their parents had learned that regulation activities needed to grow and change with their children's development.

"The breathing exercises that work for Connor just make me more fidgety," Lily explained to her mom one evening. "But when I do jumping jacks first, then I can do the breathing stuff."

This insight captured something important about nervous system support: what works at one developmental stage or for one nervous system may not work for another. Effective regulation activities must be matched not only to individual nervous system profiles but also to developmental stages, cognitive abilities, and personal interests.

Creating age-appropriate regulation toolkits allows children to build skills progressively while having access to strategies that actually work for their current developmental level and nervous system needs.

Ages 3-6: Foundational Regulation Activities

Young children are just beginning to develop awareness of their internal states and need regulation activities that are concrete, sensory-based, and often co-regulated with caring adults.

Sensory-Based Regulation for Young Children

Deep pressure activities: Heavy work that provides proprioceptive input helps young nervous systems organize and regulate.

- Bear hugs and sandwich games (child lies between pillows while adult provides gentle pressure)
- Animal walks (bear crawls, crab walks, frog jumps)
- Pushing or pulling heavy objects (laundry baskets, weighted wagons)
- Wall push-ups or "moving the wall" games
- Playing in rice bins, sand tables, or play dough

Vestibular regulation: Movement activities that provide input to the inner ear system support regulation and attention.

- Slow swinging (forward-back or gentle side-to-side)
- Rocking in rocking chairs or on exercise balls
- Gentle spinning (always follow the child's lead and stop before dizziness)
- Sliding down slides or rolling down hills
- Balance beam walking or jumping activities

Tactile regulation: Touch-based activities that provide organizing sensory input.

- Texture exploration bins with various materials

- Finger painting, water play, or sensory art projects
- Brushing activities (with soft brushes on arms or back)
- Playing with kinetic sand, therapy putty, or stress balls
- Warm baths with different bath accessories

Breathing and Body Awareness Games

Young children need concrete, playful ways to learn about breathing and body awareness since abstract concepts are difficult at this age.

Animal breathing: Making breathing exercises fun and relatable through animal themes.

- Bunny breaths (quick sniffs followed by long exhale)
- Snake breathing (long, slow hissing exhales)
- Bear breathing (slow, deep breaths like a sleeping bear)
- Butterfly breathing (gentle breaths while fluttering arms)

Bubble activities: Using bubbles to make breathing visible and fun.

- Blowing bubbles to practice controlled exhaling
- Catching bubbles to encourage tracking and attention
- Pretending to be bubbles floating slowly through the air
- Making different sized bubbles with different breath strength

Body part games: Helping young children develop body awareness through play.

- "Simon Says" with body awareness (touch your nose, wiggle your fingers)
- Freeze dance with body position awareness
- Yoga poses named after animals or objects

- Tension and release games (squeeze tight like a ball, then melt like ice cream)

Five-year-old Emma loved the "robot and rag doll" game where she would march around stiffly like a robot, then completely relax and flop like a rag doll. This simple activity helped her understand the difference between tense and relaxed states in her body.

Co-Regulation Activities for Young Children

Young children primarily regulate through relationships with caring adults, so many effective activities involve shared experiences.

Reading and storytelling: Calm, connected activities that support regulation through relationship.

- Cuddling while reading books about feelings and emotions
- Making up stories about characters who have big feelings
- Using puppet shows to act out regulation strategies
- Interactive books that involve movement or sensory elements

Musical regulation: Using music and rhythm for both activation and calming.

- Singing lullabies or calm songs together
- Dancing to release energy, then transitioning to quiet music
- Playing simple rhythm instruments
- Creating family songs about regulation strategies

Creative expression: Art and creativity as regulation outlets.

- Drawing or coloring while listening to calm music
- Creating art projects that represent different feeling states
- Building with blocks or other construction materials
- Playing with play dough or clay while talking about feelings

Simple Mindfulness for Young Children

Mindfulness for young children must be concrete and brief, focusing on present-moment sensory experiences rather than abstract meditation concepts.

Five senses games: Helping children notice their immediate sensory environment.

- "I spy" games focusing on different senses
- Listening walks to notice different sounds
- Texture treasure hunts
- Taste testing games with different flavors
- Smelling jars with different scents

Present moment activities: Simple activities that bring attention to the here and now.

- Watching clouds move across the sky
- Feeling tree bark or grass with hands
- Listening to their own heartbeat after running
- Watching a pinwheel spin in the wind
- Feeling warm sunlight on their skin

Ages 7-11: Building Nervous System Awareness

School-age children can begin to understand their nervous system patterns and learn more sophisticated regulation strategies while still needing concrete, engaging approaches.

Developing Internal Awareness

Emotion identification activities: Helping children recognize and name their internal states.

- Feeling faces charts with more nuanced emotions

- Body scanning activities to notice physical sensations

- Emotion journals with drawings and words

- Role-playing different emotional states

- Creating personal emotion vocabulary lists

Trigger recognition games: Helping children identify what situations challenge their regulation.

- Detective games to investigate what makes regulation hard

- Creating lists of "green light" and "red light" situations

- Drawing maps of easy and challenging environments

- Keeping simple logs of what affects their mood and energy

- Family discussions about individual differences in triggers

Energy level awareness: Teaching children to recognize and communicate their energy states.

- Energy level check-ins using numbers or colors

- Creating personal energy level charts

- Identifying activities that give energy vs. activities that use energy

- Planning daily schedules around energy patterns

- Learning to communicate energy needs to adults

Intermediate Regulation Strategies

Breathing techniques for school-age children: More sophisticated breathing exercises that children can use independently.

- Counted breathing (4 counts in, 4 counts out)

- Square breathing (breathe in, hold, breathe out, hold)

- Flower and candle breathing (smell the flower, blow out the candle)
- Hand breathing (tracing fingers while breathing)
- Breathing with visual aids like apps or videos

Movement regulation for school-age children: Physical activities that children can do independently or with minimal adult support.

- Yoga sequences designed for children
- Running or walking meditation
- Dance parties for energy release
- Stretching routines for tension relief
- Sports or playground activities for regulation

Mindfulness practices for children: Age-appropriate mindfulness that builds present-moment awareness.

- Guided imagery exercises
- Mindful eating with different foods
- Nature observation activities
- Body scan exercises
- Loving-kindness practices for self and others

Problem-Solving and Coping Skills

School-age children can begin learning systematic approaches to handling challenging situations.

The regulation toolkit approach: Helping children build their personal collection of strategies.

- Creating visual toolkits with pictures of helpful strategies
- Practicing different tools for different situations

- Rating which tools work best for them
- Adding new tools as they learn and grow
- Teaching children when to use which tools

Social regulation strategies: Helping children manage regulation in social situations.

- Practice scripts for asking for breaks or help
- Identifying trusted adults in different environments
- Learning to recognize social overwhelm early
- Strategies for handling peer conflict
- Building confidence in social self-advocacy

Academic regulation support: Strategies specifically for school and homework challenges.

- Study environment optimization
- Break scheduling during homework
- Test anxiety management techniques
- Focus and attention strategies
- Communication with teachers about needs

Nine-year-old Marcus created his own "regulation menu" with drawings of different activities he could choose from when feeling overwhelmed: "When I'm feeling yellow (getting stressed), I can do wall push-ups, use my fidget toy, or take five deep breaths. When I'm feeling red (very upset), I need to go to my calm corner with my weighted blanket."

Ages 12-15: Teen-Appropriate Regulation Strategies

Middle school and early high school students need regulation strategies that honor their growing independence while addressing the increased complexity of adolescent emotional and social challenges.

Advanced Self-Awareness Skills

Pattern recognition and analysis: Helping teens understand their own regulation patterns in sophisticated ways.

- Keeping detailed regulation journals
- Identifying environmental factors that affect mood and energy
- Tracking patterns across different contexts (home, school, social)
- Understanding how sleep, nutrition, and exercise affect regulation
- Recognizing seasonal and hormonal influences on mood

Emotional complexity understanding: Supporting teens in navigating more complex emotional experiences.

- Learning about mixed emotions and emotional layering
- Understanding the difference between emotions and thoughts
- Developing vocabulary for subtle emotional states
- Recognizing emotional triggers and patterns
- Learning about emotional intensity and duration

Social-emotional awareness: Building understanding of how relationships affect regulation.

- Recognizing which relationships are energizing vs. draining
- Understanding social anxiety and its physical symptoms
- Learning about peer pressure and its effects on decision-making

- Developing awareness of social roles and expectations
- Building skills for handling social conflict and drama

Sophisticated Regulation Techniques

Advanced mindfulness practices: Mindfulness approaches appropriate for teen cognitive development.

- Longer meditation sessions with guided instruction
- Mindfulness apps designed for teenagers
- Walking meditation and mindful movement
- Mindful technology use practices
- Integration of mindfulness into daily activities

Cognitive regulation strategies: Teaching teens to work with their thoughts and thinking patterns.

- Recognizing anxious or negative thought patterns
- Learning cognitive reframing techniques
- Understanding the connection between thoughts and feelings
- Developing realistic self-talk strategies
- Learning to challenge unhelpful thinking patterns

Physical regulation for teens: Exercise and movement approaches that appeal to adolescents.

- Finding personally meaningful physical activities
- Understanding how exercise affects mood and attention
- Learning to use movement for emotional regulation
- Developing consistent exercise routines
- Using physical activity for stress management

Independence and Self-Advocacy Development

Personal regulation planning: Helping teens take ownership of their regulation needs.

- Creating personal regulation plans for different situations
- Learning to anticipate and prepare for challenging situations
- Developing backup plans when primary strategies don't work
- Building confidence in their ability to handle challenges
- Learning when to seek additional support

Communication and advocacy skills: Building teens' ability to communicate their needs effectively.

- Learning to explain their regulation needs to others
- Developing scripts for requesting accommodations
- Building confidence in self-advocacy
- Learning to set boundaries around their needs
- Practicing assertive communication techniques

Thirteen-year-old Sarah with autism learned to recognize her social energy patterns: "I know that I can handle about two hours at social events before my nervous system gets overwhelmed. Instead of pushing through and having a meltdown later, I've learned to make plans that honor my limits. My friends understand now that it's not about them—it's just how my brain works."

Ages 16-18: Preparing for Independent Regulation

High school students need regulation strategies that will serve them in adult environments while building the self-awareness and skills needed for lifelong nervous system health.

Mastering Personal Regulation Systems

Comprehensive self-assessment: Helping teens understand their complete regulation profile.

- Detailed understanding of personal triggers and patterns
- Recognition of optimal conditions for different activities
- Awareness of recovery needs after challenging experiences
- Understanding of how different environments affect functioning
- Integration of regulation needs into life planning

Advanced strategy integration: Building sophisticated regulation toolkits for adult environments.

- Developing regulation strategies for work and academic environments
- Learning to modify strategies for different social contexts
- Building flexibility in approach based on changing circumstances
- Creating backup systems for when primary strategies aren't available
- Integration of technology tools for regulation support

Crisis prevention and management: Building skills for handling regulation challenges independently.

- Recognizing early warning signs of regulation breakdown
- Having detailed plans for preventing crisis situations
- Knowing how to access professional support when needed
- Building resilience for recovering from difficult experiences
- Developing realistic expectations for regulation capacity

Life Skills and Environmental Management

Environmental design skills: Teaching teens to create regulation-supportive environments.

- Understanding how to modify living spaces for optimal regulation

- Learning to evaluate environments for regulation support vs. challenge

- Developing skills for advocating for environmental modifications

- Building awareness of how different environments affect performance

- Creating portable regulation supports for various environments

Relationship and social skills: Building capacity for adult relationships while honoring regulation needs.

- Learning to communicate regulation needs in romantic relationships

- Building skills for maintaining friendships while managing regulation needs

- Developing professional relationship skills that honor nervous system differences

- Learning to set boundaries in various types of relationships

- Building capacity for both independence and interdependence

Future planning integration: Incorporating regulation needs into life planning.

- Considering regulation needs in college and career choices

- Understanding how to access accommodations in adult environments

- Building financial awareness of regulation support costs
- Creating long-term plans for maintaining nervous system health
- Developing realistic expectations for adult independence

Mentorship and Community Building

Peer support and mentorship: Connecting with others who understand neurodivergent experiences.

- Connecting with neurodivergent peer groups
- Finding adult mentors who model successful neurodivergent living
- Building relationships with others who share similar challenges
- Learning from others' regulation strategies and experiences
- Contributing to community support for other neurodivergent individuals

Seventeen-year-old Jordan described his regulation toolkit: "I have different strategies for different situations now. For studying, I need instrumental music and my standing desk. For social situations, I prepare by doing some deep breathing and I know which friends I can talk to if I'm feeling overwhelmed. For work, I've learned to take short breaks every hour and I use an app to remind me to check in with my stress level. It's taken me years to figure out what works, but now I feel confident about managing my ADHD in college."

Family Activities That Support Everyone's Nervous System

The most successful regulation activities are often those that can be adapted to support different family members' needs simultaneously.

Nature-Based Family Regulation

Outdoor activities that provide universal regulation benefits:

- Family walks or hikes that can accommodate different energy levels

- Gardening projects that provide sensory input and connection to nature

- Beach or lake activities that offer various sensory experiences

- Camping or outdoor adventures that reduce technology stimulation

- Outdoor sports or games that can be modified for different abilities

Seasonal regulation activities: Using natural seasonal changes to support family regulation.

- Fall leaf collection and sensory play

- Winter snow activities for proprioceptive input

- Spring planting and growth observation

- Summer water play and outdoor exploration

Creative Family Regulation

Art and creativity projects that support different nervous systems:

- Family art projects that can accommodate different skill levels

- Music activities that provide both stimulation and calming

- Building projects that offer proprioceptive input

- Cooking and baking activities that engage multiple senses

- Drama and storytelling that support emotional expression

Movement-Based Family Activities

Physical activities that provide regulation for various nervous system needs:

- Family dance parties that can be high or low energy
- Yoga or stretching routines that family members can modify
- Sports activities that can accommodate different abilities
- Walking meetings or discussions for kinesthetic processors
- Playground activities that provide vestibular and proprioceptive input

Adapting Activities for Different Sensory Profiles

Successful regulation activities must be adapted to match individual sensory processing patterns and preferences.

For Sensory-Seeking Children

High-intensity activities that provide the input seeking nervous systems crave:

- Intense physical activities like jumping on trampolines
- Heavy work activities like carrying weighted objects
- Loud, energetic music and movement
- Textural activities with various materials
- Activities that provide intense but safe sensory experiences

For Sensory-Avoiding Children

Gentle, low-intensity activities that don't overwhelm sensitive systems:

- Quiet, calm activities in low-stimulation environments
- Gentle touch activities that respect tactile sensitivities
- Soft, predictable sounds like nature recordings

- Visual activities that aren't overstimulating
- Activities that allow for personal space and control

For Mixed Sensory Profiles

Flexible activities that can be adjusted based on current sensory needs:

- Activities that can be made more or less intense
- Options for different types of sensory input within the same activity
- Activities that allow children to self-regulate intensity
- Multiple versions of the same activity for different sensory states
- Activities that provide choice and control over sensory input

Building Your Family's Regulation Activity Collection

Creating an effective collection of regulation activities requires understanding your family members' individual needs while building a sustainable system that grows and changes over time.

Assessment and Planning

Understanding individual and family needs:

- Assessing each family member's regulation patterns and preferences
- Identifying activities that appeal to different personality types
- Considering practical constraints like time, space, and budget
- Planning for different seasons and life circumstances
- Building flexibility for changing needs over time

Implementation Strategies

Making regulation activities practical and sustainable:

- Starting with simple activities and building complexity over time

- Creating systems for remembering and accessing different activities

- Building activities into daily and weekly routines

- Teaching family members to suggest and lead activities

- Celebrating successes and learning from activities that don't work

Growth and Adaptation

Evolving your activity collection over time:

- Regularly reviewing and updating your collection of activities

- Adding new activities as family members grow and change

- Retiring activities that no longer serve family needs

- Learning from other families and professional resources

- Building family traditions around successful regulation activities

Your Family's Regulation Success Story

The Murphy family's regulation journey illustrates how activities can evolve and grow with family development. What started as desperate attempts to help Connor during preschool meltdowns became a sophisticated family system that supported everyone's nervous system needs.

By age twelve, Connor had developed his own toolkit of regulation strategies that he could use independently, while still benefiting from family activities that supported everyone's wellbeing. His sister

Lily had found her own preferred activities that matched her ADHD needs, and their parents had learned to create family experiences that honored everyone's differences while building connection.

"Now we have family regulation time on Sunday evenings," Connor's mom explained. "Everyone does their own thing—I might read, Dad listens to music, Connor uses his sensory swing, and Lily does art projects. We're all in the same room supporting our nervous systems in our own ways. It's become one of our favorite family times."

The goal of age-specific regulation activities isn't finding perfect solutions that work forever, but rather building your child's capacity to understand their own nervous system needs and develop the skills to support their regulation throughout their changing developmental journey.

When you provide age-appropriate regulation activities that match your child's current developmental level while building toward future independence, you're giving them tools they'll use for life. Most importantly, you're helping them understand that taking care of their nervous system is normal, important, and something they can learn to do successfully for themselves.

References

Aron, E. N. (2013). The highly sensitive person: How to thrive when the world overwhelms you. Kensington Publishing Corp.

Barkley, R. A. (2015). Attention-deficit hyperactivity disorder: A handbook for diagnosis and treatment (4th ed.). Guilford Press.

Barrett, L. F. (2017). How emotions are made: The secret life of the brain. Houghton Mifflin Harcourt.

Brown, B. (2017). Rising strong: How the ability to reset transforms the way we live, love, parent, and lead. Random House.

Coogan, A. N., & McGowan, N. M. (2017). A systematic review of circadian function, chronotype and chronotherapy in attention deficit hyperactivity disorder. ADHD Attention Deficit and Hyperactivity Disorders, 9(3), 129-147. https://doi.org/10.1007/s12402-017-0221-7

Corbett, B. A., Mendoza, S., Abdullah, M., Wegelin, J. A., & Levine, S. (2006). Cortisol circadian rhythms and response to stress in children with autism. Psychoneuroendocrinology, 31(1), 59-68. https://doi.org/10.1016/j.psyneuen.2005.05.011

Delahooke, M. (2019). Beyond behaviors: Using brain science and compassion to understand and solve children's behavioral challenges. PESI Publishing.

Dunckley, V. L. (2015). Reset your child's brain: A four-week plan to end meltdowns, raise grades, and boost social skills by reversing the effects of electronic screen time. New World Library.

Feldman, R. (2012). Bio-behavioral synchrony: A model for integrating biological and microsocial behavioral processes in the study of parenting. Parenting: Science and Practice, 12(2-3), 154-164. https://doi.org/10.1080/15295192.2012.683342

Foster, R. G., & Kreitzman, L. (2017). Circadian rhythms: A very short introduction. Oxford University Press.

Gerdes, M. R., Schneider, M., & Talay-Ongan, A. (2012). Motor development in children with autism spectrum disorders: A systematic review. Research in Developmental Disabilities, 33(4), 1213-1232. https://doi.org/10.1016/j.ridd.2012.02.015

Gotham, K., Brunwasser, S. M., & Lord, C. (2015). Depressive and anxiety symptom trajectories from school age through young adulthood in samples with autism spectrum disorder and developmental delay. Journal of the American Academy of Child & Adolescent Psychiatry, 54(5), 369-376. https://doi.org/10.1016/j.jaac.2015.02.005

Grandin, T. (2006). Thinking in pictures: My life with autism (Expanded edition). Vintage Books.

Greene, R. W. (2014). The explosive child: A new approach for understanding and parenting easily frustrated, chronically inflexible children. Harper Paperbacks.

Herrington, J. D., Maddox, B. B., Kerns, C. M., Maddox, B., Merchant, S., Schultz, R. T., & Miller, J. S. (2017). Amygdala volume differences in autism spectrum disorder are related to anxiety. Journal of Autism and Developmental Disorders, 47(12), 3682-3691. https://doi.org/10.1007/s10803-017-3206-1

Hull, L., Petrides, K. V., Allison, C., Smith, P., Baron-Cohen, S., Lai, M. C., & Mandy, W. (2017). "Putting on my best normal": Social camouflaging in adults with autism spectrum conditions. Journal of Autism and Developmental Disorders, 47(8), 2519-2534. https://doi.org/10.1007/s10803-017-3166-5

Kaplan, B. J., McNicol, J., Conte, R. A., & Moghadam, H. K. (1989). Dietary replacement in preschool-aged hyperactive boys. Pediatrics, 83(1), 7-17.

Lupien, S. J., McEwen, B. S., Gunnar, M. R., & Heim, C. (2009). Effects of stress throughout the lifespan on the brain, behaviour and cognition. Nature Reviews Neuroscience, 10(6), 434-445. https://doi.org/10.1038/nrn2639

Maslach, C., Schaufeli, W. B., & Leiter, M. P. (2001). Job burnout. Annual Review of Psychology, 52(1), 397-422. https://doi.org/10.1146/annurev.psych.52.1.397

Maté, G. (2003). When the body says no: Understanding the stress-disease connection. Vintage Canada.

McEwen, B. S., & Sapolsky, R. M. (1995). Stress and cognitive function. Current Opinion in Neurobiology, 5(2), 205-216. https://doi.org/10.1016/0959-4388(95)80028-X

Menon, V. (2011). Large-scale brain networks and psychopathology: A unifying triple network model. Trends in Cognitive Sciences, 15(10), 483-506. https://doi.org/10.1016/j.tics.2011.08.003

Miller, L. J., Anzalone, M. E., Lane, S. J., Cermak, S. A., & Osten, E. T. (2007). Concept evolution in sensory integration: A proposed nosology for diagnosis. American Journal of Occupational Therapy, 61(2), 135-140. https://doi.org/10.5014/ajot.61.2.135

Ne'eman, A. (2010). The future (and the past) of autism advocacy, or why the ASA's magazine, The Advocate, wouldn't publish this piece. Disability Studies Quarterly, 30(1). https://doi.org/10.18061/dsq.v30i1.1059

Perry, B. D., & Szalavitz, M. (2007). The boy who was raised as a dog: And other stories from a child psychiatrist's notebook. Basic Books.

Porges, S. W. (2004). Neuroception: A subconscious system for detecting threats and safety. Zero to Three, 24(5), 19-24.

Porges, S. W. (2011). The polyvagal theory: Neurophysiological foundations of emotions, attachment, communication, and self-regulation. W. W. Norton & Company.

Porges, S. W. (2017). The pocket guide to polyvagal theory: The transformative power of feeling safe. W. W. Norton & Company.

Ratey, J. J., & Hagerman, E. (2008). Spark: The revolutionary new science of exercise and the brain. Little, Brown and Company.

Schore, A. N. (2003). Affect dysregulation and disorders of the self. W. W. Norton & Company.

Schore, A. N. (2019). The development of the unconscious mind. W. W. Norton & Company.

Shaw, P., Malek, M., Watson, B., Greenstein, D., de Rossi, P., & Sharp, W. (2012). Trajectories of cerebral cortical development in childhood and adolescence and adult attention-deficit/hyperactivity disorder. Biological Psychiatry, 74(8), 599-606. https://doi.org/10.1016/j.biopsych.2013.04.007

Siegel, D. J. (1999). The developing mind: How relationships and the brain interact to shape who we are. Guilford Press.

Siegel, D. J., & Bryson, T. P.. (2012). The whole-brain child: 12 revolutionary strategies to nurture your child's developing mind. Bantam.

Steinberg, L. (2013). The influence of neuroscience on US Supreme Court decisions about adolescents' criminal culpability. Nature Reviews Neuroscience, 14(7), 513-518. https://doi.org/10.1038/nrn3509

Van der Kolk, B. A. (2014). The body keeps the score: Brain, mind, and body in the healing of trauma. Penguin Books.

Vygotsky, L. S. (1978). Mind in society: The development of higher psychological processes. Harvard University Press.

Walker, M. (2017). Why we sleep: Unlocking the power of sleep and dreams. Scribner.

Wargocki, P., & Wyon, D. P. (2017). Ten questions concerning thermal and indoor air quality effects on the performance of office work and schoolwork. Building and Environment, 112, 359-366. https://doi.org/10.1016/j.buildenv.2016.11.020

Winner, M. G. (2007). Thinking about you thinking about me: Philosophy and strategies to further develop perspective taking and communicative abilities for persons with social cognitive learning challenges. Think Social Publishing.

Yerkes, R. M., & Dodson, J. D. (1908). The relation of strength of stimulus to rapidity of habit-formation. Journal of Comparative Neurology and Psychology, 18(5), 459-482. https://doi.org/10.1002/cne.920180503

www.ingramcontent.com/pod-product-compliance
Lightning Source LLC
Chambersburg PA
CBHW062150080426
42734CB00010B/1628